NYGÅRD!

CHILD OF LAMPOSAARI

The Inspiring Story of Hilkka Nygård

LINDA MCINTOSH

CHILD OF LAMPOSAARI
The Inspiring Story of Hilkka Nygård

Falcon Flight Publishers
30 Hamilton Meadows Dr.
Winnipeg, MB, R2Y 2K2

FIRST EDITION PUBLISHED 2011
By Falcon Flight Publishers

Photographs courtesy the Nygård family.

Library and Archives Canada Cataloguing in Publication

McIntosh, Linda, 1943-
Child of Lamposaari : the inspiring story of Hilkka
Nygård / Linda G. McIntosh.

ISBN: 978-0-9866575-1-1 [hc.]
ISBN: 978-0-9866575-0-4 [pbk.]

1. Nygård, Hilkka, 1923-2010. 2. Nygård, Hilkka, 1923-2010--
Childhood and youth. 3. Nygård, Hilkka, 1923-2010--Family.
4. World War, 1939-1945--Finland--Biography. 5. Finns--Manitoba--
Winnipeg--Biography. 6. Immigrants--Manitoba--Winnipeg--Biography.
7. Finland--Biography. 8. Winnipeg (Man.)--Biography. I. Title.

FC3396.26.N94M45 2010   971.27'43004945410092   C2010-904368-5

Book Design by Alix Reynolds/ Kurio Studio
www.kuriostudio.com

Printed and bound in Canada by Friesens Corp.

Dedicated to the memory of
Hilkka Kanerva Nygård
who understood the true meaning
of unconditional love.

Acknowledgements

Hilkka Nygård made me laugh, made me cry, and filled me with gratitude for all the blessings life gives us. Her courage and fortitude inspired those around her to find joy and wonder in every aspect of their existence. "In all things, thank God" was a command by which she lived. To her, bad things were not inherently bad in and of themselves. Rather, they were learning experiences from which one gained wisdom and increased understanding. She thanked God for these learning experiences while, at the same time, she prayed for relief from the trauma they inflicted.

The details of her life, revealed through many conversations leading to the creation of this book, consisted of more than simple recitations of historical data and chronological events. Our talks were wide ranging, leaping from one era to another, interspersed with personal observations, expressions of faith and philosophical commentary. The love she felt for her children, grandchildren and great-grandchildren was strong and unconditional. They were the most important things in her world and she would have done almost anything for them. They loved her deeply in return and filled her life with meaning and purpose. Her descendants recognized the legacy of character and Finnish *sisu* that had been passed down to them. As her grandson Kristopher stated in a poem he wrote for his grandparents when he was a boy,

And all the while I can see
you were thinking ahead for me . . . .
Your influence is always there
even if I'm not aware . . . .
From you to them and them to me
and one day to my own you see . . . .
For the knowledge great, the love supreme.

I cannot thank Hilkka enough for sharing with me the mystery and adventure of her days. She pulled out memories from the deepest recesses of her heart, and honoured me with their revelation. Not everything thus revealed, of course, is recorded in this book. Some recollections are too private, too personal to publicly disclose. For taking me into her intimate realm, I am grateful. Her untimely death shortly before this manuscript was fully complete was a sorrow for all of us, but her unwavering faith that she would be with her Lord when her days on earth were ended gave us occasion for rejoicing.

Liisa (Pirjo-Liisa) Nygård Johnson, Hilkka's daughter, has been the driving force behind the making of this book. She was the one who persuaded her mother to put her story down on paper, and who argued with her over specific details, dates and names until both mother and daughter could agree that they had the fact under debate correctly recalled. She was the one who invited me to be the author of this tale and thus provided us with the opportunity to have lots of visits together.

How can I possibly explain all that Liisa has done to encourage the progression of this project? Since for much of the time during the writing, Hilkka was in the Bahamas, Liisa was in Manitoba and I was in the wilds of northwestern Ontario, Liisa became the coordinator of material for the book. The e-mails, long distance phone calls, the "back and forthing" of Hilkka's information—these happened in large part because of Liisa's determination. How do I express my delight at the good times we shared during our working sessions? Liisa fed her mother and me innumerable incredible delicacies, brimming with natural ingredients and enticing flavours. She made us green smoothies and homemade soups. She brought boxes of photographs to our home in the northern woods so that we could sort through them and select ones for these pages, and we poured over them for hours discussing the circumstances leading to the creation of each image. When we had finished sorting all those pictures, she found more boxes and went through each one of them! The early morning swims, the singing, the long talks that put us behind schedule, the laughter over silly jokes (Liisa's jokes were silly, mine were intellectually stimulating) made the whole exercise a pleasure.

To Peter Nygård, for his contributions and support throughout, and for his deep and constant devotion to his mother, thank you for making this story a reality. You said she was the wind beneath your wings, but she felt that you had helped *her* to soar. Her eyes lit up when she talked of you. Because of you, opportunities and exciting experiences were made available to the whole family, and your mother was enormously pleased that this was so.

To my husband Don McIntosh, who kept things humming along when the book took precedence over our normal routines, thank you for always being there, and for making each day fun!

To those thousands of wives and mothers who emigrated from Finland and who have given Canada a rich example of *sisu*, even though they as individuals are not the subject of this writing, collectively I thank them.

Linda McIntosh, Autumn, 2010

FOREWORD

The original purpose of Hilkka's memoirs was to provide her grandchildren, great- grandchildren and future descendants with an historic account of her journey of eighty-seven years. Through the years, our children have been intrigued by her life stories and have sought to learn the recipes and customs that have endeared "Gramma Hilkka" to them. As they learn of their grandmother's life, it was our intention that they would also learn of the forces of history that molded the Finnish people and imbued them with unique characteristics inherited from ancestors reaching far back into ancient times.

Compiling the details inspired us to offer these memoirs for a wider audience when it became obvious that Hilkka's story is in many ways also a story of thousands of immigrant mothers who, as brave newcomers to Canada, persevered through a multitude of struggles, hardships and language barriers en route to establishing themselves and their families as productive citizens of Canada.

Mom is just one of the thousands who have taken this journey and her story is certain to induce reflection and memories in others who identify with that time in their lives.

She began relating her story in the fall of 2008 to the author, Linda McIntosh, and it was on the verge of completion when illness delayed production to 2009. It was intended that she would be present to launch this book but sadly, her journey on this earth, despite a strong will to live, ended on January 12, 2010 when she joined her Heavenly Father.

It is with the deepest gratitude to Hilkka and Eeli, our parents, that we have been able to experience the Canadian Dream. Their courage and wisdom in the orchestration of the events in our lives, which have brought us to this point, are gifts which are immeasurable.

As is the case in many families, the life of our mother, Hilkka, has touched all generations of our family in a most profound way. Her memory lives on daily through the hearts she warmed with her compassion, through the lessons she taught us with her example, and will be forever preserved through these pages.

Thank you for joining us to meet The Child of Lamposaari.

Most sincerely,
Liisa (Nygård) Johnson and Peter Nygård

TABLE OF CONTENTS

Section Three:
Canada: The Immigrant Years 1952

Section Four:
Winnipeg, The Building Years 1952-1997

Section Five:
All Right Together 1997-2010

"Always a Child of Lamposaari"

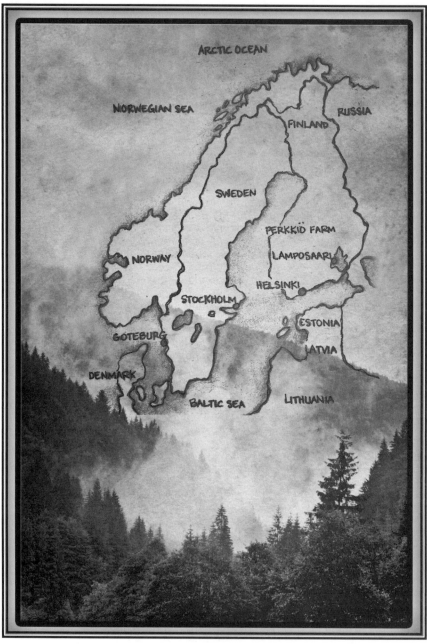

Map of Finland and Sweden showing:
Helsinki, Finland • Stockholm, Sweden • Goteburg, Sweden
Lamposaari, an island in Lake Saimaa, Finland and the
area of Finland where Perkkiö was located.
Russia is to the east of Finland.
Norway is to the west of Sweden and to the north of Finland.
The Arctic Ocean is to the north of Norway and Finland.

PROLOGUE

More than eight thousand years before the birth of Christ, at the end of the Scandinavian Ice Age, the first humans made their way to Finland from Asia to the east and other regions to the south.

These early Finns were primarily stone-age hunters and gatherers about whom very little is recorded. It was known that they created saunas by digging pits into the sides of sloping ground or small hills. The air in the pits was warmed by stones which were heated with fire and then doused with water to produce steam; and the Finns dwelt in these warm dugouts during the long cold northern winters. The Finnish sauna has endured to this day and almost every Finnish home has some version of it.

The ancient Finns were thought to be a mystical people, whose belief in the gods of the spirit world guided their actions and gave them power to prevail against adversity. This provided the Finns with an indomitable will to do what needed to be done, fearlessly and without weighing the cost. This Finnish temperament, like the sauna, also endures to this day. It is called *sisu*, and it is a noted characteristic of the Finnish population.

Living as they did in daily contact with the natural world around them, the ancient Finns came to feel deeply connected to the earth; and this love of nature and the outdoors is one other thing that has stayed with them as a people throughout the millennia, and it is something for which they are still known today. The clear cold lakes and vast evergreen forests, the soft mosses and lichens, the abundance of wildlife—all these spell "home" for those modern Finns whose souls contain some deep ancestral memory of the days when they lived free from constraint.

From those ancient beginnings, the Finns developed into an independent self-sufficient people whose adaptation to northern life has been superlative. One of the earliest recorded references to these extraordinary people was made around the year 98 A.D. by the Roman historian, Tacitus, who talked about "a savage and primitive people" called the Fenni who lived "on the uttermost shores of the Baltic Sea." In writing of the Fenni, Tacitus stated:

> In wonderful savageness live the nation of the Fenni, and in beastly poverty, destitute of arms, of horses, and of homes; their food, the common herbs; their apparel, skins; their bed, the earth; their only hope in their arrows, which for want of iron they point with bones. Their common support they have from the chase, women as well as men; for with these the former wander up and down, and crave a portion of the prey. Nor other shelter have they even for their babes, against the violence of tempests and ravening beasts, than to cover them with the branches of trees twisted together; this is a reception for the old men, and hither resort the young. Such a condition they judge more happy than the painful occupation of cultivating the ground, than the labour of rearing houses, than the agitations of hope and fear attending the defense of their own property or the seizing that of others. Secure against the designs of men, secure against the malignity of the gods, they have accomplished a thing of infinite difficulty; that to them nothing remains even to be wished.

The actual recorded history of Finland began in the 12th century when Christian missionaries began operating there. From the 12th to the 19th century, Finland was ruled by Sweden. The eighteenth century was one of hardship for the Finns. Famine and disease decimated their population, taking the lives of a third of their numbers. Invasions by Russia resulted in war and the subsequent Russian occupation of Finland, the loss of yet more Finnish lives and the ultimate surrender by Sweden of the south-eastern portion of Finland to the Russians in 1808.

In the 19th century, after being ceded to the Russian Empire by Sweden, Finland existed (from 1809-1917) as the autonomous Grand Duchy of Finland, under the ultimate authority of the Russian Tsar.

The city of Helsinki was founded in 1550, and became the capital of Finland in 1812, when the Tsar decided to move the capital designation to that site from the city of Turku.

In 1856 the Saimaa Canal was built which increased Finland's trading opportunities, specifically the ability to export timber and other resources to Western Europe more easily. The Canal was a major boost to Finland's economy. Raw goods were not the only Finnish exports. The country also became known internationally for its artistic and creative works, and also acquired a respected reputation for its glasswork, textiles and furniture design.

In 1907 Finnish women were given the right to vote in national elections and the right to run for elected office, making Finland the first country in the world to give women full national political rights. (New Zealand and Australia had given women the right to vote, but had not yet given them the right to run for office.) That same year Finnish women became the first in the world to win seats in a national parliament.

In 1917, Finland became an independent republic. The Republic of Finland is a Scandinavian country that borders Sweden on the west, Norway on the north, Russia on the east and the Gulf of Finland on the south.

After World War I, Finland was the only country to repay its war debt to the United States of America in full, establishing for itself an international reputation for integrity and reliability.

In November 1939, Russia once again attacked Finland. Russia was concerned that its capital city of Leningrad, located only 32 kilometers from the Finnish border, was vulnerable to attack from the west through Finland. The conquering of Finland was not as easy a task as Russian leader Joseph Stalin had envisioned. Finland's small army of only 200,000 soldiers fought tenaciously and skillfully. Accustomed to winter conditions, the Finns, wearing white camouflage and speeding on skis through the hills and snow, held the mighty Russian Army—representing a nation over fifty times larger than Finland—at bay for over three months in what came to be known as the Winter War. Twenty-two thousand Finns died in the Winter War, and in the end Russia claimed a large part of the Viipuri province in southeastern Finland.

In June 1941, a defiant Finland joined with Germany as a co-belligerent to attack Russia in what the Finns called the Continuation War. The Finns recaptured their lost territory, but caused difficulty for Britain which by then was at war with Germany and had allied itself with Russia to defeat Hitler. The world was at war, and Britain had to stick with its allies, so it declared itself at war with Finland even though Finland firmly rejected the Nazi ideology. The Continuation War ended in September 1944. It had taken 85,000 Finnish lives; Finland had to pay huge reparations, which it did in full, and was forced to surrender large amounts of territory to Russia. The entire population which lived in the land that was turned over to Russia—almost half a million people—chose to leave their homes rather than live under Soviet rule. As refugees, being Finns in their hearts, they settled in the land that still belonged to Finland.

A final peace treaty was made between Russia and Finland in 1947. Russia began a concerted, but ultimately unsuccessful, attempt to conquer Finland by converting its populace to Communism.

When the Soviet Union collapsed in 1991, the 1947 treaty between Finland and Russia ended and a more agreeable treaty was established in 1992. In 1995 Finland joined the European Union; in 2000 Tarja Halonen was elected the first woman President of Finland; and in 2002 the Finnish currency was replaced by the Euro.

As the calendar turned to 2010, the population of Finland was 5.2 million, the vast majority of whom were Christians by faith and Lutheran by denomination. Of 182 countries ranked by the United Nations in 2009, in terms of the quality of life of their citizens, Finland ranks in the top twenty as the twelfth best place to live.

INTRODUCTION

In 1951, with an oppressive communist influence and activism swirling around and throughout his beloved Finland, Eeli Nygård, a baker, refused to place his signature on a paper which would pledge him to the Communist movement. Openly rejecting the ideology being so aggressively encouraged in his native land was a dramatic first step towards the Nygård family's journey to Canada.

With a growing sense that it would not be long before the Soviet domination of Finland was complete, and seeking to escape a potential communist regime, the Nygård family (Eeli, his wife Hilkka and their two children Pekka and Pirjo-Liisa) fled to Canada several months later, in 1952, to start a new life. Carrying a trunk and two suitcases containing all their worldly possessions, the family settled first in the small rural community of Deloraine, Manitoba and later in Manitoba's capital city of Winnipeg.

Hilkka Nygård's inner strength, her personal courage and her fierce determination to have her children become independent and self sufficient in a free society, are a tribute to her and to all Canadian immigrant mothers, to the lands they left behind and to the great country to which they came.

This is her story.

SECTION
ONE

LAMPOSAARI
THE CHILDHOOD YEARS
1922 - 1936

Hilkka (left), Aili (right), inseparable sisters

CHAPTER ONE

Muukonniemen Koulu

Hilkka turned her wooden boat into the waves, the muscles in her small arms straining as she pulled heavily on the oars. Rowing hard to the left, she turned her craft at a sharp right angle and plunged it forward. "In a storm," her father had taught her, "go straight into the wind past your target and then tack back by turning the boat so that the wind is behind you." With the wind now at her back, she relaxed her grip on the oars, and wiping the rain from her eyes with her aching hands she gauged the distance to shore.

A blast of strong wind whipped up icy spray from the lake and sent it splashing over the edges of the boat, soaking and chilling the six young children sitting inside it. None of them cried out either in shock or in fear as they were repeatedly drenched by the waves crashing around them. Life on the island had taught them to reserve their energy and strength for more practical purposes than displays of hysteria. Besides, they were used to the lake and familiar with its ways.

Hilkka looked to the prow where her little sister Aili sat huddled and shivering, crouched down on the bottom of the boat, her hooded cape partly obscuring her pale face and solemn eyes. Water dripped from the folds in the hood and trickled off Aili's nose and chin, continuing its downward trek over the cape and onto the wooden slats at her feet. Noticing Hilkka's glance, Aili smiled and nodded confidently to indicate her trust in her older sister's ability to get them safely to the opposite shore. Hilkka's tenacity and determination to succeed were well understood by everyone in the boat. More than that, her passengers also knew that her strong sense of duty and responsibility would not allow her to waver in meeting the challenge before her. It was not just for her rowing expertise that Hilkka Valtonen had been chosen to be the one at the oars.

The boat was a large sturdy one, and the Valtonen family had been able to depend on its steadfast reliability in all kinds of weather. They had painted it white with green trim, matching the colours of their house and sealing the wood against rot and water damage. It was, understandably, a proud possession. The boat was big enough to easily contain six or seven people, and thus was one of the boats used each school day (when the water was open) to take children from the island to the main land to attend school.

As on all school days, besides Aili and Hilkka, the white boat held the students' belongings—lunch pails with food for their mid-day meal, brown pouches holding their books and felt slippers, a bucket for bailing, a rope. No life jackets were carried on board—the island children had been swimming since they could walk and life jackets were not common to their way of life.

The mainland, Hilkka judged, was still about a quarter of a kilometer away. Turning back was out of the question. They were much farther from the island than they were from the shore before them. All that she could do was to let the turbulent water toss their little craft to and fro until the wild wind decided to settle itself for a rest. And indeed before long she felt the wind begin to blow less harshly and the drenching rain ease its assault. The storm was abating and she judged that it would be safe to continue towards her destination.

The waves were still rolling and the little boat was still being tossed back and forth as Hilkka resumed rowing. Hilkka was not afraid of nature's elements. She had experienced sudden squalls before and knew how to work with and through them. It was a testament to her confidence and skills at the oars that she maintained a steady course to the shore until she was able to row the boat into the sand. Scrambling out on to the beach, the children joined together to pull the boat out of the water and land it securely so that it would be safe and ready for the return trip home at the end of the day. They had made it to school on time, despite the indignities of the weather. For Hilkka especially, arriving on time was important because she prided herself on never being late. With her reputation for being prompt intact, she scurried with the rest through the rain to begin the school day.

The icy air and sharp wind were harbingers of the cold Finnish winter that would soon be upon them. In the dead of that winter, when the lake was solidly frozen, the children would ski to school. It was great fun to swish across the snow-covered ice and slide on their long narrow boards, marveling at the white world around them. They would call out to each other and laugh along the way. The skiing was more than just a fast way to travel. It was delight. They would arrive at school, rosy-cheeked and breathless, growing in health and strength without even being aware of it.

In the seasons between the summer water and the winter ice, crossing the lake was a dangerous undertaking. As the ice began to form in the fall, or melt in the spring, one of the men from the mill would go ahead of the children on the lake, thumping and poking the ice with a big stick to see if it was strong enough to hold people. The children walked in a row behind him and would turn back without question if he ordered them to do so. Being sent off the lake because of thin ice wasn't necessarily a joyful indication that there would be no lessons that day. While on occasion school had to be missed because of ice conditions or severe weather, most often thin ice meant waiting on the shore in the cold for the big tugboat to arrive. When it got to the island, the students would board and the heavy vessel would break through the thin ice and take them across to the mainland where they would be met and escorted to the school, watched over and protected. Watching out for each other was something that was woven into the fabric of their lives.

Hilkka was not one of the students who wanted to miss school, however. She adored everything about her school from its very name, Muukonniemen Koulu (*koulu* meaning "school"), to her teachers, Matti Suorsa and Aili Suorsa. Aili Suorsa was the daughter of a famous writer, and she infused her students with a deep appreciation of literature. Hilkka was one of those fortunate children who loved to learn. She was especially good at working with numbers, and she was adept with words, often writing little stories and attaching comical or fanciful poems to gifts she gave.

The day at Muukonniemen Koulu always began with the singing of "Maammelaulu" (*maamme* meaning "our land", and *laulu* meaning "song"). "Maammelaulu" had, through long use, obtained unofficial status as the song to be sung to proclaim loyalty to the country, and the students sang it proudly each day before beginning their lessons.

Oi maamme, Suomi, synnyinmaa,
soi, sana kultainen!
Ei laaksoa, ei kukkulaa,
ei vettä, rantaa rakkaampaa
kuin kotimaa tää pohjoinen,
maa kallis isien.
Sun kukoistukses kuorestaan
kerrankin puhkeaa;
viel' lempemme saa nousemaan
sun toivos, riemus loistossaan,
ja kerran laulus, synnyinmaa
korkeemman kaiun saa.

(English translation by Clement Burbank Shaw)

Song of Our Land
Our land, our land, our fatherland
Sound loud, O name of worth!
No mount that meets the heaven's band
No hidden vale, no wave washed strand
Is loved, as is our native North.
Our own forefathers' earth.

Thy blossom, in the bud laid low,
Yet ripened shall upspring
See! From our love once more shall grow
Thy light, thy joy, thy hope, thy glow!
And clearer yet one day shall ring
The song our land shall sing.

After the singing of this anthem, the Lord's Prayer was said. The prayer would remain in Hilkka's mind and heart throughout her life and become a source of comfort and strength to her in good times and hard. The anthem and prayer were followed by an hour of Bible Study and Biblical History. Island students, most of them Lutherans, knew their religion and respected the Church's Sacraments of Baptism and Communion and the rites of Confirmation and Marriage which gave them spiritual dimensions that were as familiar to them as the earthly realm around them. Becoming old enough to take part in the Lord's Supper was considered a serious and solemn rite of passage. In such an environment, beginning the school day with an emphasis on a power larger than themselves seemed a natural thing to do.

Geography, History, Mathematics, Penmanship, Language Arts, Physical Education, and Home Economics came next, and Hilkka loved them all. Her natural curiosity and high intellect drew her to explore each subject in detail and with great enjoyment. She worked hard as well to please her teachers and to be well behaved. She was thrilled when Matti Suorsa patted her on the head and said, "Hilkka is such a levelheaded girl", and she couldn't wait to tell her parents of the compliment.

At home in the evening, the Valtonen girls would kneel at a wooden sofa they used as a desk and do their homework. Their parents demanded that their homework take priority over everything else, because they valued the opportunity their girls had to become well educated. Hilkka was always quite happy to settle down with her studies since, for her, learning was pleasure.

Muukonniemen Koulu
Hilkka Valtonen, third from left, front row

CHAPTER TWO

Most of the Time

Hilkka was a good girl most of the time. She truly tried to stay out of trouble. But she was no stranger to spanking, for despite her best efforts, she seemed to find herself in trouble quite often . . . not really bad trouble you must understand; just little troubles like playing in places she wasn't supposed to be and doing little things just to find out what it was like to do them. Because she was curious and adventurous, she was drawn to intriguing and fascinating things, which unfortunately were often things that she had been cautioned to avoid. She also found it exceedingly difficult to resist physical challenges or dares, and would jump and climb and take chances that she shouldn't. She had learned from experience that spankings were usually the consequence one paid for taking silly risks.

Still, when excitement beckoned, Hilkka somehow forgot about spankings. She remembered the spectacular ones she'd received of course. She had been given a good walloping when her father found out that she and her friends had been running on the rolling logs that floated into the saw mill landing. All of the island children had been warned not to play at the saw mill when the logs were being loaded and Hilkka truly never meant to go to the forbidden site; but there was an amazing giant garden swing in the deep shade of the forest, a sort of a magical place which drew little children and young lovers to it like a magnet. When children were gliding back and forth on the swing, the nearby water and the logs bobbing and dancing upon it were both visible and inviting. The lure of all that floating wood was irresistible and despite the warnings, the children would sometimes sneak down to the water and jump from one rolling log to another.

It was hard to keep one of the forbidden log-walking episodes from her father, since the evidence had been hard to miss. Poor little Aili, then only six years old, had been in on the fun with Hilkka, but lacking the older children's agility, had fallen between two logs into the lake, which was bitterly cold at that time of year. Unable to get a solid grasp on her hands, Hilkka and her companions had to pull Aili out of the water by the hair. This proved to be no easy task, for Aili's hair was shorter than Hilkka's and she had no long braids to act as ropes for the rescue operation. Frantic that they would be found out and get in trouble the children tried to squeeze the water out of Aili's hair, to no avail. They pulled off her long woolen stockings and tried to squeeze the water out of them too, again to no avail. Putting the wet stockings back on her was difficult, for they were made of raw wool and held up with garters, both items difficult to work with when wet.

Father, naturally, found them out, and Hilkka was spanked, not just for going on the logs, but also for having led her younger sister into mischief. It was her duty to set a good example and she had failed to do so. Aili, having allowed herself to be so easily led into said mischief, and for being on the logs, was also spanked. It was a hard lesson for both girls, for Aili loved to follow Hilkka around, doing everything her older sister did, and Hilkka always had fun being the leader, not wanting to spoil adventures by being timid.

"Hilkka," her mother had explained, "being timid and being cautious are not the same things. You must learn the difference to be safe." Try as

Lamposaari friends sitting on the Valtonen steps.
Hilkka (left), Aili (right)

she might to heed her parents' warnings, Hilkka sometimes let caution fly away with the wind. When she and her companions played near the large piles of sawdust that stood near the sawmill, for example, she would forget everything except the fun that could be had by jumping into them. As high as a house, the piles were wonderful places in which to play. One could slide or roll down the sides of the piles, or burrow and hide inside them. The sawdust piles, however, could be extremely dangerous. Sharp sticks remained in the residue of the sawed wood, which at best could scratch and cut flesh, and at worst could inflict serious, permanent damage to a body; and inhaling the dust was harmful not just to the lungs but to the entire respiratory system. The sawdust piles were forbidden places to play. When Hilkka played there anyway, she was spanked.

The problem was that for every act of mischief she cast aside another one would surface, because everywhere Hilkka turned there was always something fascinating to discover. She was intrigued by the intricate wooden structures her father created in the mill yard. As part of his job he was required to assemble freshly cut lumber into stacks to dry. Built so that each piece of lumber was supported by another in such a way that air could freely circulate round them all, the drying stacks were engineering and architectural delights. Their box-like shape and great height made them look like houses. Even the boards placed at the top of the pile were sloped like rooftops so that rain and snow would flow off the wood, rather than settle into it. Such places cried out to be explored by curious and imaginative children, of which Hilkka was surely one. Squeezing through the slats and climbing up and over the rough planks inside the lumber stacks was a great deal of fun, and when playing hide-and-seek with her friends, there was no better place in which to hide. Going into the interior of a lumber stack was a dangerous thing to do, however. A heavy piece of wood becoming dislodged from its place could cause a crushing collapse of the entire structure and a rain of damaging, even deadly, blows to a tiny body. Hilkka's father had therefore forbidden her to play in the stacks. When temptation overcame her, she was invariably caught—and spanked.

Her smarting bottom and bruised dignity would eventually dissuade her from further wrongdoing, but over time the memory of the fun she had earning those spankings was what remained uppermost in her mind.

Hilkka was learning lessons in humility. The adventures had been fun but the consequences were not.

CHAPTER THREE

At Home with the Valtonens

One should not presume however that Hilkka Valtonen was by nature a naughty or badly behaved child. Despite her many misadventures and resultant spankings, she was a loving, helpful and obedient daughter. Her parents, Aleksanteri and Selma Valtonen, both worked for the lumber company that was the island's sole employer. Her mother worked inside the mill, operating a machine that emptied the sawdust into containers that were then sent to be added to the great sawdust piles.

Her father, besides working in the mill yards, also took care of the mill manager's horses, grooming and exercising them, and taking the reins to drive the horses with buggy or sled when the manager wanted to travel around the island. Hilkka thought the manager's house, which was close in proximity to theirs, was like a palace, a magnificent dwelling that deserved to have stables of horses and someone to care for them.

Aleksanteri was very fond of the horses, as indeed was his whole family. The horses in return were at ease with the Valtonens and in warm weather they would frequently wander over to their nearby home and trustingly poke their faces into the open windows looking for a lump of sugar or carrots. Hilkka loved to hold out her hand and feel the soft nibbling and nuzzling of the horses' moist mouths as they took the treats she offered them—such big teeth and yet so gentle a touch!

There were times, though, she knew from bitter experience that one needed to be careful around the horses. She would not soon forget the time that Pirkko, one of the most beautiful of the horses, had nearly crushed her hand. She and her friends had been playing baseball on the road, when the horse came trotting down with its master. The other children scurried to one side and out of the way, but Hilkka in her haste tripped and fell—right in the horse's path. Pirkko's hoof collided with Hilkka's hand as he came up against her. His touch on that occasion was far from gentle, but Pirkko had meant no harm. From her pain and injury, however, Hilkka learned to be cautious around animals and to treat them with a somewhat fearful respect.

The Valtonen home was a nurturing place, where the children grew up confident in the love and devotion of their parents. Living on Lamposaari isolated the family somewhat from the distractions, pressures and stresses of the mainland, and as a result they bonded closely with each other. Indeed

Selma and Aleksanteri Valtonen

Hilkka (left) and Aili (right) in front of their home on Lamposaari.

the whole island community was like one big family. Everybody worked at the sawmill, where logs were transformed into lumber. Everybody knew and relied upon and cared about everyone else. There were no cars on the island. They really weren't needed. There were a few horses, and the manager had a buggy, but people were used to walking and were healthier for the activity. One man had a bicycle but it was considered more of an instrument for fun, not transportation. All the roads were made of sawdust which proved to be an excellent and readily available medium for the purpose. The beaches were of soft sand, clean and luxurious in texture. There on the beaches the children would play and run into the lake to swim. Swimming was a skill that to the children of Lamposaari was as natural as breathing. There existed such a sense of trust and security on Lamposaari, and its natural beauty was so intoxicating, that the people who lived there had rightly dubbed it "Paratiisi" or "Paradise" Island.

True, the island was not completely self-sustaining. Residents had to travel by boat to the mainland for many essentials, but the distance wasn't far—only a little over a kilometer to the closest shore—and the scenery was breathtaking. Lamposaari was just one of many islands on Lake Saimaa, Finland's largest lake, near the western border of Russia. A glacial lake more than 4,000 square kilometers in size, Saimaa presented boaters with views of incredible beauty from every vantage point. Although they were not fully conscious of it, living in this peaceful place had a profoundly positive influence upon the Valtonen children.

Their family dwelling was humble, consisting of two rooms, the main room which was a kitchen/sitting room combination and another room— the room that wasn't the kitchen—where they all slept. The wooden couch that was used as a sofa and desk by day, when topped with a straw-filled mattress at night, became a sleeping platform for Selma and the two younger daughters. Aleksanteri slept in a separate bed in the corner of the bed room. Hilkka's sister Iida, older than Hilkka by ten years, now slept in the cozy loft in the attic of the shed beside the house, leaving a bit more room in the sleeping room for the rest of the family and providing Iida with some of the privacy so desired by young women of her age. A wood burning cook stove stood near the kitchen entrance and a ceramic fireplace warmed the sitting room. An out house had its obvious purpose.

Everyone in the Valtonen family took their baths at the public sauna, where all islanders went to cleanse the impurities from their bodies. The sauna contained a fire-fed heater which held rocks heated to a great intensity. Bathers tossed water on to the hot rocks to create steam. The children thought it was fun to hear the water hiss and pop as it hit the stones and turned to instant vapour. The steam thus created caused the bathers to perspire, opening the pores of their skin. Slapping and scrubbing the skin with a bouquet of wet birch branches with their aromatic leaves still attached (*saunavihta*) helped to stimulate circulation and exfoliate the skin.

In the communal sauna the women sat on one side of a partial wall and the men sat on the other. The women usually wore towels and if the men had to scoot past them for any reason, the men would hold their *saunavihta* strategically placed to cover themselves so as not to offend the women. Eventually women and men were assigned separate days to use the sauna because many of the seasonal mill workers who were strangers to the island began to use the sauna, and being unfamiliar with these workers' ways and leanings, it seemed a wise and cautious thing to allocate separate days for each gender.

Hilkka loved going to the public sauna. To enter, one had to pay an attendant by passing money through a tiny little opening. Aili and Hilkka knew that as soon as the money had disappeared through the opening, they would be given a bottle of red soda to drink after their sauna. This was to prevent dehydration, but when they were little they didn't know that and they didn't care. They just liked the red soda.

On the mainland, many families had their own family saunas, and there would come a day in her future when Hilkka would learn and understand more about the mystical significance and power of these structures; but for the time being she knew only that she felt shiny clean and relaxed after her bath, and that she enjoyed the delicious aftertaste of the sparkling soda in her mouth.

The public sauna was in a complex that contained the sauna itself and the dressing room for the sauna. Attached to those facilities were the wash house where people did their laundry and the communal baking ovens where they all made regular bread and specialty breads like Finnish coffee bread (*pulla*). The islanders shared many parts of their lives with each other, as small communities often do.

The house itself contained four small apartments, two on each floor. The Valtonens had one of the ground floor apartments. Everyone on the island called the house the "White House" because it's broad expanse of wood was painted a gleaming white. The window sills and shutters, by contrast, were deep green, as were the window boxes which in summertime Selma planted with brightly coloured flowers. Inside the house, potted geraniums sat on the window sills, lending splashes of colour to the white exterior during both summer and winter. Everywhere there were lilac bushes, daisies, tiger lilies, roses, perennials of all kinds and they, added to the beauty of the pines and the birches and the nearby beaches with their rows of boats left trustingly on the sand, gave the whole place a comfortable and settled appearance.

The family moved eventually to a second location when a new mill manager assigned Aleksanteri a change in responsibilities. Since his duties no longer included having to care for the horses, Aleksanteri didn't need to be near the manager's house any more; and so the Valtonens moved to a building which had eight apartments, each slightly larger than the one they were leaving. Their new home was located high up on a hill, giving the family a magnificent view of the land below, and even better, it was close to the outside well with its bucket, rope and cold clear drinking water.

Evidence of Selma's homemaking skills were everywhere in the house. She had sewn the curtains which graced their windows. She had hand crafted the rugs which covered their floors. She had made the rugs out of old rags which she had torn into strings and then loomed into breathtakingly beautiful designs, creating area rugs and long runners that were works of art. Hilkka loved the patterns and colours in the rugs and would go down to the shore with the women in the spring time to help clean them and see the colours refreshed. The spring time cleaning ritual was something the island women shared. It seemed to Hilkka that all the mommies and grammas on the island would gather at the big dock, where they would proceed to scrub their loomed and braided rugs with homemade lye soap and stiff brushes and then rinse them in the lake. She loved the sight and smell of the cleaning and the sound of the women's voices as they visited outside in the spring sunshine after the long Finnish winter.

The Valtonen girls were responsible for the housework in their home during the summer when school was out, and they worked hard to try and do a good job. The sawmill provided electricity for light to the island houses from six in the morning until ten at night. Selma would wake up first at six a.m., light the wood stove, prepare the coffee and then wake the girls by shaking them by the toes. Selma and Aleksanteri would have a cup of rich dark coffee and a piece of bread with butter and go immediately to work. The children would then do the dishes and clean the rooms, after which they

The tradition continues.
Aili and her daughter Lea wash rugs at the dock,
keeping the spring time ritual alive.

would begin lunch preparations. Lunch was served when the parents arrived back for their mid-day meal at eleven a.m. The food was always the same. Every day for years they had boiled potatoes and sauce made out of pork fat, onions, flour, water and salt, accompanied by the ever present strong Finnish coffee. The parents came home at eleven, ate quickly and returned to work. The girls cleaned up and then they had some free time, with strict rules as to how they must behave.

Occasionally, they would get a bit rambunctious and playful while they worked. This sometimes led to disastrous results. One day, while they were tending to their chores—Hilkka to making the beds and Aili to doing the dishes—Hilkka tiptoed up behind Aili and threw a bed sheet over her head. Unfortunately Aili was carrying a stack of dishes at the time and they went crashing to the floor, breaking and shattering all around them. As they cleaned up the bits and pieces of china that were now just fragments in a pile of debris, Hilkka resigned herself to the spanking that she knew was coming her way, and which she further knew she deserved.

The children had great respect for their father. He was stern and strict but he was devoted to them and always fair in his treatment of them. The rules he set for them were clearly understood and justly administered. Their father was the head of the household, and when he came home from work and entered through the doorway, he became king. Aleksanteri Valtonen was a handsome man, very tall and sturdy with a commanding presence. He always had a hot toddy when he came home from his day's heavy labour at the sawmill. Made with boiling water, spirits and spices, the drink was poured into a glass-lined silver cup.

Aleksanteri would sit in his chair at the head of the table and stir the drink in his cup with a small silver spoon. The children always wondered what was in that cup to make him enjoy it so, and one day he let them have a tiny sip as a special treat. Hilkka liked the taste very much. The spices and the sweet hot whiskey left a delicious sensation in her mouth, but Aleksanteri wouldn't allow them anything more than that one little taste. "When you are older," he told them, "you will be able to have your own hot toddy, but for now you are too little." When dinner time came, Aleksanteri always sat at the head of the table, and always had his utensils laid out for him in the same way for every meal. He was served first, as was his due. He was, after all, the one ultimately responsible for the safety and care of the family. He had his routines and traditions, and set for his daughters an example for leadership and familial respect that stayed with them throughout their lives.

Aleksanteri was exceedingly careful with the household money and frugal and thrifty in his buying habits. There were few, if any, frivolous or impulsive purchases. Aleksanteri always bought things that would be durable and lasting, and shoes for his daughters were always bought just a little bit too big so that the girls' feet could "grow into them." Hilkka's eyes shone with delight when he returned from one particular trip to the mainland with a pair of soft leather lace-up boots for her . . . but the shine faded a bit when she tried them on. They were a size nine, many sizes too big for her tiny feet. She wore them faithfully for many years. They were of such a fine quality that they never wore out, and her feet never did grow into them. Throughout her life those dainty feet were to remain a size smaller than the beautiful leather boots her father brought to Lamposaari for her.

In the summertime, Hilkka and Aili played ball games with their friends, jumped rope and played at each other's houses. The White House in which the Valtonens lived was a favourite place for the others to come to play, as was the beach where they could swim on especially hot days. Hilkka remembered how she had learned to swim when she was very little. Iida had encouraged her to put her tiny hands on the bottom of the lake and walk on them, and then to "walk with her hands" while *not* touching the bottom.

With the warm sun shining and the water softly lapping on the shore, Hilkka would sometimes sit quietly day-dreaming and then she would write poems about her dreams. Her poems were lovely, but she didn't always share them with other people. They were her secret thoughts, private and personal.

The children were usually in bed by eight p.m., a source of some irritation to Hilkka who frequently wanted to keep on going until the electricity was turned off and the oil lamps turned on. Most of the time however, she would be sound asleep well before ten p.m., as would be everyone else in the family, so the oil lamps were seldom used.

Prayers were always said at bedtime, and then, once everyone was tucked safely in under their covers, they would sing out to each other in the dark: "Good night Mommy Darling . . . Daddy Darling . . . and Aili Darling . . . Hilkka Darling." Then, having addressed the Lord and each other with love, they would sleep.

The children had a nighttime curfew, and Selma and Aleksanteri were strict about them adhering to it. One evening Hilkka was playing hide and seek with her friends when her father called her in. Wanting to finish the game, Hilkka whispered to one of her playmates to tell her father that she wasn't with them. Aleksanteri received the message, but Aleksanteri wasn't stupid. He knew that Hilkka was hiding so that she wouldn't have to come in. He turned without a word and went back into the house, locking the door behind him.

When Hilkka finally finished her playing and decided that it was time to go home to bed, she was met with the locked door and knew that she was in big trouble. She knocked. She knocked again. There was no answer. She knocked on the wooden door once more, growing more apprehensive each time her hesitant tapping went unacknowledged.

Aleksanteri finally opened the door and told Hilkka to go and fetch a birch switch. Hilkka knew that the birch switch was going to be used for a spanking, and that she was going to be the recipient of its stinging slap. Obediently she did as she was requested to do. She searched out the gentlest of branches and peeled off the branches that she felt would administer the most pain and returned with the switch to her father. She was told to go back and get a better, more effective switch. This she did, once again peeling off branches, but not quite as obviously as she had done before. Her father couldn't help but laugh at her perseverance and determination to minimize any trauma that might come her way. Even though both of them knew that the punishment should have proceeded—children need to learn that actions have consequences after all—both father and daughter recognized the humour of the moment, and Aleksanteri realized more than ever that his daughter was becoming a realistic, clever and courageous young lady. Aleksanteri could see the big picture. The punishment that day was not meted out.

Aili and Hilkka on a return visit to Lamposaari many years after their childhood there.

Aili (left) and Hilkka (right) in front of the Valtonen family home.

Aili (right) and Hilkka (left) in front of the mill manager's house.

CHAPTER FOUR

Selma

Hilkka's mother had been forty years old when Hilkka was born and forty-two when Aili came into the world. She and Aleksanteri had previously buried an infant son and a two year old daughter who had died of pneumonia. When Selma was pregnant with Hilkka, Aleksanteri had hoped his dear wife was carrying another boy, because he wanted to have a son in his family. When Hilkka was born, however, and he saw that he had another daughter, he was overjoyed to have her and he blessed Selma for giving him such a beautiful girl. Hilkka quickly became her father's favourite, but Aleksanteri never spoiled her, and never showed her favouritism over her two sisters. No brothers for his daughters ever arrived in the Valtonen household, but Aleksanteri was content with his family and proud of his children.

For Selma, her three daughters brought continuous joy and helped numb the pain of having lost her two other children. Iida, who had not died, and Hilkka and Aili, who came to her later in life, were therefore precious to her. Selma spent many peaceful and tender moments in her rocking chair, holding her two littlest girls on her lap and singing hymns and folk ballads to them.

As the girls grew, and took on chores, they became a genuine blessing. She could not, for example, have managed her mainland farm garden without them. The mainland garden had been Selma's idea, but she could not do it alone. By being frugal and careful with her spending, she had saved up a little money and at her request Aleksanteri rented a bit of land on the mainland from a farmer who needed to augment his income.

The garden became a source of nutritious food for the family and together they would row over to the mainland to plant and tend the vegetables. They grew mostly potatoes and root vegetables on the farmer's land, things which could store well over the winter; and near the house on Lamposaari they had a small garden with carrots and green onions. The forests and meadows also provided nourishment for the family. Selma would take her children with her into the wild places to help her pick mushrooms and berries. Each girl had a little mug of her own to fill with berries and they were allowed to eat – literally – the fruits of their labour. Hilkka especially loved the sun-ripened juicy berries with their sweet full flavour. Selma would later make pies from the fruit and jams to fill their larder for the winter.

Hilkka and Aili were not supposed to touch the newly preserved fruit, but they did anyway. On one occasion, they each smuggled a glass jar of sweet fruit out of the kitchen and hid them under their father's big bed. When no one was looking they gobbled up the entire contents of the jars, leaving the empty glasses and spoons under the bed, intending to sneak back later to get them, wash them and put them away in the cupboard. Unfortunately for them Selma was faster in her cleaning than Hilkka and Aili were in getting rid of the evidence, and when she was sweeping the bedroom, she discovered the two empty glass jars and two sticky little spoons.

The two precious girls who came to Selma later in life,
Hilkka in back, Aili in front.

It was a compliment to Selma that her daughters liked her preserves so much, but rules had been broken, and Selma's expressions of disappointment at their disobedience hurt the girls more than anything else could have.

Hilkka did not fail her parents in her diligent attention to the tasks she was given to help with the household, and despite her sometimes impulsive misbehaviour, she had developed a good work ethic.

If there were spankings for misbehaving, there were also rewards for being good. The children were not given an allowance per se, but they were given a small amount of money now and then to purchase a treat. It wasn't much, but if they saved it up they could buy something special. For Hilkka there was one delicious treat that she always loved. When the farmers came to the island from the mainland to sell their produce in the Tori (Farmers' Market), they would also bring with them wagons full of berries and baked goodies. Hilkka would run with her money to buy a "piggy." Oh, they were so good, those piggies! The large soft jam busters shaped like piglets and filled with sweet jam, the flavour of which would burst into her mouth when she bit into the center, were absolutely wonderful. She would try to eat her piggy slowly to savour the taste as long as she could, but invariably she would gobble it up with unseemly haste because it was just "so good."

Fortunately, the beloved piggies were not part of Hilkka's regular diet, since a trip to the dentist was both infrequent and expensive. Food at home was hearty and plain and typical of island fare. There were no cows or goats on the island, so milk came from the mainland in large cans. In these milk cans, rich cream floated to the top and skim milk sank to the bottom. Selma would use the milk in many combinations of cream and skim, and Hilkka especially enjoyed a cold drink in which the two were stirred together.

While there were no cows or goats around, nor were there turkeys or other fowl to be found, there were some animals on Lamposaari. Selma had a pig to which she fed cooked potato peels. Although she discouraged the children from treating the animal like a pet, it nonetheless was given a name, Liisa. That Liisa's ultimate destination would be to be slaughtered for meat was known and accepted by the family.

Aleksanteri was one of the men on the island who slaughtered and butchered pigs for his own family and for others. The children understood that when he shooed them away and took out his gun and his big knife there would be one pig less on the island and more roasts and chops and hams in the cold cellar. The cold cellar was deep in the ground and was shared by several families. Filled with blocks of ice cut from the lake in winter which were kept frozen by a covering of sawdust, the cellar's air was cold and close to freezing all summer long. There the families stored foodstuffs they wished to keep fresh and it worked well for them all.

After a pig was butchered, every part of it was put to use for the humans who had raised it. The head was boiled and from it Hilkka's mother made head cheese, which was not actually a cheese, but rather a jellied meat dish. Despite the grisly way in which it was prepared, the resulting concoction was delicious and good for building strong fingernails and bones. Pig's feet and knuckles, high in protein and surprisingly low in fat, were slow-cooked with onions in large pots. Using the lentils that she kept in the cupboard, Selma made hearty pea soups from ham bones. Lard rendered from the pig was used for baking and, when mixed with lye made from wood ashes, for making soap. Hams and bacon were cured, and sausage and ground meat were prepared and set aside for the family to enjoy.

CHAPTER FIVE

Holy Days

There were other delicious treats that came the girls' way throughout the year. Sometimes at Sunday school the children would be given sweets to eat, which made the religious lessons something to look forward to. Hilkka needed no incentive to attend Sunday school, though, and the treats she received there were simply extra reasons to enjoy the lessons she was taught. Hilkka was blessed with the ability to read something once and remember it; and both her regular school and the Sunday school gave her ample opportunity to explore ideas and literature.

There was no church on the island, but there was a good-sized congregation of Lutherans, and the Valtonens were among them. Most Sundays, their services and Sunday school were led by a devout Christian man who lived on Lamposaari, and on special Sundays, the Lutheran pastor from the mainland would come. Palm Sunday was one of those days, as was Easter Sunday.

In preparation for Palmusunnuntai, as Palm Sunday was known, Hilkka and Aili would gather pussy willow branches and decorate them with streams of coloured crepe paper. These switches, which were called *virpovitsa*, were carried with them when they went to their Godmother's house on Palm Sunday.

On Palm Sunday morning Hilkka and Aili would get up early and dress in their most beautiful clothes. They had light green soft wool dresses with little flowers embroidered on them. They wore long smooth cotton stockings instead of the scratchy woolen ones, hand knit with raw wool, which every-one wore in the winter. With their legs deliciously encased in their smooth cotton stockings, Hilkka and Aili put on their good shoes. What a delight it was to dress up in these wonderful garments, to put on such delicate shoes and stockings! Dressing up was always saved for special days and was there-fore a thrill for the island girls.

Most days, and always in cold weather, they would be dressed in rougher clothing; woolen underwear (*villa-alusvaatteet*), long woolen stockings held up with garters (a sure sign of spring was the sight of woolen stockings being rolled down to the ankles!) with long wool pants (*pitkät villahousut*) on top of them. Woolen dresses were worn on top of both of these items. When they were outside, they wore heavy felt outerwear and felt boots, with knitted hats and mittens. In wet weather the felt boots were replaced with leather ones, which were not nearly as warm, but which didn't soak up water the same way felt did. Hilkka and Aili had boots made of red felt which were the envy of their classmates, since Selma was an expert at creating colours from reci-pes using vegetable dyes. (Her one disaster was an attempt to turn Hilkka's grey stockings into a soft yellow. They turned instead into a hideous orange. Hilkka hated the colour, but had to wear the stockings anyhow because too much effort had gone into their making to not use them.) To make stockings and other woolen clothing, Selma would buy lamb's wool from a mainland shepherd, spin the fleece into wool, dye and shrink the wool and knit the gar-ment. These clothes formed the basic daily wardrobe worn by the Valtonens and most of the other families on Lamposaari.

The soft light wool from which the girls Easter dresses were knitted made them, therefore, a most significant part of the Easter week celebra-tions. After getting dressed, Hilkka and Aili brushed their blond hair with extra care. Aili would put a pretty bow in her hair, while Hilkka added ribbons at the ends of her braids. It was usually cold early in the morning at that time of year—they were after all north of the 60th parallel—and sometimes there would be ice on the road as they hurried to their Godmother's house to give her their decorated pussy willow branches. They would be welcomed into the warmth of the home and once inside, they would stretch out their branches, and gently whisking them to touch their Godmother, they would recite a traditional poem which said:

virvon, varvon vitsallani
tuoreeks terveeks
tulevaks vuodeks
vitsa sulle, muna mulle

For freshness, for health
for the coming year
The branch for you,
The treat for me

With this verse and the good wishes it contained, the children handed their branches to their Godmother. Having presented their *virpovitsa*, they knew that when they returned on the next Sunday, which was Easter Sunday, they would be given a treat. And so it would happen. On Easter Sunday they would return and would indeed be given a special treat—a chocolate egg, which had inside it a ring to wear on their fingers. Hilkka could never figure out how that ring could get inside the egg. Pastor had told them that Easter was a miracle and so she guessed that a ring inside an egg was part of the miracle.

During the week leading up to the Easter celebration, the children prepared decorated eggs with the help of their mother and school teacher. Selma would boil eggs in water which was coloured with the peels of red and yellow onions. Once they were hard cooked and deepened to a rich colour, Hilkka and Aili would decorate them at school with water colour paints, creating individual designs and pictures on the shells that were, as their parents told them, "*kaunis* . . . beautiful." These eggs were displayed with pride at Easter and would last all year, the inside contents drying up and disappearing as the months passed.

Good Friday, at the end of the week, was a quiet and solemn day, but Easter Sunday was a feast day, and everyone was in a good mood. Father would go out to play cards with his friends and come home before dinner with little pouches full of red and pink candies for his daughters, candies that melted in one's mouth without having to be chewed. While he had been out, a delicious ham had been cooked, filling their small home with delicious aromas and moist warmth. Everyone dressed in their very best clothes for the evening meal and the family sat down together as if they were all guests. Easter was one of Hilkka's favourite holidays. When the girls were finished eating, they would go to the corner of the table, as they did after all their dinners, cross their hands on the table in front of them, and give thanks to God for the food they had just eaten. They would then thank their parents and be excused.

Perhaps her very most favourite holiday, though, was Christmas. The baby in the crèche and the young mother bending over him was a magical vision that stayed in her memory all year and the thrill of Joulupukki (Santa Claus) arriving could not be outdone by anything else in the world. The children would be on the watch from early in the evening, for Santa's elves would peek first into the windows to see if the children were at home and being good, and then Santa would knock loudly on the front door of the house.

The children would be beside themselves with excitement. It was Santa! With a sack of gifts!!! Sometimes Santa looked suspiciously like someone they knew, and sometimes Santa arrived a bit later than they had expected him because other homes had given him generous cups of whiskey. Ah, but he always came and he always brought presents for them, and in turn they gave him goodies to eat, but they gave him no whiskey to drink. Mother did not allow that, for she said that Santa still had a long way to travel.

Christmas dinner was always served on Christmas Eve. Succulent ham was cooked, as well as meatballs in gravy, herring salad, traditional casseroles, potatoes, turnips, carrots, rice, liver, *piirakka* (potatoes or rice baked in a rye flour crust), and rice pudding with sweet mixed fruit sauce. The family sat to dinner, as they did at Easter, in their very best clothes. Before the festive meal was eaten, Father read aloud the Christmas story from the big Bible. He had a deep, full voice and the magic inherent in the story came to life as he read. The meal was consumed with great delight, and when they were finished and full to bursting, it was to the children that the task of cleaning up was assigned. After giving their thanks at the corner of the table, they moved swiftly to complete their duties in the kitchen, since they were not allowed to open their gifts until everything was done to restore the room to order.

Then finally, they were allowed to light the little candles they had earlier tied carefully to the branches of the Christmas tree. The tree itself hung from the ceiling over the table that was in front of the window. The hanging tree was unique to many Finnish and Scandinavian people because the rooms in their houses were traditionally small with little space to place a tree inside the dwelling. There in the evergreen branches, among the red apples, gingerbreads and tiny flags from countries of the world with which they had decorated their tree, the lighted candles gave off a soft glow and honeyed scent. With the fragrance of the pine needles and the aroma of the roasted ham still lingering in the air, Hilkka would inhale deeply and be filled with utter contentment.

Christmas day itself was generally a quiet, peaceful sort of a day. Books and magazines were always among the gifts opened the night before, and the family members would lounge about the tiny home, reading all day and eating leftovers. For all of these reasons, Hilkka counted this to be her most favourite holiday.

CHAPTER SIX

Leaving Lamposaari

As she grew older, Hilkka began to tire of her braids. Long braids might have been all right for her when she was younger, but now she was older and she wanted a stylish short hairdo, one that was more grown-up looking. Only little children wore braids. Her parents, however, didn't share her enthusiasm for the idea, and told her that she couldn't get her hair cut. She was, they said, "too young to wear a grown-up hairdo."

Determined to make her dream come true, Hilkka went to the place where they cut people's hair, and had her long braids cut off without anyone's permission. When she saw the results of this action in the mirror she was aghast. Where was the image of a sophisticated and fashionable young woman she had expected to see? The face she saw looking back at her from the mirror must surely be distorted by some quirk of reflection! The creature in the glass looked horrible! The hairdo was a disaster, and there was nothing she could do about it. The deed was done and the braids could not be glued back on. She was ashamed of her appearance, and worse still she had yet to face an angry and disappointed father. She had been disobedient and foolhardy. Grown-up looking or not, Hilkka was still young enough to get a spanking, which she did get.

Hilkka's determination to get her hair cut was just one signal that she was indeed beginning to seek her own way in the world. Seeing that, Aleksanteri began to worry that she would end up working in the sawmill like so many other island children had done, because there was no other work on the island. He understood her intellect and great curiosity and he knew that a life as a labourer in the mill would dry her up and she would never realize her true potential. He knew this from personal experience, and he didn't want it for her. When she was fourteen, and therefore finished her formal education, Aleksanteri told her that he thought she was too smart to spend her life working in the mill and that he wanted her to move to the mainland, to Finland's capital city of Helsinki, to seek employment.

Hilkka was extremely upset by her father's words. Leave Lamposaari? How could she leave Lamposaari? She loved it there. She knew everybody. She had many, many friends, and they had their own ways of having fun and being happy. She couldn't understand why he would want her to leave. Didn't he love her and want to have her around? When her father told her of his plans for her, Hilkka ran with tears in her eyes to the nearby woods, where she hid and sobbed until her eyes were red and swollen and she could cry no more. She had shed countless tears and yet still her heart was heavy with great sorrow.

In time she would understand it was in fact her father's deep love for her that made him want her to have more opportunity than she could find in the sawmill—opportunity to grow and create and achieve, to have dreams and be able to fulfill them—but when she was just fourteen years old and getting ready to leave all that was familiar and comfortable and precious, it was hard to understand. As her life unfolded, however, there were to be many occasions on which she would realize that her father was a wise man.

The journey away from home was made easier by the fact that Hilkka's older sister Iida had married a captain of one of the tugboats which plied the waters near Lamposaari. Iida and her husband lived on the mainland on a small farm in the countryside. They owned some livestock—a few horses and cows—and grew a variety of crops and vegetables. Iida's home was familiar to Hilkka, since she had visited there during the summer with her parents and Aili. It was Iida and her husband who had alerted Aleksanteri, through a mutual friend, that there was a couple in Helsinki who could provide the perfect place of employment for Hilkka. The couple, Anselm and Iida Käkelä, needed a housekeeper and a caregiver for their baby daughter Seija.

Nervously Hilkka prepared for the train trip to Helsinki. Her sister Iida had loaned her a uniquely and beautifully hand-crafted wooden carrying case, which Hilkka would be the first to use. Iida's generous gesture touched Hilkka deeply because the case was the work of a master craftsman who was a true artist. It was lined with velvet, hinged on sloping sides and secured with leather straps and belts. The wood with which it was made was polished to a high shine, and it was big enough to contain all of Hilkka's belongings. With such a magnificent carrying case in her possession, Hilkka's nerves were somewhat calmed. Her luggage at least would have a look of sophistication and culture, and perhaps as passersby glanced to admire it, they wouldn't notice that Hilkka's knees were quaking as she sat beside it.

The day before Hilkka was to leave Lamposaari, she and her father sat side by side on the outdoor steps in silence for a long, long time. Both recognized that Hilkka's carefree childhood was swiftly coming to a close and both grieved its passage. "Oh, that one could stay young forever and never have to grow up and leave home!" was Hilkka's thought. "Oh, that one's precious children could stay little and innocent forever and never have to face the world on their own!" was Aleksanteri's thought. In mute and mutual misery they sat together, immersed in their private thoughts and wondering what tomorrow would bring for Hilkka.

Aleksanteri and Hilkka

The next day, when it was time for Hilkka to leave, she clung tightly to her mother and sister as if she would never see them again, and they all wept until their faces were wet with tears. Then Hilkka and her father left by boat for the mainland where Aleksanteri threw off his customary frugality and bought his daughter a stylish new coat and hat. Traveling by bus to the train station in Lappeenranta wearing her new outer garments, Hilkka tried not to be nervous about the journey ahead of her and the life waiting for her at the end of it.

In Lappeenranta, Aleksanteri purchased a magazine entitled *Lukemista Kaikille* (Reading for Everyone) and gave it to Hilkka, instructing her to hold on to the magazine in her hand when she got off the train in Helsinki, because it was an item by which her future employer would identify her. Her father then embraced her and put her on the train to Helsinki. Hilkka watched out the window as the train pulled out until she could see him no more.

And so, in 1936, at the age of fourteen, Hilkka Valtonen journeyed to Helsinki, leaving her beloved Lamposaari and her childhood behind her.

SECTION
TWO

FINLAND
HELSINKI & PERKKIÖ
1936 – 1952

CHAPTER ONE

The Käkeläs

Hilkka held the magazine her father had given her throughout the train ride, clutching it so tightly that it became moist and limp because of her perspiring palms. She arrived at the Helsinki station to find Anselm Käkelä waiting for her. He approached her as she disembarked. Having noted the magazine and recognizing her nervousness, he smiled gently and introduced himself, asking politely if she was Hilkka Valtonen. Shyly she replied that she was, and he, smiling again to ease her anxiety, lifted and carried her wooden case from the platform. They took the street car—a new experience for Hilkka—to the family's comfortable, albeit small, apartment.

Reaching the apartment and seeing the smiling wife, Iida, and little baby girl Seija helped Hilkka relax. Here was the familiarity of a home and family, something that she understood. Iida, the wife, she discovered, was a kind lady and the little baby was adorable. She was told that her duties would be to look after the baby during the day while Iida was at work, and that she was also to take telephone messages for Anselm. Hilkka thought that she could manage the job without too much difficulty.

Although the tiny apartment was crowded the household members managed. Hilkka slept in the corner of the Käkelä's bedroom and the baby's bed was beside the parents. A nephew slept in the kitchen.

Iida worked in a shop where she made silk lamp shades and Anselm repaired slot machines in gambling establishments. Both parents worked hard and were planning towards a secure financial future. Since Hilkka would be answering the business phone, Anselm gave her instructions in proper business telephone etiquette, demonstrating how to be thorough and professional in words and tone. Hilkka was by nature courteous and polite, and she recognized immediately that being professional essentially meant being considerate and helpful. As she took messages for Anselm from those wanting repairs to their machines, carefully recording customers' phone numbers for him so that he could return their calls, her confidence in being able to acquire new levels of expertise grew; and her shyness at encountering new people began to fade.

Iida Käkelä liked to cook, and she was justifiably proud of her culinary skills. When she came home at the end of her working day, she would cook dinner for the household while Hilkka cared for the infant. Hilkka found this routine more than acceptable, since it spared her the task of preparing the evening meal, but she would linger in the kitchen all the same, because she was also keen to learn new recipes from Iida. Many of Iida's recipes eventually became part of Hilkka's own cuisine.

Iida enjoyed finding herself in the role of mentor. She took Hilkka under her wing and passed on to her many of her own homemaking skills and traditions. It was Iida who taught Hilkka to make a bed with sharply creased hospital corners on the bed sheets. Hilkka loved the tight and tidy look of the bed when it was made in this fashion. She became meticulous in paying attention to this detail, and would eventually pass down the art of presenting a well made bed to her children and grandchildren and even her housekeepers.

Hilkka with the Käkelä baby in Helsinki.

The year that Hilkka turned fifteen was a year in which she stepped into the adult world in a wide variety of ways. Of great spiritual significance to her was the moment that she was confirmed in the local Lutheran Church.

A personal confirmation of faith in Christianity is a rite of passage for Finnish Lutherans, and occurs for most baptized adherents when they begin to mature or reach "the age of reason", usually in the year of their fifteenth birthday. Confirmation (*Konfirmaatiomessu*) has its roots in the Bible's New Testament when the Holy Spirit was received by Christians through the laying on of apostolic hands. In the Lutheran Church, the Pastor lays his hands on the head of the person seeking to be confirmed and it can be a highly emotional moment for many who kneel before him. The act of confirmation was, for Hilkka, much more than a mere coming of age.

Confirmation does not happen automatically. This public profession of faith must be preceded by intense and thorough instruction in the tenants of faith. Hilkka, eager as always to study and learn as she did in Sunday school back on Lamposaari, was given the opportunity, while living with the Käkeläs, to attend Confirmation classes (*rippikoulu*) in the evenings. She was greatly excited about her lessons and worked diligently to prepare herself for the ceremony to come, and for her first Communion (the taking of bread and wine commemorating Christ's sacrifice of His body and blood, as instructed by Him to His disciples at the Last Supper) which would be part of the service. She memorized the Apostle's Creed (*Apostolinen Uskontunnustus*) which declared her belief:

I believe in God, the Father Almighty, Maker of heaven and earth.
And in Jesus Christ, His only Son, our Lord; who was conceived by the
Holy Ghost, born of the Virgin Mary; suffered under Pontius Pilate,
was crucified, died and was buried. He descended into hell.
The third day He rose again from the dead;
He ascended into heaven and sitteth on the right hand
of God the Father Almighty;
From thence He shall come to judge the quick and the dead.
I believe in the Holy Ghost, the Holy Christian Church,
the Communion of Saints, the Forgiveness of Sins,
the Resurrection of the Body, and the Life Everlasting. Amen.

This creed she was never to forget. Its words, along with the words of her beloved Lord's Prayer, were to sustain her throughout her life.

Traditionally the girls who were being confirmed wore white garments, to symbolize the purity of their faith. Iida, who was helping Hilkka prepare for the day, took her to the department store to purchase a white confirmation dress and matching shoes and stockings. Hilkka tried not to feel too much pride at the beauty of her clothing, but it was impossible not to be pleased at the image reflected back at her from the mirror as she dressed for her confirmation. In most cases when the *rippikolu* lessons were complete and the confirmands received first Communion, their families were present to share the special event with them. With Hilkka's family so far away, it was Iida Käkelä who greeted Hilkka after the service with four tulips and it was Iida Käkelä who took her to the photographers to record the day.

It was a great celebration, physically and spiritually, and was one more step on Hilkka's journey to maturity

Sixty two years after Hilkka's confirmation, in 1999, at the first Lutheran Church of Venice, California, far away from Finland, Hilkka's great-granddaughter Courtney kneels to be confirmed as Hilkka had done so many decades before.

In 2003, sixty-six years after her own confirmation, Hilkka joined in celebration with her granddaughter Scarlet as she received her first communion in the Catholic Church in Kitchener, Ontario. Left to right, Gramma Hilkka, Auntie Liisa and big sister Alia with Peter's daughter Scarlet on her special day.

Hilkka on her confirmation day.
1937

CHAPTER TWO

The Beginning of Always

Hilkka enjoyed living with the Käkelä's and she grew to love their little girl, but her mind was wandering and she knew that she needed more challenge and excitement in her life. As she became used to the city, and she became more and more familiar with stores and shopping, she thought that she would like to work in a store. She felt that she would be good at selling things and servicing customers. She liked to see people being happy because they were able to buy something they needed or wanted.

There was a store on a corner near the apartment where she lived with her employers, run by a Swedish couple, the Lundels, who spoke both Swedish and Finnish. Hilkka liked going into the store and she gradually struck up a friendship with its owners. One day the Lundels asked her if she could help them out. They needed someone to help in their home, housekeeping, cooking and caring for their two girls who were in kindergarten. Best of all from Hilkka's perspective, they also needed someone to help out a bit in the store, and they felt that she would be able to do all of those things well. Would she be interested in working for them? Do fish swim in the ocean? Hilkka jumped at the chance!

Taking the job entailed learning to speak Swedish, since many of the store's customers were Swedish and liked to be served in that language. So Hilkka, fast and eager learner that she was, learned to speak Swedish. Picking up that second language opened more doors for her.

One of those open doors led to her first experience with kissing a boy. Still young and inexperienced with the opposite sex, and ignorant of sexual matters, Hilkka accepted an invitation to attend a dance with a Swedish boy who had met her through the store. Hilkka had a good time at the dance, enjoying the music, the whirl of activity and the company of the young man who had escorted her. He walked her home and as they came to her door, he asked if he could have a goodnight kiss. She said yes, he could, and she leaned forward expecting a light brushing of his lips on hers. To her utter shock and horror, as she said later, "He put his whole mouth in my mouth—even his whole tongue!" Having experienced nothing like this before, Hilkka was so stunned and surprised that she immediately gagged and then ran upstairs and washed out her mouth. It was her first and last date with the hapless lad. "I guess," she recalled, "I was pretty naive."

As Hilkka kept watching for opportunities to progress, she spotted a newspaper ad, seeking trainees for HOK Dairy Stores. Both her previous employers (the Käkeläs and the Lundels) provided her with glowing recommendations, and with those references, her application to enter the HOK training program was accepted. Hilkka was thrilled to be part of the dairy division of such a prestigious company.

The HOK company had a bakery division as well as a dairy one, and the bakery division, responding to requests from the military, had began a recruiting drive for new employees who were needed especially to bake bread for the Finnish military. A training program was promised for these new employees. The bakery division offered more money than the dairy stores, so Hilkka applied for a position with that division, was accepted, and became a bakery trainee.

By now Hilkka had turned sixteen and with the higher wages she was earning, she was able to get her own small—very small—apartment above a store. The tiny dwelling place had room for only a bed, a table and a lamp. But it was hers alone, and it was enough.

At the bakery she worked at a long table, making bread. She had not made bread on Lamposaari. It was something that her mother had always done, so the task assigned her in the bakery was a new one for Hilkka. She enjoyed her job, the aroma of the bread and other baked goods, and the people who worked with her. One woman in particular was especially kind to the "new girl" and went out of her way to help Hilkka learn her job. Such small things made life pleasant for Hilkka at the bakery and she was happy.

In addition to the satisfaction she felt because of her working conditions, the knowledge that her baking would help feed brave Finnish soldiers, who were preparing for an impending war with Russia, gave her pride and purpose in her work. When Finland was attacked, as anticipated, by the Russian Red Army on November 30, 1939 and the war began, Hilkka and the others in the bakery supplied endless loaves of nourishing and life-sustaining bread to the Finnish war effort. The Finnish soldiers were strong and hardy outdoorsmen, expert skiers whose swift passage over treacherous terrain was legendary. In their white snowsuits they were perfectly camouflaged for winter battle and they blended so well with the landscape that they were all but invisible to the enemy. The Russian attack on Finland came to be known as the Winter War, and the Finnish army became widely respected for its skill in winter warfare. Hilkka was proud to be helping feed these remarkable men who were defending her country.

Hilkka returns to Lamposaari to visit.
Left to right, Helmi (family friend), Hilkka, Aili, Selma

Hilkka Valtonen was a very pretty girl, an innocent who was just beginning to blossom into womanhood and who was blissfully unaware of her charms. The two men who worked near her in the bakery found her to be thoroughly delightful and were captivated by her beauty and her fresh and natural ways. They flirted with her and kept glancing her way as they worked.

Hilkka started to notice the men in return. One of them in particular she thought was especially good-looking. He would talk to her as they worked and they would laugh together. Hilkka discovered that she enjoyed being in the same place as this man. She didn't recognize the growing attraction between them. One day, he came over to her table, and bending slightly, softly kissed her arm. "You have flour on your arm, right there" he murmured, and Hilkka felt a warmth spreading through her that she had never felt before. He asked her if she would like to go out with him to a bar after work and she stammered and replied that she didn't go to bars. He bowed slightly, accepting her reply and he went back to his workplace, with a little bit of flour clinging to his mouth and chin. Hilkka was confused by her feelings, and by her reaction to his kiss.

Later while Hilkka was filling a cup for a drink of water, the other man who worked nearby sidled over to her and said rather loudly, "Boy you sure have nice breasts!" Hilkka wasn't the least bit confused by her feelings about this fellow. She had a cup of water in her hand and she tossed the water at his face without any hesitation. She was now old enough to know that even though she did have nice breasts, it was rude and overly familiar of him to say that to her. She heard a roar of laughter coming from the other side of the room, and turning around she saw the good-looking fellow who had kissed her arm doubled over howling with glee as his adversary was soundly put in his place by this delicate creature he so admired. Hilkka smiled herself, pleased with her ability to take charge of the situation.

Still laughing, Eeli Nygård, the baker who had kissed Hilkka Valtonen's arm and set her heart racing, came back to Hilkka's table and said, "I know you don't go to bars, but would you have dinner with me?" Hilkka needed breathing space. She couldn't say "No." The man had become irresistible. But she couldn't say "Yes." She wasn't ready. Everything was happening too fast. Besides she had nothing suitable to wear to dinner. So she said, "Ask me again in two weeks." And so he did. And she was ready.

Mrs. Lundel, her former employer at the Swedish store, had given Hilkka some richly coloured red wool material which was shot through with angora threads. Hilkka had taken the cloth to a tailor and was having it made into a dress, which would be completed within the week. She knew that this dress would look stunning on her, and that Eeli would like what he saw when she appeared in it. During the two weeks that she had asked Eeli to wait before inviting her out, Hilkka also made an extravagant and luxurious purchase. She bought an elegant black wool coat with a bell shaped skirt and Persian lamb trim on the hem, cuffs and collar. With her new red dress and her contrasting stylish black coat, Hilkka looked like a fashion model, and Eeli did indeed like what he saw.

Eeli Nygård as a young man.

When he came to pick her up, she noticed again, as she had before, what a nice clean good looking man he was, how well groomed, how politely he took her arm to guide her through the walkway. He took her to Restaurant Tenho, a sophisticated establishment that had white linen cloths on tables beautifully set with sparkling glasses and polished silverware. He ordered food for them from an elegant menu. And then they just sat there staring at each other. The food arrived and they stabbed away at it. It was delicious fare, well prepared, but they couldn't seem to eat. The food was hardly touched. Finally he reached across the table and took her hand in his. They sat like that for the rest of the evening, just sitting there at the table silently stroking each other's fingers and palms in wonderment, as if neither one of them had ever touched another person's hands before. Hilkka was seventeen. Eeli was twenty-six. The waiters didn't interrupt them. It was plain to all that they were smitten.

Hilkka had never felt her heart go "thump" before. She didn't know it was possible to be so suddenly and completely in love. Leaving the restaurant he once again took her arm, but there was much more than mere courtesy in his touch this time. Now he was protective, as if he were taking care of her, a precious thing to be kept safe from harm. He was tender in the way he held her arm, the arm he had playfully kissed not so very long ago; before he realized that he had fallen hopelessly in love with the woman walking by his side.

It was the autumn of 1939. The war had not yet come, but everyone in Finland was alert and braced for an impending Russian attack. The streets were dark because of this expectation and no street lights shone. Eeli walked Hilkka to her apartment, and knowing that it would still be fairly dark in the early morning, he offered to come back and walk her to work. The measure of his devotion was evident when one realized that Eeli lived close to the bakery with another bakery worker. To pick up Hilkka he had to walk past the bakery to get to her apartment and then double back with her on his arm. He did this just to be with her and to make sure that she came to no harm on her way. She in turn was deliriously happy to be holding his arm, feeling his strength and the warmth of his body.

Arriving at the bakery the morning after their dinner date, Hilkka and Eeli were surprised to find everyone upset and in possession of gas masks. "Haven't you heard?" they asked in amazement, "the Russians are going to drop poison gas on Helsinki!"

Like most establishments in Finland, the bakery was well prepared for facing such an attack, but the alleged takeover turned out to be an unfounded rumour. Hilkka and Eeli had been spared the trauma because they were so absorbed in each other that they couldn't notice anything else going on in the world around them. Oblivious to rumours and fear, they were overwhelmed by the first heady and glorious moments of love. To the end of her life, Hilkka would never forget what it felt like to be newly in love with Eeli Nygård.

It was a given that the two would marry. When Eeli proposed, the two young lovers walked miles in the winter cold to the jewelry store to purchase their rings and as a special gift from Eeli to Hilkka, a delicate lady's watch. Hilkka made the lengthy trip wearing silk stockings—lovely to look at but not warm enough for Finland in January—but was so in love and excited at the prospect of marrying Eeli that she didn't even feel the cold. Fortunately her legs and feet didn't freeze, giving credence to the song writer who wrote, "I've got my love to keep me warm . . . . "

Before announcing their engagement to others, Eeli sat down and carefully wrote a formal letter to Aleksanteri Valtonen, asking for permission to marry Alexsanteri's daughter Hilkka. Aleksanteri replied in like formal fashion, writing back to give permission for Hilkka Valtonen to be "joined in Christian Marriage with Eeli Nygård."

On January 15, 1940 Eeli and Hilkka announced their engagement to no one's surprise, and everyone was happy for them.

Because they were now engaged, the company policy dictated they had to work different shifts at the bakery. That separation, plus the fact that the Russians were now dropping bombs on Finland, made it difficult for the young lovers to see each other as often as they would have wished.

Throughout the turmoil, chaos, confusion and danger of the Winter War, Eeli Nygård was a vital part of the support system for the Finnish army. So steadfast was he in his commitment to feeding the troops that after the war ended on March 13, 1940, he was given a military medal of bravery, presented to him by the Finnish government for risking his life in time of war. Hilkka, who also risked her life by working to prepare bread for the military in time of danger, was awarded a civilian medal for bravery.

Eeli still lived with his fellow bakery worker in the house near the bakery. His room mate had a girlfriend and Eeli and Hilkka would socialize with the other couple when their schedules allowed them to do so. They were comfortable companions who enjoyed each others company, joking and laughing with the joyous abandon of carefree children. Despite the war, Hilkka was young and in love, with good friends and a satisfying job, and she had never been happier.

Hilkka Valtonen married Eeli Nygård on June 24, 1940 in the Mikael Agricola Lutheran Church in Helsinki, Finland. She was seventeen. He was twenty-six. They were to spend the rest of their lives together.

Hilkka wore a beautiful wedding dress and veil which was borrowed from her new sister in law Aili who had worn it at her own wedding not long before. Aili also arranged for the photographer and the flowers. The bride and groom walked home, the veil billowing in the wind around them as they made their way to their future together. It was a day to be treasured and indeed it was. As faithful Lutherans, Hilkka and Eeli pledged before their God to love and care for each other to the end of their days. It was for each of them a solemn vow, which they kept.

The Commemorative Medals for Bravery awarded to
Hilkka Valtonen and Eeli Nygård.

Mr. and Mrs. Eeli Nygård,
June 24, 1940

Hilkka, radiant on her wedding day.

CHAPTER THREE

A Smile & a Tear

Eeli and Hilkka took up residence in a small apartment on Josefatin Katu (Joseph Street). There they settled into marriage and began to forge their life together. Passionate in their love for each other and full of wonder at the newfound joys of physical union, they sought opportunities to overcome the vagaries of war and experience romance at its sweetest. They wanted to make love in the moonlight, beneath the soft light of the evening sky, with the fragrance of night blossoms and freshly cut grass all around them. This of course was not realistic during the dark stillness imposed on citizens because of the anticipated Continuation War with Russia, and the immediate impact of a world at war all around Finland. They couldn't even open their window to the outside city, since all windows in Helsinki were blacked out at night.

Seeking to create an illusion of moonlight, Eeli and Hilkka draped Eeli's blue silk shirt—a prized garment—over a standing lamp. The light thus produced was indeed very much like moonlight and its warm glow was just what the couple had been seeking. What they hadn't been seeking was the peculiar smell and oily smoke that came from burning cloth, melting silk and a smouldering lamp shade. The evening remained an exciting one, but in a somewhat different context than originally desired. Abandoning their amorous intentions, they rushed to extinguish the fire before it did more damage than simply ruining a favourite shirt. They would later smile as they recalled the incident, because the delight of getting to know each other as husband and wife made each day and every happening an adventure.

One terrible sorrow broke the happiness of Hilkka's days as a married woman. Aleksanteri Valtonen had a sudden stroke which left him paralyzed on one side of his body, and this once strong man was left disabled and unable to function as he had in his younger years. Pride made him attempt to continue as he had before, but he finally had to accept the fact that he needed Selma to care for him, to wash him and to help him dress. He had no wheelchair, so he dragged himself around the house and yard, still overseeing the running of the household with determined will.

Hilkka went to see him. To see her father, the powerful loving force that had guided her childhood, the working man who provided well for his family, who used to sit at the head of the table and sip his hot toddy and spank her when she did wrong . . . to see him thus reduced pained her heart. They spent time together talking and reminiscing. She told him of her life in Helsinki with Eeli, and how happy she was. Aleksanteri nodded with pleasure hearing her speak of these things, and Hilkka was to treasure these intimate moments with her father.

Not long after Hilkka returned to Helsinki, a blazing destructive fire broke out on Lamposaari. It burnt down the mill, and forced the Valtonens to re-locate to the mainland. They found a safe place to stay there, in the eastern part of Finland, but when the Russians invaded and occupied eastern Finland, Aleksanteri and Selma moved once more to the west coast of Finland to avoid being in Russian territory. Eventually they were able to return to Lamposaari, which was not occupied by Russia. By this time Aleksanteri was weakened and physically vulnerable.

The Winter War had ended with Finland reluctantly giving up a considerable amount of its eastern border to Russia as part of the peace agreement. All across the Finnish nation, a feeling of grave injustice and anger prevailed at this loss of Finnish territory; and the bitterness Finns felt towards Russia and the entire Soviet Union was palpable. The Continuation War, which continued Finland's efforts to defeat Russia and reclaim its lost territory, was on the horizon. Eeli had chosen to join the Air Force, where he was serving as both air and ground crew.

He wasn't part of air or ground crew very long however, because the military kept running short of bread and Eeli was told that his skill as a baker would now be considered an essential service! Eeli took this service seriously. When the Continuation War finally began in 1941, in the midst of World War II, even when the bombs were bursting in Helsinki, Eeli did not run to the bomb shelters. He kept on working even at risk to his own life. It wasn't all that he did for the war effort of course. As a man on the ground, Eeli would always be there to help when a bomb landed in the city, and that was often a sorrowful and tragic event.

In 1940, during the Second World War, while Finland shared the fundamental values and philosophies held by Great Britain and the United States of America, it had also shared a common objective with Germany—to defeat the Soviet Union. Although the Soviets and Germans had previously been allies, in 1940 the two powers were at war with each other. In August of 1940, Germany had approached Finland for permission to access Norwegian waters through northern Finland in order to be able to launch an attack from there on Russia. The Finns would, in exchange, be allowed to purchase weapons from the Germans to better fight the Soviets in what everyone believed would be their next inevitable attack on Finland.

While the Finns, who firmly opposed the Nazi ideology, did not officially align themselves with Germany, they allowed the Germans to fight the Soviets on Finnish land. On June 25, 1941, Soviet Bombers attacked Helsinki, and Finland joined with Germany to attack Russia. The Finns thus recaptured the territory they had lost to Russia during the Winter War, but their actions forced the British to honour their alliance with Russia. Being friends of neither the Soviets nor the Germans, the Finns had hoped that the Germans would defeat the Soviets and the British would then defeat the Germans, but with Britain siding with Russia, Finland decided that negotiating peace with Russia was the practical and thus preferable way to go.

The Second World War did not end until May 31, 1945, and in the final analysis much of the 1940 Winter War peace agreement between Finland and Russia remained intact and the former Finnish territory, briefly recaptured by Finland, was still ceded to the Soviets.

Chapter Four

The Mommy House

After only three months of marriage, Hilkka had become pregnant. She had gone to work at an HOK store selling bread and dairy products (basically milk, cheese and eggs), and she had risen quickly to become second in command at the store. The work was satisfying and worthwhile, but when she reached her fifth month of pregnancy Eeli insisted that she stay home. She recognized that he was right. He was worried about her safety and that of their unborn child in an atmosphere of war. She quit her job and concentrated on preparing for a safe birth. The regular hospital had been moved to a safer location because of the bombs which had threatened it, and a maternity hospital had been set up in what had formerly been a luxury spa frequented by the wealthy and famous. (It was later to become a veterans' home.) Pregnant women were encouraged to go to the expectant mothers' wing (dubbed the "Mommy Home") of the "spa" when they were near their due date. There, nurses would watch over them until they went into labour. This was a safe house for mothers to be. They were washed, scrubbed, shaved, and generally made ready for birthing even before they went into labour. There was no way that any babies were going to be lost during childbirth because of the Continuation War!

Hilkka went to the Mommy Home as her due date approached. When she went into labour she was carefully escorted across the grounds from the expectant mothers' safe house to the maternity building which contained the birthing rooms. Never had she experienced such incredible pain. It was terrible. Surely no one could live through such agony! She thought she was dying. Hilkka had never really been taught the facts of life and had learned them as she went along. She knew that giving birth was painful—but this! This was beyond pain. This was the most horrible experience of her young life and she thought it would never end. When her son was finally born, she was exhausted and sapped of strength. She lay back on her bed and she was given her baby. While she was familiar with older babies and infants, Hilkka had never actually seen a newborn child in its first moments of life. She didn't know that babies came out of the womb covered in body fluids and blood, with the freshly severed remnants of dripping umbilical cords hanging like amputated limbs from the middle of their abdomens; that they were wrinkled and splotchy, often bald, and generally howling. She cradled her baby and kissed his wet forehead, wondering if he would always be so ugly and what Eeli would think when he saw this child.

The baby had his hand in his mouth and she reasoned that he was hungry already—a good sign, she thought. Perhaps he would plump out a bit and not look so scrawny. Eeli came to her with roses in his arms. He was delighted to have a son, and as they admired him, his fingers, his toes, his tiny hands and perfect ears, he got better and better looking. Hilkka had good rich milk. Her breasts were always full and the baby flourished. They called him Pekka Juhani (Peter John) and they loved him with all their hearts.

Peter John Nygård

Hilkka spent ten days in the maternity hospital. As she overcame the pain and trauma of childbirth, and held her warm and beautiful boy to her breast she felt profoundly content. Despite the tension of war and the difficulties it brought with it, she held new life in her arms and saw a future that was full of promise. A son. A family. She was able to wander into the garden which had been part of the luxury spa and there she would eat strawberries, sweet and juicy and full of nature's goodness. The earth offered up health and hope.

The peace she felt in the maternity hospital was shattered when Eeli brought her and Peter home to their sixth floor apartment on Josefatin Katu (Joseph Street). The alarms were ringing as they got to the building and they had to run down to the bomb shelter for protection. Poor Hilkka took her baby son from the hospital where he was born and ran with him straight into a bomb shelter! What a homecoming! Luckily the only food Peter needed was nourishment from Hilkka, so there was no fear that he would be hungry even if they were trapped down there for several hours. "Lucky little boy" Hilkka thought, "at least you will have food." She hugged her child close to her as the alarms continued to ring. "Welcome home darling Pekka," she whispered softly into his tiny ear, "welcome home."

When the parents and their new baby finally got up to their apartment, one of the first things they did was to make sure that they had everything ready for a fast escape when the next alarm bells clanged. The elevators always shut down when the alarms went off, so everything that they packed to take with them in an emergency evacuation would have to be carried down six flights of stairs. It was important, therefore, to be conscious of what was essential to their needs and what was extraneous to them. The packed bag of essentials was always waiting ready by the door, containing enough supplies to see them through a few days in the bomb shelter if their stay underground was to be prolonged for any reason. Peter would be quickly slipped into a thick sleeping bag, better than a blanket since it completely enveloped him in the warmth generated by his own body.

Like so many who lived in Finland and in other war torn countries, having to be constantly braced for chaos and destruction became part of the way of life. Just because such tension became a familiar part of the daily routine, however, it didn't make it any easier to bear.

The Nygårds moved with their baby boy to a somewhat larger two room apartment on Braahen Katu, and before long Hilkka was pregnant again.

This time she was ready, both mentally and physically, for the delivery and postpartum period. In the meantime, taking care of her infant son and guarding her own health for the protection of the baby she carried within her, all the while dealing with the vagaries of war, created for Hilkka many demanding and challenging days.

Planning ahead for the birth of their second child, Hilkka and Eeli had made arrangements for Hilkka to be taken to a teaching hospital in Helsinki, where nurses were both trained and employed. The facility was older, and had a reputation for providing reliable and trustworthy care. Hilkka and Eeli had confidence that this would be a safe delivery site for their second child. Gramma Johanna Nygård (Perkkiön Mummo), Eeli's mother, would come to be with Peter and help run the household when Hilkka's due date came near.

Gramma Nygård arrived on schedule and her welcome presence in the apartment did much to ease the family's concerns about the amount of time that Hilkka would have to spend away from her husband and son while she was in the hospital. When Hilkka finally went into labour, Eeli was busy working in the bakery making bread for the troops. Her contractions were in the early stages and so, with Peter safely in his grandmother's arms, Hilkka planned to catch the street car to take herself to the hospital. Plans of course often go awry. En route to the street car stop, she stumbled and fell, scraping and opening a wound on her leg which began to bleed profusely. The leg was of secondary concern to her more immediate one of getting to the birthing room safely, so she ignored the injury and carried on her way.

Arriving at the hospital, in labour and with a bloody leg, Hilkka steeled herself for the oncoming ordeal of childbirth. To her great and overwhelming relief, the pain she experienced during this second delivery was not as terrible as the first one had been. It was at the very least bearable, and mercifully, not prolonged. On October 31, 1942, as the war raged on, Hilkka gave birth without fear to a perfectly exquisite baby girl. The old hospital had a comfortable fire going in the open fire place, and its warmth and the tenderness of the nurse who bathed her newborn daughter and placed the baby in her arms, provided Hilkka with contentment and assurance right from the start. It had become the practice, during the war, to baptize babies the minute they were born, and so, with the Red Cross nurse pledging herself as Godmother, Hilkka's tiny daughter was named Pirjo-Liisa Nygård, and became a child of God. Hilkka's heart overflowed with gratitude for her many blessings.

She was no longer a novice at this business of having children. Now she had a daughter as well as a son, and to her both were uncommonly beautiful. The hospital staff brought Hilkka a steaming bowl of creamy carrot soup, a delicious and nourishing broth with which to revive her energy and start her milk flowing.

From that day forward, Hilkka revelled in her children and when from time to time she would look down at the jagged scar she would carry forever on her leg, it offered up only memories of a momentous occasion.

When Hilkka came home with the new baby, she walked into the kitchen and found little Peter sitting on the floor with a babushka on his head, surrounded by pots and pans which he was banging and clanging together like a cymbalist in an orchestra. She knew that Gramma Nygård worried about Peter getting an ear infection and the babushka was to protect his ears from the cold, but he looked so funny that Hilkka had to laugh. Gramma laughed with her, and Peter laughed too although he wasn't quite sure why. It just seemed right to join in because it was such a happy sound and they were looking at him with smiling eyes. Gramma was thrilled with the baby girl and eagerly gathered her into her arms to hold. Peter was fascinated with the new baby, with her tiny little fingers and toes, and her soft hair.

Eeli's heart was full to bursting with the pride that he felt in his family and his love for Hilkka grew ever deeper.

Johanna Nygård

CHAPTER FIVE

Bombs on Helsinki

The Nygård's apartment was a good one with two rooms, an alcove for the kitchen and a separate bedroom. With Hilkka not working, however, it became too expensive for their budget, and so they moved to a less expensive one room apartment on Kotkankatu. There were now four of them in one room instead of three of them in two rooms. This posed no major problem for them since they had grown up with small spaces and the building they were in was secure and well built.

Security was important to the family. The war was still on and the bombs were still falling. The emergency bag continued to stand ready by the door in case the air raid sirens started to wail, and the way to the bomb shelter was well known.

There was a water tower nearby, which provided water for Helsinki residents. It was a strategic target for the enemy and those buildings close to it were at risk of being damaged by attacks on the structure. The Nygård's apartment was not far from this tower and Eeli worried about their proximity to it. As his concern began to grow, a compelling event caused him to make a difficult decision in order to keep his family safe. The alarms had begun to shriek and as was their practice, Hilkka had scooped up Liisa in her arms and dashed downstairs to the underground shelter. Eeli was in the process of getting Peter and himself ready to follow them when the building immediately next door to them was struck. The blast shook their apartment like an earthquake and all the windows shattered inwards, covering both Eeli and

Peter with splinters and shards of flying glass. When Peter's eyes widened with shock, Eeli, not wanting his little son to be afraid, told him that a bus had bumped into the building, but that it had driven away.

That incident was the final in a series of frightening events that convinced Eeli that his wife and children could no longer remain in Helsinki. Their apartment was in need of repair and the bombing had intensified. So when Liisa was two and Peter was three, Hilkka took them away from their father (who remained in Helsinki as part of the war effort) and went to live with her husband's parents on the Nygård's farm homestead, Perkkiö, in north central Finland, where the three of them would remain for the better part of a year.

The move was a challenging one for Hilkka. A few years before, when she had left Lamposaari and her childhood home, she had been moving towards a future that was optimistic and promising, and had only herself to worry about. Now, leaving her city apartment and the comforting presence of her husband, she had not just herself to worry about, but also two young children for whom she was responsible, and the future was one of ominous uncertainty.

Eeli, Pekka, Pirjo-Liisa and Hilkka Nygård during the war years.

CHAPTER SIX

Perkkiö

Hilkka prayed for safety as she pulled her children to the railway station on a sled, and kept them close to her side all through the journey north. When they finally stopped at the Seinäjoki railway station, she was able to get them all on a bus which could take them part way to their destination. The bus let them off about ten kilometers from Perkkiö, the Nygård farm, and Hilkka began looking for a way to finish the last leg of their journey. By now, on top of all the tension and travel (or maybe because of it), she and the children had become ill, a factor that Hilkka, usually so healthy, had not anticipated. Trying to ignore her weakness and exhaustion, she managed to search out a man who had a horse and a sleigh and who, for a fee, agreed to take the young family to the Nygård farm. She paid the fellow and she, Peter and Liisa clambered aboard the sleigh. About five kilometers into the trip, the sleigh's long wooden tongue broke and they could go no further. With the help of friendly neighbours, people came to their rescue and took them to Eeli's parents.

Perkkiö was a landholding that had been acquired by Eeli's parents, Johanna and Eeli Nygård Senior, in December 1935. They were the first inhabitants of the land. Johanna, with the help of her eldest daughter and some hired farm hands, dug the fields and planted the crops and gardens. As a skilled and reputable seamstress, Johanna would travel to her client's homes to fit and sew garments for them. (It was the custom in that time and place, for shoemakers, tailors and others in similar trades to go house to house to work, rather than having customers come to a shop.) Grampa Nygård, Eeli Senior, was a good salesman and direct seller who would market his and Johanna's wares from his horse drawn wagon, as he drove from town to town. Widely respected for his mathematical abilities, Grampa Nygård was able to work out almost any problem, or perform almost any task requiring mathematical skill.

The Nygårds of Perkkiö were self-sufficient, strong people, not wealthy by any means, but always caring and welcoming, especially to their son's family who was coming to them from so far away.

Hilkka arrived at her in-laws house very late at night, sick, cold and worried about her children, especially Liisa who had become quite ill.

With the warmth and love given them by Eeli's parents, however, they were soon well and settled into a secure home life. The farm itself was a small one, with vegetables, grains and a few animals. The house was tiny, with only three rooms, but the five occupants were cozy within its walls and were glad to be in a safe place.

Hilkka and the children slept in a room with Gramma Johanna Nygård. There were two beds and a sewing machine in the room. (The room also served as Johanna's sewing room as well as her bedroom.) Hilkka and the children slept in the larger of the two beds, on a mattress stuffed with straw and covered with a fur cover. Gramma slept in the smaller bed, next to her sewing machine. Grampa Nygård slept on a mattress on the floor in the other room.

Grampa Nygård was an amputee, who didn't recognize that he was a courageous and inspiring man. When gangrene caused by diabetes had attacked his legs many years before, his legs had been amputated, one just above the knee and the other slightly higher. He had custom made leather covers that served as shoes for his stumps, and he shuffled about on these, holding canes in each hand.

When gangrene later attacked his fingers he was without medical help nearby; but knowing what had to be done to prevent the spread of the gangrene and save his life, he had performed his own amputation, cutting off his finger as deftly as any surgeon. Eventually most of one whole arm was affected and its final complete amputation, thankfully, was performed in a hospital.

Grampa Nygård was amazing. Disabled? Not in his opinion. Complain? Not that anyone ever heard. With his one good arm and leather pads on the stumps of his legs, he walked, climbed stairs, drove horses and did his work. In partnership with each other, the Nygårds had begun a small informal garment industry. They didn't think of it as a garment industry of course. They just were doing whatever they could do to make ends meet, but they were, in fact, true entrepreneurs, seeking to generate income to sustain themselves by providing useful goods to paying customers. Gramma Nygård, as designer and seamstress, would obtain discarded cloth from used military uniforms and prepare it for recycling. She would then make assorted garments, aprons and other household items from this material. Grampa, as marketer, would fill a trunk with her homemade articles and place it on a horse-drawn flat board trailer. He would climb on to his buggy seat at the front of the flatbed with agility and speed (and without any help), and travel to nearby communities to sell his wife's creations. He would frequently let Liisa and Peter sit up there with him in the second buggy seat behind the horse, and when he got to his destinations he would let them stay at his side while he sold things, as if the children were important allies in any transaction he made.

An essentially private man who kept his emotions and personal feelings to himself, Grampa Nygård was a faithful Christian who knew his hymnal from cover to cover and could quote scripture at length. With their quiet example of steadfast faith, Gramma and Grampa Nygård had a profound influence on subsequent generations of their family.

Grampa Nygård (Perkkiön Vaari), with his daughter Ellen (Eeli's sister), son-in-law and grandchildren.

Later, when it was safe for Hilkka and the children to return to Eeli and their apartment on Kotkankatu in Helsinki, Grampa Nygård would sometimes come to visit them, traveling by boxcar because he did not fit on the seats in the passenger car, and climbing the three fights of stairs to their apartment using his arm and the leather padded stumps of his legs to propel himself upwards. He would sleep on the floor as was his custom and it never occurred to any of them at the time that his abilities were extraordinary. He did set an example for resiliency and determination that his son Eeli emulated. Those characteristics were similar to characteristics Hilkka possessed because of her own unique upbringing, and were a vital part of the mutual attraction Eeli and Hilkka felt for each other.

Living in Perkkiö with her husband's parents during the war gave Hilkka an understanding of the man she had married that could not have been obtained in any other way. She became truly a part of this extended family. Although she was an island girl and a city woman, and was not used to living on a country farm, she was eager to learn and willing to do anything to help the household. Grampa Nygård loved Hilkka because she was such a good cook, and Hilkka's efforts in the kitchen endeared her as well to Gramma Nygård, who was of a more serious nature than her husband and less demonstrative in her enthusiasm.

To her surprise Hilkka learned fairly quickly to be a good farmer and to excel at doing most farm chores, except for milking a cow. Milking a cow properly was a skill that she never quite mastered, and the cows seemed to know that they had the upper hoof, so to speak, and instinctively resisted making her task any easier.

Hilkka would dig potatoes, chop wood, anything that would be helpful to Gramma and Grampa. She frequently wore a bathing suit while working outside in the summer heat, and felt very comfortable and cool in it. She was distressed to find out that some of the neighbouring farmers were shocked at her attire, saying that it was inappropriate for her to be revealing so much of her body. Hilkka felt badly that some people would think she was showing off her body while she was sweating in the garden digging potatoes. Still young herself, she was constantly being surprised by the things she was learning about human nature. A bathing suit is not something that she would have worn to go shopping in the city, but surely, in context, wearing such a garment at home while working in the yard on a hot summer day would be acceptable. "And why," she wondered, "were the neighbours watching me work in the garden?" Still, not wanting to cause any embarrassment for her husband's parents, Hilkka began to cover up more sedately when outside.

She also tried, with some limited success, to learn to ride a bike. Eeli's mother rode a bike all over the place, easily and smoothly, even taking her grandchildren for rides on the back of her bike. Hilkka's own wobbly attempts to do the same were less than impressive, but her efforts were respected and applauded by those who loved her.

Liisa and Peter loved the many months they spent as little children living with their grandparents at Perkkiö. They had a wonderful time. The war was far away. No sirens forced them to flee to underground shelters. No shattered windows spewed glass around and on them. They played endlessly outside, exploring the countryside and making discoveries that they were certain no one before them had ever seen.

There were moments, though, when the realities they had lived with since birth crept back into their lives. Liisa was found one night standing on the back step yelling out at the moon to go away. She yelled at the moon the way the farmers yelled at their cows. "Go away, Moon!" she kept calling out, and when Hilkka asked her why she was wishing away the moonlight, Liisa replied that the moon was shining light down upon them on the ground, and the bombers would be able to see them.

Despite such occasional intrusions into the tranquility of Perkkiö, Hilkka was pleased with the effect the Nygård farm was having on her children. They were becoming strong and sturdy and had natural outlets for their lively curiosities. They did get into a little bit of mischief now and then. Perhaps on occasion they got into more than just a little bit of mischief, but they were Hilkka's children after all and she, remembering her own childish mischief, had some compassion for their misadventures.

There were times, however, when even Hilkka's compassionate understanding was sorely tried. There were lambs on the farm—gentle little animals whose wool was regularly sheared to be sold or spun. Both children loved the lambs and were fascinated watching the wool come off their tiny bodies at shearing time. One day, when Johanna was busy at her chores, she didn't notice just what it was that was keeping her grandchildren so well-occupied and happy. She just noted with pleasure that they seemed to be having a good time and were getting along well with each other. What she failed to recognize was that Peter and Liisa were about to try something new, which was not usually a good sign.

Playing lamb seemed like such a good game. They didn't mean to be naughty. Wasn't Liisa sometimes called a "sweet little lamb"? Peter knew he could shear just as well as any farmer, and indeed he discovered that he could. He made this discovery by shearing off Liisa's soft blond curls, letting them drift like feathers to the ground. This was great fun for them both. Hilkka shrieked when she saw them, and her two little children looked up at her with wide innocent eyes. Peter stood with the shears in his hands and Liisa sat before him with a shaggy half-shaven head. Hilkka knew that if Eeli had been there he would take off his leather belt and spank them with it, across their buttocks and the back of their legs, but Hilkka didn't spank as often as Eeli. Perhaps she remembered a young girl on Lamposaari who cut her own beautiful hair, not just through childish play, but in active disobedience. She did not spank either Peter or Liisa, although both of them knew she was deeply disappointed in their behaviour. As she tried to trim what was left of Liisa's hair into some sort of tidy appearance, she reminded herself that her children's bright minds and desire to discover their potential was something for which a mother should be grateful. Wanting to be good, Peter and Liisa never again played with the shears. They just looked for other things to do.

Farm life, like island life, held potential for accidents and injuries, and the family soon learned where caution was required on the homestead. Three year old Peter had found a little hatchet, and he was using it to chop a hole in a tree stump. While he chopped, Liisa was scooping out the debris from the hole with her hand. Peter was chopping faster than Liisa was scooping and it wasn't long until the hatchet came down on her hand instead of on the stump, and the blood began to pour. Liisa, not much more than a toddler, ran to the house screaming, "Get a rag! Get a rag!"

The rag, having been quickly produced, had just been washed in a big black pot which hung on a giant tripod over a blazing fire pit. The pot was filled with scalding water and lye soap in which the household linens were being boiled until they became sparkling white and thoroughly cleansed. Hilkka ripped a strip off the clean cloth and wrapped it around the bleeding hand as she cuddled her sobbing toddler. To this day, Liisa bears a scar on the top of her index finger . . . a tangible memory of Perkkiö and adventures with her brother.

Hilkka tried not to worry, but as a mother she could see danger every-where. She was determined that she would not raise her children in an atmo-sphere of fear and worry, and she knew she had to strike a balance between teaching them realistic caution and allowing them freedom to take reasonable risks. This was to be her challenge throughout her life—to encourage her children to be both unafraid and realistic.

The big black pot which hung outside had many uses. Aside from boiling linens, it was also used to boil meat from carcasses they killed on the farm, and to make soap. The soap was made with the lard which came off the carcass and with wood ashes from the fire.

There were recipes for making everything from soap to butter and cheese. A creamer stood in the little room where the food was prepared, and the buckets of fresh cows' milk were poured into it, splashing to the bottom in a wide ivory-coloured stream. The creamer would spin the milk until the skim milk and cream were separated from each other. As soon as they were separated, Johanna would give the children each a cup of warm milk to drink.

And the butter! Oh the butter! The butter churn agitated the rich cream which came from the cows' daily milkings, until it thickened and became a delicious creamy butter. When that butter was spread on Hilkka's fresh baked bread, there was nothing on earth that tasted better—except perhaps a taste of bread and butter topped with Johanna's uncultured cheese, which made a squeaky sound when chewed, and which Liisa pronounced to be "yummy."

These simple foods—milk, cream, butter and cheese—were gifts from the milk of the cow. These gifts were pure and natural, the ultimate nourishment for the children's growing bodies. Their other foods were also simple—meat, potatoes, vegetables—all grown organically on the Nygård's small farm. This healthy diet was a far cry from what people were experiencing in the city, where butter and other foodstuffs were being rationed. Eeli's decision to send his wife and children to the north was proving to be a wise one in so many ways.

There was a brook on the farm from which water was drawn for household uses. Drinking water was scooped with a dipper and pail from a pond fed by a spring. The water was heavy with iron which would form a film on the surface and had to be cleared away before dipping, but the water itself was ice cold and sparkling clear, and tasty. (Many years later, as adults, Peter and Liisa returned to Perkkiö and drank fresh water from the brook.)

Mummo (Gramma) Johanna had told the children that the farm's hens sat on their eggs to keep them warm so that they would hatch. Thinking to speed up the hatching by making the eggs really warm, Peter and Liisa put

Peter drinking from the puro
(brook) at Perkkiö.

heated stones from the sauna in the nests and egg baskets. While the eggs were being thus "warmed" little Peter would carry the chickens to the horse barn to eat the grain that had spilled on the barn floor, so that they would grow fat and lay more eggs. The children soon learned, by personal observation and through the reception of stern lectures, that though their intentions were positive, the results they were producing were, to say the least, negative.

The stones were returned to their spot in the sauna, a small wooden building which held a special significance for the family. Saunas in Finnish households, then and now, hold a unique place in Finnish history and culture. In ancient times saunas were built into the sides of hills and used as winter dwelling places, shelters so warm that one could undress within them even in the depths of a cold Nordic winter. The principle behind these early saunas was a simple one. Inside the small shelter, a wood fire was lit in a stone fireplace and rocks placed over a fire box on top of the fireplace were heated. When the rocks became hot, they would make the air inside the sauna warm (a dry sauna). People could increase the air's heat and humidity by throwing water on the hot rocks, creating steam (a wet sauna). The smoke was let out of the sauna but the heat would remain inside for up to twelve hours, and the sweet aroma of wood smoke still lingered in the air. The heat caused the people inside to perspire and thus their skin was cleansed, their bodies purified, their aching muscles soothed and their stress relieved. After sweating heavily for a period of time, adherents would then immerse themselves in cold water or snow and bring down the internal temperature of their bodies, and close the pores. The sauna was an integral part of personal hygiene and bathing.

The sauna has evolved and is available today in many different forms, but the initial principle behind it remains the same. Its physical benefits are well known throughout eastern and western societies, and it is praised as a therapeutic treatment for many bodily ailments. What began as a Finnish custom and a bathing necessity for Finns has become popular all around the world.

Hilkka had been taking baths in a public sauna all her life. In Perkkiö she began to realize the sauna's history and came to understand other aspects of the old tradition. Hundreds of years before her time, the sauna had a mystical character. Oh, it cleansed the body, to be sure; it created warmth in winter—that cannot be doubted; it helped soothe aching muscles and congested chests—all constant users had experienced those benefits. But how many outsiders knew that long ago brides were ritually washed and cleansed, and thus made pure, in the sauna? How many knew that babies were born in its moist warm air? How many knew that the dead were prepared for burial there? Who remembered that sometimes the spirits of the dead took up residence in the sauna and that the fires built therein were in part a tribute to the spirits and in part a fiery altar to a generous God? How many still quoted *"saunassa ollaan kuin kirkossa"* (you should be in the sauna as in a church.) The sauna was a spiritual place where both life and death were respected.

The family sauna at Perkkiö was more than just a steam room to the Nygårds. It held a life-giving force, for it was in a sauna that Eeli had been born. As had so many Finnish women before her, Johanna had chosen a sauna to give birth to her son because of its clean and sterile environment. Equally important to her was the fact that the sauna was warm and moist like a mother's womb, and it would lessen the shock of being born for the baby when it emerged from the shelter of her body and came into the air. Was there also a sense that the sauna might be a holy place? Eeli had taken his first breath in a sauna, and spent the first hours of his life lying comfortably naked on his mother's breast, inhaling the warm moisture laden air.

The Nygård's family sauna at Perkkiö had such a lasting impression on the children that many years later, living in his Bahamian home at Nygård Cay, far from Finland, Peter had his grandparents' sauna carefully disassembled, and its weathered logs carried across the ocean to become part of a re-constructed "Perkkiö Sauna" on the beach at Nygård Cay. To honour his father, Peter timed the completion date for the sauna to coincide with Eeli's December 23rd birthday. The whole family—from Eeli the oldest, who had been born in a sauna, to his great-granddaughter Courtney, then only three—took part in the traditional family bathing ritual. Even though the family no longer lived in Perkkiö, Finnish customs were being kept alive at Nygård Cay.

Tragically, not long after, someone overloaded the sauna fire box with too much wood, and left the door open. The wind fanned the flames and within a very short time, the sauna was burnt to the ground, and with it the history and memories it contained. It was to be one of the few times that Hilkka would ever see her grown son cry.

But that would all take place many years in the future. For Hilkka and her children, living in Perkkiö during the war years, the sauna was still an important part of the homestead.

When the bombing lessened and their apartment was repaired, Eeli felt it was safe for Hilkka and the children to return to the Kotkankatu apartment. It was with a mixture of joy and sadness that they left the farm in Perkkiö. They had been grateful for the safe shelter Gramma and Grampa Nygård had given them and had grown very fond of the elderly couple during their long sojourn with them. Glad as they were to be returning home, they knew they would miss Eeli's parents and the homestead greatly.

Little Liisa, however, was to return on her own to Perkkiö within the year. She was about three years old when she developed a case of whooping cough, a highly contagious upper respiratory infection, which prevented her from attending the local day care centre.

Knowing that the city air, with its industrial elements and bomb residue, was unhealthy for their daughter, and fearful that their son would also become afflicted with the disease, Hilkka and Eeli decided to send Liisa back to the farm to heal. This was a difficult, almost unbearable, decision for Hilkka, but she knew it was the right one. Never before had she been separated from one of her children. To send Liisa north when she was so little and so sick was frightening to her mother, but Liisa looked forward to seeing her grandparents again and Peter was in nursery school so he wouldn't be quite as lonely for his sister as he might have been otherwise. Hilkka knew two things: that Liisa needed isolation and the fresh unpolluted country air, and that Peter must be protected from getting the disease. Arrangements were hastily made for Gramma Nygård to come to Helsinki, pick up Liisa and take her back with her to Perkkiö.

Liisa lingered in Perkkiö for many months during her recuperation, and her attachment to the place deepened as the days went by.

Johanna Nygård adored Liisa and the child came to be an important part of her life. Liisa in turn loved her grandmother very much, and at night when she lay sleeping in Johanna's arms, she felt her grandmother's strength and warmth surrounding and healing her. Gramma Nygård was a religious woman, with a deep faith in God and Jesus Christ. She took immense pleasure in telling Liisa Bible stories and singing hymns to her. Johanna's Christian devotion had a profound influence on the little girl, which would remain with her as her own life progressed.

Liisa gradually regained her health and with it the energy that her illness had sapped from her. As her lungs cleared and her strength began to return, Liisa started to play outside again, as she had done when her brother Peter was there.

One day while outside alone, she followed the farm's meandering cows into the nearby woods and became lost. She didn't understand the perils of being lost in the woods nor was she afraid, because she was enjoying her walk with the cows. Johanna, on the other hand, was frantic when Liisa couldn't be found. Calling out her granddaughter's name over and over, Johanna looked everywhere trying to find Liisa. Not finding her anywhere on the farm, Johanna finally ran into the woods to search. Her heart was pounding and she was praying to the Lord with every breath she took to keep her precious little one from harm.

When she came at last to find Liisa happily wandering around in the forest, she scooped her up in her arms, hugging her tightly and covering her with kisses. She carried Liisa out of the woods on her back, piggy-back style, and Liisa remembers the whole event as an exciting adventure. It was fun being carried on Gramma's back! For her part, Johanna could have done without such excitement and without such a scare, and she fervently praised God for having kept the child safe in His Heavenly care.

Johanna was still making clothing out of old khaki material, but she also loomed beautiful material from wool. She used some of the material she had loomed to make a dress for Liisa. With an eye for design, Liisa got her hands on the scissors and cut decorative little holes all up and down the dress. She thought it looked really pretty and was quite proud of her efforts. It wasn't the design her grandmother had in mind, but it was one of many early indications that the Nygård children had a zest for the fashion industry. (Many years later, as an adult, Liisa was to become a direct seller of her own fashion line under her company name Pirjo-Liisa Fashions, Ltd.)

When Liisa bid her second farewell to Perkkiö, the memories of the sickness that had sent her there faded, and she carried away with her instead a lasting sense of serenity and security that formed an integral part of her character as she matured.

After attending the wedding, in Finland, of former Winnipeg Jets hockey player Markus Mattson, David, Kristopher and Allison visited the Perkkiö homestead. Here they walk with their Finnish cousins down the path to their great-grandparents' sauna.

The magic still exists even though the structure is old.

Eeli and Hilkka join the carpenters and workmen reconstructing the Perkkiö sauna at Nygård Cay. The logs are from the original structure that existed in Finland.

CHAPTER SEVEN

Kotkankatu

Life was not free of some of the frustrations that came along with raising children. Peter and Liisa were constantly finding ways to get into mischief. They were always eager to find things out, and impulsive in their quest for new experiences and discoveries. There was a short period of time between when Eeli left for work and Hilkka came home from her shift, and during this period, Peter and Liisa were left alone in the apartment. The children had rules that they were to obey, and they did, but their parents didn't anticipate the number of things that their lively and curious youngsters could do without violating any stated rules.

They were not to leave the apartment until their mother got home from work, so the apartment became their playground. In a storage cupboard in the kitchen area they found old newspapers and odds and ends of the kind of "useful stuff" that was part of wartime recycling. There were lots of crepe paper sheets in the cupboard. Crepe sheets were used for overnight guests during the war because there was a shortage of cloth and most families could not find or afford a second set of sheets to use for company. Peter and Liisa discovered that if you threw crepe sheets out of a fourth floor window, they would billow out and sail through the air like parachutes and if they got stuck in the treetops they would flap about like giant birds. Depending on where the sheets landed they would become canopies or umbrellas or would lie like snow on the ground.

They also threw the old newspapers out of the window. They threw them spread out flat. They threw them folded. They threw them crumpled up. It was great fun watching things fly through the air.

When Hilkka came home and saw the newspapers and crepe sheets lying outside, and found the apartment floor littered with paper, she was aghast. More than anything else Hilkka endured a fearful recognition that her precious children could have fallen out of the wide open fourth floor apartment window. The very thought made her knees weak and her blood run cold. Thus, on this occasion, Hilkka's spanking ability was well demonstrated. She made her children lie down on the sofa, and spanked their little bottoms hard, on their bare skin, and they never forgot it.

Later a man came to their door with a bandage on his forehead. It turned out that one of the crumpled up newspapers thrown by the children had a piece of metal in it and this, as luck would have it, had hit the gentleman as he had walked by the building, cutting his skin as it did so. He had come to complain to the parents, and the complaint didn't do anything to lessen Eeli and Hilkka's being upset. The reader can be certain that Peter and Liisa never again threw anything out a window.

Some time later a fire started in the storage cupboard. It was quickly extinguished before it spread out of control, and it should be noted for the record that on that particular occasion the children were completely innocent of any wrongdoing. Sometimes excitement could occur even without their initiative!

Having learned that it wasn't wise to throw things out the window, the children began to explore other items that attracted their attention. They wanted to know how things worked, how things were made and how things could be used. They were always taking the lids off boxes and tins to look inside, examining the contents and figuring out what to do with them. Everything they saw was a mystery that needed to be solved and they busied themselves with discovering the intricacies of the world around them.

Hilkka had to go out to the downstairs grocer one day to get potatoes. After the luxury of the Perkkiö garden which had provided such an abundance of root vegetables, it was frustrating for Hilkka to have to stand in line to get even a limited supply of grocery rations. However, standing in line was a necessity if she was to get nourishing food for her growing children.

While she stood patiently waiting for her chance to get the potatoes, those growing children of hers were alone in the apartment, and Peter was examining the family's furniture. A recently purchased new chair was of great interest. A pair of scissors pressed very easily into the soft material and exposed the stuffing and springs below . . . He had wondered what was inside them. What were they stuffed with that made them so soft? Now he knew.

Poor Peter! Eeli was not happy when he learned of his son's latest escapade, and was about to spank him soundly when Liisa burst into tears. "Please don't spank him!" she begged, "please don't spank Peter! He just wanted to see what Daddy put in the chair when he made it!" The children thought Daddy made everything. Eeli softened under the spell of Liisa's pleas, and spared Peter his wrath.

During another occasion in that short period of time the children were left alone between their parents' shifts, Peter opened the door and let in a burglar. Hilkka came home and found Liisa and Peter standing in the middle of the room with a strange man. The fellow told Hilkka that he was a soldier who was serving in the army with her husband and that he was bringing her greetings from the front. Eeli, of course, was not at the front. He was at that very moment starting his shift at the bakery.

Without letting on that she knew she was being told a lie, Hilkka nodded and murmured a quiet acknowledgement. As she spoke she gazed around her to see if anything obvious was missing. The most important thing in the apartment was a little desk which held all of the family's food coupons. The desk seemed to be locked and no one except Hilkka and Eeli knew how to open it, which they actually did fairly easily with a particular turn of a knife. For anyone other than them, however, the little desk was inaccessible. Looking about it was plain to Hilkka that the apartment had been searched. Things were strewn about and the floor was covered with papers. It was clear to her that the stranger had been looking for money and government coupons. (The government gave coupons to families that they could trade for food and other rationed supplies. Unscrupulous dealers could make a lot of money selling coupons on the black market to buyers who could afford to pay high prices to obtain a large supply of limited goods.)

Hilkka's heart was pounding. With two children to feed, she didn't want to risk losing any food coupons. She didn't let on that she knew he was lying, and Peter and Liisa instinctively knew to stay quiet. Eventually the man left. Hilkka, trembling with fear, glanced around the room and noticed that the intruder had left behind his intended loot—the radio, with the cord wrapped around it and a suit case with a variety of marketable foodstuffs, including the fresh butter Eeli's sister Aili had brought them from the farm.

Hilkka ran down the stairs after the man left and screamed for help. The caretakers in the building called the police, and Hilkka ran back up the stairs to comfort her children. When the police came to investigate, she was still so upset and frightened by the incident that she was afraid to open the door and let them in to ask questions and search the apartment.

The thief was eventually apprehended and Hilkka had to go to court to testify against him. She was nervous doing this, but her children had been put in danger and so she steeled herself to the task. In court it became apparent that this was a fellow who had committed a number of robberies, taking advantage of women and children living alone, as so many were in wartime, to steal money and valuables for himself. He had told the police that he had only been in the Nygård's apartment because he and Hilkka were lovers! Hilkka was horrified to hear this, but the police indicated that his story was not in the least credible.

Peter and Liisa added another bit of wisdom to their growing repertoire . . . never open the door to strangers.

Peter and Liisa during their days of adventure at Kotkankatu.

Peter, all grown up, returns with Hilkka to the Kotkankatu apartment with its infamous window.

The war ended in 1945 and the Finnish people were once more able to walk down the street without apprehension or fear of mortal danger. Hilkka, Eeli, Peter and Liisa continued to live in the apartment on Kotkankatu until 1949, and enjoyed a period of relative peace.

Summers were spent visiting Perkkiö or the surrounding area where Eeli's sisters, Bertta and Ellen and their husbands and children, farmed successfully. It is interesting to note that Eeli's nieces and nephews seemed to have inherited the same entrepreneurial spirit that Liisa and Peter had acquired. The cousins grew up to launch successful companies in clothing, footwear, furs, food products and other assorted business operations. Perhaps this spirit might have emanated from the tenacity and determination to succeed that Eeli's father had demonstrated with his horse and wagon so long ago.

Lamposaari was also a great holiday destination. There, the children would play and explore, as their mother had done when she was a girl. Hilkka would watch her children pick berries, swim, go to the sauna and drink the red soda, investigate the sawdust piles and other forbidden places, and best of all visit with their grandparents! Liisa would sit on Aleksanteri's bed and keep him company while he was being fed. In fair weather, Aleksanteri's bed would be moved outside to a shady spot under the trees so that he could benefit from the fresh summer air. Through the eyes of Peter and Liisa, Hilkka could see her own childhood days re-created.

Hilkka walking with her children near the
Helsinki Railway Station after the war.

In Helsinki, performers entertaining the public in outdoor theaters and band shells in the parks and urban forests were common in the summer months, and dancers would sweep gracefully across outdoor wooden dancing floors which were set up on public lands. The Nygård family would often attend the theatres and concerts, and Eeli and Hilkka would dance outside in the fresh summer air.

Holidays would also afford Hilkka the chance to spend hours reading books of all sorts and sizes. She was a passionate reader who savoured the quiet moments she could break out of her busy days to vicariously experience the settings, the eras, and the lives of the characters in the literature she chose.

Hilkka, Eeli and the children were lovers of the outdoors and took many camping holidays to Finland's wilderness regions, revelling in the beauty of the forests and lakes that surrounded them. They would frequently row over to a small island on a clear lake and set up camp. Their parents would create hammocks for each child by tying the ends of a folded blanket to two closely spaced trees. Peter and Liisa would lie nestled securely, safe and cozy in the resulting suspended pouches while Eeli and Hilkka rowed out with their nets to catch fish for a shore meal, which would then be cooked over an open flame on the island's rocks.

On stormy days, Eeli would drag their row boat out of the water and lay it on its side by a tree. He would then gather evergreen boughs to build a temporary shelter for the family, and they would all huddle, cozy and dry, beneath the curving branches he carefully arranged. Sitting together on the soft springy mosses of the island's sandy soil and inhaling the heady fragrance of wet cedar and pine while watching the sky darken and burst forth with a drenching rain, a stormy camping day became as pleasant and memorable as a sunny one.

Hilkka and Eeli made every outdoor adventure a happy and exhilarating experience for their children. Because they did this, Peter and Liisa would always appreciate and respect the earth and its natural elements, and the bond they forged among the four of them became exceptionally strong.

The traditions with which Hilkka had been raised were passed on to Peter and Liisa, who in turn would eventually pass them on to the next generation. Christmas, for example, still called for a decorated tree inside the house. It might no longer hang from the ceiling, but it was inside the house all the same. As Aleksanteri had done before them, Liisa and Peter read the

Visiting relatives in the summer, 1950
Left to right: front row Aili's son Heikki, Peter, Liisa
Middle row: Aili holding Seppo, Selma, Auntie, Hilkka
Back row: Aili's husband and a visiting cousin.

story of the Christ Child's birth aloud from the Bible before the festive dinner. They couldn't open their gifts until after the meal was finished and all the
dishes were cleaned up. Like their mother before them, the children washed
the dishes really quickly on Christmas Eve. So many things that Hilkka taught
her children would remain part of them for the rest of their lives.

Hilkka went to work again at the HOK Company where Eeli had become a master baker. Eeli and Hilkka were fortunate to work for this company. As an employer, HOK was ahead of its time in recognizing the corporate
advantages of having a satisfied work force, and the Nygårds were beneficia-
ries of this recognition. Twice a year, the company held a "Mini Olympics"
competition for the employees and their families. These were not tame affairs, since the Finnish people were athletic and highly competitive. Eeli won
many awards in Track and Field events, and Hilkka, not surprisingly given her
upbringing on Lamposaari, was a consistent winner in swimming contests.

In the winter, the whole Nygård family participated in the cross country
marathon, and Peter and Liisa kept a credible pace with their parents. They
skied whenever they could—it seems that most Finnish children can ski as
soon as they can walk—and were invigorated while swishing and swooping
through forests and over hills on their long boards. The constant physical
activity was good for the children and they flourished.

The Nygårds were joined in most of these activities by many friends, chief among them being Reino and Meeri Helgren. Reino and Eeli belonged to the Chess Club, where Eeli excelled as he did in track and field, and he was frequently the chess champion, winning many awards testifying to his skill. He took great pleasure in singing with Reino in the HOK male choir. Hilkka and Meeri, throughout the year, regularly participated in the Ladies' Swim and Exercise class.

Life was good.

Bakery manager Eeli Nygård and his bakery staff.

Eeli Nygård, far right, playing at the HOK Chess Club.

CHAPTER EIGHT

Into Each Good Life . . .

Even good lives have occasions when tears will flow. In the natural order of things, death will eventually part people from the ones they love, and so it was with Hilkka. In 1948, Aleksanteri Valtonen contacted pneumonia and died. He was not yet sixty years old.

This was Hilkka's first intimate acquaintance with death and it left her stunned and heartbroken. She traveled to her parents' home to perform the last gesture she could for her father—to help with his burial. Since the bodies of the dead were often kept for up to two weeks in a cold cellar to allow family members to pay their respects, Hilkka had time to make the journey to Lamposaari, and her employer kindly gave her leave from work so that she could do so. Aleksanteri's funeral was the traditional grave side service of Christian burial and Hilkka, joining in grief with her mother and sisters, laid her dear father to rest in the Lappeenranta Church Cemetery.

When it was all done, friends and relatives had a coffee hour at the grocery store near the Valtonen's home. And just like that everything was over. Aleksanteri was gone. He was somewhere else, out of her reach. His influence on all aspects of her life had been profound, and she would love and respect him as long as she lived.

The Nygård family continued to prosper and by 1949 Eeli was in a management position in the bakery, and Hilkka was manager of one of the HOK dairy stores. They moved from their tiny apartment on Kotkankatu to a condominium at Hämeentie 156, a beautiful modern suburban develop-

Aleksanteri's gravestone, Lappeenranta Cemetery

ment not far from a green park and the Olympic Village and Pool being built for the upcoming 1952 Olympics. The HOK Company continued to show its generous support for employees by assisting Eeli financially with the acquisition of the Hämeentie premises.

Peter and Liisa began to attend the Käpylän Koulu, a comprehensive lyceum school with a specific orientation towards students interested in the natural sciences. After lessons, they played at the beach across the road from their condominium, near the famous Arabia Ceramic Factory. Built in the 1800's at this site because of its proximity to the Russian market, the Arabia Ceramics Factory, by the outbreak of the Second World War, had become the largest producer of porcelain in Europe, producing world renowned art, pottery, domestic and utility wares, sanitary wares, tiles and even bricks. Playing in the shadow of the Arabia Factory, Peter and Liisa once again saw manufacturing as a positive and worthy enterprise.

Eeli also understood the many benefits of entrepreneurial endeavours. He wanted eventually to own his own bakery. He could visualize the sign above the bakery door. "Nygård's Bakery" it would say. It would be clean and big and bright and he would bake specialty breads and cakes that would attract customers from far and wide. He dreamed of this and planned for it as he continued to become more and more a reputable master of his trade.

Ominous forces were threatening the fulfillment of his dream however. The Soviet Union still had its sights set on Finland and the Continuation War, which had been intimately intertwined with the events of World War II, had not lessened the Communist desires to place Finland under its power.

After the Second World War was over, still determined to dominate the rest of Finland, the Communists embarked upon the "Russification" of Finland, an intense effort to infiltrate everyday Finnish life and spread the Communist influence throughout Finland. By 1950 many Finns had capitulated and had begun to embrace the Soviet philosophy. Others, like Eeli Nygård, abhorred the idea that such an ideology might one day rule his beloved nation.

As time went on, becoming an independent business owner in Finland was an increasingly difficult thing to achieve. Independent entrepreneurs were not encouraged and big collectives were becoming the order of the day. Finland sought desperately to appease Russia, the domineering giant next door. Eeli noticed that countries all around them were bowing to communist Russia, and that many Finns were submitting, indeed acquiescing, to Russia's communist influence. Eeli Nygård did not appease well. When the communists came to his company to get him to sign up as a member of the party, he refused. He sensed that his refusal to pledge allegiance to the concept of a communist regime would probably seal his fate, and that his chances of succeeding in business in Finland were fast fading away. Even so, he couldn't sign.

Eeli decided that he and his family would have to leave their beloved Finland while they could still do so as free citizens. He believed that if things continued as they were developing, it would take less than five years for Finland to be fully and officially a communist state under Russian authority. It was vitally important to him that he and his children be able to grow and create and achieve as they would be able to do in a free land. He could not risk their future on the ever-decreasing hope that Finland would be able to escape the threat of communism.

In 1951, Eeli and Hilkka began to discuss going across the ocean to North America and emigrating either to the United States or to Canada. When Peter and Liisa were around and listening, they would conduct their conversations in Swedish so as not to alarm them, and to keep their plans secret from others.

By now, Eeli's sister, Aili, had met and married an American mining engineer, William Hill, from Nashwauk, Minnesota in the United States, and at first Eeli and Hilkka considered going there to live, but when they were told that the quota of immigrants being allowed into the United States from Finland had already been met, they took a look at other options available to them. Canada, Australia and New Zealand were receiving immigrants from Finland, and all three countries held appeal for them. Canada, however, with its northern clime so like Finland's, seemed to be the most appropriate, and so Canada was chosen to be their new homeland. They looked at a map and it appeared that Winnipeg, Manitoba, in the middle of Canada, was pretty close to Minnesota in the USA—at least it looked as if it were a relatively short distance in the midst of the vast expanse of the North American continent.

It was a terrifying thought to leave behind everything they knew and loved; to travel to live in a strange country in which their language and customs would be foreign to others. What if they were never to see Finland again? What kind of work would they be able to find across the ocean?

Gradually the nervousness dissipated to be replaced with optimism about this wonderful new land, the true north strong and free, which promised for them the opportunity for a prosperous future. In Canada, all they would have to do was to work hard to succeed.

CHAPTER NINE

Letting Go

Finally, when the plans were all in place and everything was organized, Eeli and Hilkka told their children that they were going to emigrate from Finland to Canada. Peter and Liisa were wildly excited and curious about the great adventure that lay ahead of them. They wanted to learn everything that they could about this land that would become their new country, and they bombarded their parents with questions about Canada and all the things they might discover there. This discussion, and the way in which the family members shared information, thoughts and ideas, was to become a template for the family meetings they subsequently held whenever weighty issues came before them. Frank and open dialogue formed part of the Nygård family culture.

Having already displayed a remarkable ability to adapt to life's changing circumstances, both Peter and Liisa were optimistic about this latest change. As the days passed, though, it became clear to them that going somewhere also meant leaving somewhere, and while their excitement and curiosity didn't diminish, they also felt an unaccustomed sense of sadness. Finland had always been their home. They had no other roots, no depth of feeling for any other place. Would saying good-bye to Finland mean that they would never return to the land of their birth? Or would there be many trips back to Scandinavia to visit and see family and familiar places? The future was unknown and unforeseeable; a mystery that would unravel as they lived through it ... which of course made everything that was happening to them even more thrilling. Even the status quo was in a state of flux.

The Nygård's application to immigrate to Canada was accepted and their journey began. A short trip to Stockholm in Sweden secured their visas. Their lovely home on Hämeentie and all their furniture was put up for sale. Hilkka, with her keen eye for design and colour, had created a home in that location that was both tasteful and elegant. Her natural talent in interior decorating and design had been given a chance to flourish in the Hämeentie residence, and she knew that she would miss the place terribly. It wasn't easy to let everything they owned be sold to strangers, but it also wasn't the first time that she had something dear to her removed from her life. She was able to let go. The important thing was that with the money from the sale of these precious things—all they really had—they were able to purchase tickets to take them across the ocean to Canada. They had passage to a free land, to start all over again and build a future for themselves and their children.

After the condo was sold, along with its furnishings, and Hämeentie had faded from their view, Eeli, Hilkka and their children went to stay at a tiny summer cottage owned by friends in Marjaniemi.

The winter snows were still deep and the cottage, nestled in a picturesque park in the countryside, appeared to float in a misty white-on-white world. (Many years later as an adult, Liisa went to see the movie *Dr. Zhivago* and her mind was immediately transported back to Marjaniemi, so similar was the setting.)

The romantic and mystical cottage in the snow, being in reality only a summer cottage, was not insulated. Lovely though it was to gaze upon from the outside, it was perishingly cold inside. Keeping warm meant wearing extra sweaters, thick leggings and two pair of woolen socks. At night all four of them slept in the same bed under piles of blankets to keep the cold away from their otherwise shivering bodies.

A little stray cat crept into the cottage for warmth, and the children were allowed to let it stay inside and snuggle down on the bed during the day, but not at night when the family was sleeping. The cat gave warmth as well as received it, and it made a pleasant, if temporary, addition to the family.

The local school was not far away, and the road to it was ploughed, and so for the brief period that the family stayed at their friends' cottage, Peter and Liisa attended the school, Marjaniemen Koulu. Their parents didn't want them to get too far behind in their studies, even though they were traveling. The children didn't mind. The little rural school house was warm.

In February of 1952, one month before the Nygårds sailed for Canada, King George VI of England died. Because he had been King of Canada, Hilkka wept at the news of his death. "Our King is dead!" she said to Liisa through her sobs and tears. So closely had Hilkka already identified with Canada that she grieved as did other Canadians for the loss of their Monarch.

They would be traveling to Canada on the EMS Stockholm, an ocean liner with the Swedish America Line. As time went on it would become more and more evident that Eeli and Hilkka had chosen a very good ship to take them to Canada. They didn't know at the time that their boat had an aura of invincibility about it. It would prove to be a survivor.

Built in 1948 in Goteborg, Sweden, the vessel was at the time the largest ship built in that country, although small by international standards. It was a sturdy boat, well constructed and comfortable. The ship later became well known in maritime history when, four years after the Nygård family set sail on her, the MS Stockholm collided with the Italian Line's SS Andrea Doria in a heavy fog off the North American coast in the northern Atlantic Ocean. The Andrea Doria sank but the crippled Stockholm managed to rescue and carry over 500 survivors from the Italian liner, along with her own crew and passengers, to safety in New York Harbour.

Many years later (on December 3, 2008) the Stockholm—now renamed SS Athena—under new ownership and rebuilt from the waterline up, was attacked by pirates in the Gulf of Aden, an important part of the Suez Canal shipping route between Yemen and Somalia. Twenty nine pirate boats were counted circling the larger ship, putting the ocean liner at great risk. When the pirates attempted to board the ship, the crew members responded by firing high pressure water cannons at them, blasting them back into the ocean. That action, plus the arrival of a U.S. naval patrol aircraft, helped the Athena escape.

The EMS Stockholm would indeed be proven to be a survivor!

When it was time to leave the summer cottage and travel to Helsinki for the next leg of their journey, however, Eeli and Hilkka were not thinking about what the future might have in store for their ship. They were consumed with thoughts of their own future and the life they would lead in a new land.

They put everything they had into one trunk and two suitcases, packing all but one good "dress-up" outfit for each of them—stylish, well tailored clothing to wear when they arrived in Canada. After all, they were not poor or downtrodden. They didn't have much left in the way of belongings, but they were still a successful family with much to offer, and they would look the part when they stepped off the boat and touched Canadian soil for the first time.

They spent the last night in Helsinki at Aili's small apartment, located near the bus station. Aili was married by this time and she and her husband had three children, one of whom was just a baby. Hilkka held and rocked the infant, her newest niece, knowing that she might not ever see this tiny child again. Her heart was heavy with grief. That night they all slept on the floor, on what they called a sister's bed (*siskonpeti*), with everyone lying on mattresses side by side.

The next morning everyone went to the bus depot to see the Nygårds off. So many of them! Choked with emotion, Hilkka began to weep. Eeli's Uncle Matti and his wife Aune and daughter Raija, came to say good-bye, and with them stood the others—Aili and her children, Heikki, Seppo and Lea—dear Aili, standing there forlornly with tears streaming down her face. Aili, her precious little sister! So many memories flooded through Hilkka's mind; the days on Lamposaari with Aili would never be forgotten. They were as fresh as yesterday. How could she say good-bye to Aili? Hilkka's heart was heavy, and her stomach hurt with the pain of saying farewell.

The bus took them to Turku. Hilkka cried all the way. Finally Eeli took her hand and said softly, "Hilkka, my darling, why are you crying? I am here beside you. I am with you. Working together will give us strength. We will be strong. Do not cry, darling Hilkka." Hearing these loving words, Hilkka stopped crying and put her sadness aside.

They went through customs at Turku where they learned to their horror that forty recent Finnish immigrants to North America had returned to Finland. This information did little to bolster their confidence about their intended move, but it did not diminish their determination to proceed. From Turku they boarded the overnight ferry (a boat named Vellamo) arriving in Stockholm, Sweden, the next morning. From the ferry landing, the Nygårds joined other Finnish emigrants who would become their traveling companions and with whom they would share the excitement and anticipation of what was to come. The weather in Stockholm was unseasonably warm, with no snow on the ground and no need for heavy outerwear. Hilkka had a twinge of concern, perhaps even a small feeling of panic, that she might have been foolish to have bought the fur coat which she was carrying across her arm.

From Stockholm they boarded a train which took them across Sweden to the west port city of Goteborg. Hilkka was surprised and impressed with the luxury of the railway car which was assigned to the emigrating group. It was not what she had expected. She noted all these places and the many new experiences in a journal, a distraction which helped to keep her tears from flowing.

In Goteborg they stayed overnight in a large hotel—another first experience for the family. By the time they had booked themselves into the hotel, and had washed their faces and hands to cleanse and refresh themselves, they were hungry. Eeli took them to a nearby restaurant to dine. Perhaps because it was so close to the ocean the restaurant specialized in serving seafood. Clearly the patrons had such a preference, because it seemed that at nearly every table customers were having fish of some sort to eat. Eeli and Hilkka noticed that many diners had ordered shrimp, and never having tasted this delicacy before, they decided to order shrimp for their own table—yet another first experience! Unfortunately the children didn't care much for the shrimp, and Hilkka herself determined that shrimp must be an acquired taste—a taste incidentally that she did eventually acquire—only to later develop an allergy to it.

At Goteborg they boarded the EMS Stockholm, which was to be their home for the next nine days while they crossed the cold Atlantic Ocean.

It was the beginning of March, 1952.

M.S. Stockholm

The two Tourist Class cabins they had acquired on the Stockholm seemed positively luxurious to Hilkka after all the family had been through. They were spacious and none of them felt crowded as they had been for so long. There were no dishes to wash, no meals to cook, no housecleaning to be done. The meals, served in a proper dining room with white linens and prepared by first class chefs, were delicious. There was entertainment for the children, and there were special activities for the adults.

At the first dinner, Hilkka and the children noticed that some other diners had ordered tomato juice to drink before they ate their meal. Hilkka had never tasted tomato juice, nor had Peter or Liisa, but the colour of the juice was appealing and everyone else seemed to like it, so they decided to try it themselves and they each ordered a glass. The children's faces wrinkled up when they took a sip of this new beverage. They didn't like it, and though they tried, they simply couldn't drink the rest of the liquid in their glasses. Hilkka also didn't care for the unusual taste, but she was too embarrassed to leave the juice behind so she forced herself to swallow the thick red contents of all three glasses on their table. That way, she reasoned, no one would discover her lack of familiarity with some of the food items on the menu.

Despite such minor embarrassments, Hilkka found the journey entrancing. The great glistening swells and the powerful crashing waves of the ocean mesmerized her. Everywhere she looked the scene was the same and yet never the same. Each wave was unique, each whitecap unparalleled. The sky above the water, like the water itself, was ever changing. The wind that rushed over the depths sometimes circled around her hair, sometimes swept down to the decks, sometimes came straight at her from its prevailing direction and sometimes was eerily still. There was something magical about the sky above an ocean, about the vast expanse of windblown air swirling above the endless rolling waves of water. Hilkka had always loved lakes and rivers. Now the ocean captivated her.

Hilkka was delighted with everything on the boat, at least until the storms hit. Storms at sea are awesome in their power and terrifying for the uninitiated. The MS Stockholm was hit by a serious storm during Hilkka's family's journey to Canada in March of 1952. The ocean liner was tossed about in violent raging winds and drenched with torrential rains. Large floes of ice were heaved up on to the deck of the ship. All passengers were requested to remain below deck, which they willingly did, hanging on for dear life while the ship lurched wildly from side to side. The tables in the dining room, for those brave enough to attend, were chained to the floor, as were the dining room chairs. Soup would spill out of the bowls as the boat rolled erratically. At times the passengers thought that the boat would surely tip over. It didn't, and eventually the storm died down. The entire Nygård family (except for Liisa who remained fit as a fiddle), along with almost everyone else on board, was now wretchedly sea sick. The frantic and irregular motion of the boat over a prolonged period of time caused extreme nausea.

At this point Hilkka really regretted her one senseless planning mistake . . . there was only one suit of clothing for each family member in the cabins. Everything else was packed in the trunk and the two suitcases which were stored in the cargo hold. She had been so upset when doing the final packing for their travels that she had forgotten to take out enough clothing for the trip across the ocean. In their cabins, she washed out what clothing she could and draped the wet garments around the room, but basically for the rest of the voyage the Nygårds dressed in the same outfit every day. Hilkka wore her black wool sweater, black wool skirt and black boots every day and every evening—even to the fancy Gala at the Captain's Dinner—until they reached their destination in Canada. The Captain's Dinner was an elegant, sophisticated affair that Hilkka remembered in detail for the rest of her life. When the white gloved waiters came marching into the darkened dining room, with flaming Baked Alaskas held high above their heads, Hilkka was mesmerized. Her childlike delight at the scene made Eeli smile.

The passengers were surprised one morning to find that the outside temperature had risen to an almost balmy eleven degrees Celsius. The ship was passing through the warmer waters in the Gulf Stream and its influence on the weather was welcomed by those aboard the M.S. Stockholm. The next morning the weather had shifted again, and the passengers found themselves shivering in bitter cold air.

With endless variety in every aspect of the trip, the days on the ocean passed swiftly and soon they were far away from Finland.

SECTION
THREE

CANADA
THE EARLY DAYS
1952

CHAPTER ONE

The Train Trip Home

When the Canadian shore became visible on the horizon, the passengers on board the MS Stockholm excitedly raced to the decks to watch the land become closer and closer. Here they were at last! The immigrants were eager to see the new land they had chosen. The Canadians returning from overseas were anxious to set foot on home soil once more. The ship's crew members were looking forward to having a break and some time off. The general mood on board was one of exhilaration. They had successfully made it through nine long days on the north Atlantic without mishap and their destination was at hand.

For the newcomers, the exhilaration faded as the land became more visible. A ship's approach to the Halifax Harbour in March is not an especially attractive one. The month provides neither the sharp clean crystal white of winter nor the green and sunny warmth of summer. The islands one must pass look ominous and bleak in March, appearing grey, stern and lifeless to the viewer. They stand stoically in the icy ocean, suffering the crashing waves that bombard them as they wait patiently for the warmth of summer and the rush of exuberant life to return to them. The harbour itself, when one arrives at it at winter's end, is grey and dirty. Salt and sand mingle with grimy snow, stained with the greasy spills from machinery and equipment. The trees that stand in sight are bare and bent, with sap not yet running and branches that are dry and weary of cold. People scurry and hurry about in thickly bundled garments, rushing to get away from the docks. The whole scene is dreary and unwelcoming. It is an ugly month in which to enter a Canadian northern harbour.

Helsinki, like Halifax, is also a northern harbour, but it is on the northwest coast of Europe, where the moderating influence of the warm Atlantic Gulf Stream and one of its branches, the North Atlantic Drift, makes the temperature in Helsinki milder than other parts of the world, including Canada, that are at similar latitudes.

The kind of penetrating chill that Hilkka felt when disembarking in Halifax was new to her. She had been further north than Halifax many times on the other side of the Atlantic Ocean and had never felt such piercing and incapacitating cold at this time of year. She used to ski in Helsinki in March wearing only a light ski suit; they had family living north of the sixtieth parallel in Finland who were probably outdoors preparing for spring at the exact moment she stood freezing on the docks in Canada. Hilkka felt that she had arrived in a place that resembled the North Pole. She could now feel grateful that she had carried her heavy new fur coat with her all the way from Sweden, where she hadn't needed it, to Canada, where she most assuredly did.

She would discover as time went on that the Canadian prairies, where she and Eeli were headed, had a climate of its own, quite different again from the coastal regions of both Finland and Canada.

Taking his shivering family into the warmth of the Halifax reception area, Eeli bought them all a hot coffee (with lots of milk in it for the children) and sought out the immigration offices to complete the necessary landing documents and purchase tickets for the next part of their journey.

They took the train to Montreal, Quebec, and as they left the coast it was still snowing and bitterly cold. They traveled north from Halifax through the Maritime provinces of Nova Scotia and New Brunswick; across the Gaspé Peninsula in the province of Quebec and then southwest along the south shore of the wide St Lawrence River.

The journey took them deeper and deeper into a lonely landscape, raw and cold. There was snow everywhere and the trees looked stunted and struggling, like those that grow in frigid northern regions. They held no appeal to Hilkka as she gazed at the scenery rushing by her. Looking out the window, though, to watch the countryside as they swept through it proved to be a welcome distraction, for the train itself had uncomfortable wooden benches—not the best to sit on for any length of time, especially on a bouncing moving train—and the passenger cars were crowded with people. The benches could be laid back for sleeping but one didn't dare lie down upon them, because as the train roared around the curves of the tracks, one could be easily tossed to the floor.

The train was terribly dusty. Hilkka, Eeli and the children had to wash their hands and faces frequently to keep them free from grime. The sounds of the engine and the train wheels clicking along the tracks reminded Hilkka of the sounds the Porkkalan Juna, the Russian trains, made as they roared through the Russian-occupied territory along the eastern border of Finland.

There was a difference, however, between those trains and the one in which the Nygårds now traveled. The Russian trains roared by Finland with all their window shades drawn. No one looked out and no one could see in. There was no visible connection between those inside the Russian trains and the countryside through which they passed.

The natural beauty of the land and the charm of the communities the Nygårds traversed were not evident at this miserable time of the year, and Hilkka had to put forth great effort to be cheerful and positive for the sake of her family. With their clean clothing packed away and no bath or shower available on the train, Hilkka—normally scrubbed and shiny clean—felt grubby and uncomfortable. She had had no bed to sleep in for several days and her head was aching. It would be wonderful to arrive in Montreal just for a break from the stress!

They arrived in Montreal, Quebec, a large historic city which had played a major role in Canada's past, but there was no time available for them to go exploring or sightseeing. They were instead just stopping briefly in the predominantly Francophone province of Quebec, "La Belle Province" (beautiful province), to change trains so that they could continue their journey to Winnipeg, Manitoba.

Many of the families they had met along the way had by now arrived at their final destinations. Bidding goodbye and good luck to their traveling companions, and receiving the same kindly wishes in return, the Nygård and Aapro families, along with one other, were the only ones from the original group of Finnish immigrants to continue west.

They had already traveled a great distance and yet they were still in the early stages of their trip. Canada's vast size was truly impressive!

At the station in Montreal, Eeli reached into his top coat pocket for the tickets to Winnipeg. He couldn't put his hand on them at first, so he searched a second time. Still not locating them, he tried a third time. Hilkka began to look nervous, but Eeli told her not to worry; the tickets, he assured her, were most likely in the pockets of the suit jacket he was wearing under his top coat, instead of in the top coat itself. He searched the pockets of the suit jacket. They held no tickets. Hilkka's nervousness turned to alarm. They had sold almost everything they had to finance this journey. If the tickets were lost what would they do?

Peter and Liisa stood silently watching with widened eyes while Eeli carefully took off his top coat, shaking it gently in case the tickets were lodged in the lining and might fall out. They were not in the coat's lining. As Hilkka took her eyes off the top coat and looked at Eeli's suit, she saw, perched precariously on the outside of his jacket, the envelope containing their precious tickets. Instead of putting them into one of his pockets, Eeli had inadvertently placed the tickets between his coat and his jacket, inside nothing at all. "Thank God," said Hilkka, "they did not slip to the ground."

After that, Hilkka herself took custody of the family's documents, paperwork and tickets, and held them for the rest of their trip west.

Their next big stop was at Port Arthur, Ontario, a city at the head of Lake Superior, one of the five Great Lakes bordering Canada and the United States. Port Arthur was later (in 1970) to join with neighbouring Fort William, Neebing and McIntyre to form the amalgamated city of Thunder Bay.

Standing on the platform of the picturesque CNR Train Station in Port Arthur they were presented with a spectacular view of Lake Superior, the largest fresh water lake in the world, and directly in front of them across the shining bay lay the huge rock peninsula known as the Sleeping Giant Nanabijou or the Great Spirit of the Deep Water Manitou. This natural rock formation was aptly named, for when viewed from afar one sees the clear shape of a man lying on his back in the water, with his arms folded across his chest. An Ojibway legend tells how Nanabijou lay down in the icy cold waters of Superior and was turned to stone for betraying the secret of a rich vein of silver found beneath the waves.

For Hilkka and Eeli, Port Arthur also caught their interest by virtue of the fact that it had the largest Finnish population outside of Finland. It was not unnatural that Finnish immigrants would be attracted to Port Arthur, since the lakehead city had many similarities to Finland. The forestry industry, the cold clear lake, the deep winter snows and the abundance of perfect places for winter skiing and summer boating . . . these were all comfortably familiar to those of Scandinavian extraction.

Again there had been no time to explore their surroundings during their brief stop in Port Arthur. They were now only a day's travel from Winnipeg, and the Nygårds and the Aapros were the only families left for the final trip to Winnipeg.

The train seemed to go on forever. They raced through steep hills and deep valleys, past towering rock cliffs, dark boreal forests, swift flowing waters and countless frozen lakes. They went through northwestern Ontario, traveling through unimaginably long stretches of wilderness in which there was no sign of civilization. Hilkka was fascinated by the magnificence and mystery of the Canadian Shield, and that fascination never left her. The Mantario and Whiteshell regions were to become some of her favourite Canadian places, and she was to spend many contented summers at Falcon Lake in that area.

At last they arrived at the Canadian National Railway (CNR) station in Winnipeg. It was hard to believe that they were finally there!

They gazed about the magnificent train station, with its tall stately columns and high domed ceiling. Built at the turn of the century to a monumental scale and in the classical tradition, the massive structure had an exquisitely balanced overall design. A large central arch and vast stone lobby sent the echoing voices of the clerks announcing the arrival and departure of trains reverberating throughout the entire station, and always in the background one could hear the muted murmur of passengers' conversations and the hissing of braking trains along the tracks outside.

They were met by officials who informed them that they must now go over to the Immigration Hall which was located beside the Canadian Pacific Railway (CPR) station, just a few kilometers north of CNR station on Main Street.

After arranging for their trunk to be taken over to the CPR station, Eeli and Hilkka, carrying their two suitcases and with Peter and Liisa in tow, struck out to walk down Main Street to the CPR station.

Coming out of the wide doors of the CN station and looking across Main Street, their first sight was a view down Broadway Avenue with its wide center boulevard and towering elms, their bare branches graceful against the springtime sky. It was a beautiful street, not just for the stately elms, but also for gracious old buildings which had obviously been built to last for generations.

The walk to the CPR station turned out to be longer than they had thought, and the melting snow, mingled with the sand used by the city to keep the streets from becoming too slippery in winter, had turned to slush on the sidewalks. Merchants along Main Street had not yet begun their spring clean-up and so, as in Halifax, the Nygårds were presented with the messy and unsightly residue of winter in the city. Hilkka's good black boots, already worn much more than anticipated on the MS Stockholm, now took a real beating. They looked as if someone had marched half way around the world in them. The Nygård family noticed signs advertising hot dogs at the restaurants and local eateries as they trudged along their way, but they didn't know what a hot dog was. There were Coca-Cola signs everywhere. The bright red colours of the signs and the clutter of the streets were in marked contrast to the more sedate appearance of Helsinki.

At the Immigration Hall they were taken to a room which contained two benches. It was a relief to sit down and set the suitcases on the floor beside them. All of them were tired and weary from their travels. Hilkka and the children stretched their arms and legs to relax and Hilkka wiggled her toes up and down inside her muddy boots for relief. Eeli and Hilkka had already decided that Eeli should apply for a job before Hilkka did, so that they would know where he was to be located before Hilkka started her own job search. Eeli immediately sought out opportunities to get started working in Canada.

They took a room at the Immigration Hall, which was starkly equipped with two military-style bunk beds and access to a communal wash room. A wash room! With warm water and soap! The very first thing the little family did was bathe. How wonderful to feel refreshed and clean once more! Hilkka's spirits lifted immeasurably as the grime of their long journey was washed away.

Canadian immigration officials were available to find jobs for immigrants who were looking for work, and the immigrants of the day, wanting desperately to become self-sufficient and independent, sought nothing more than that opportunity to work. Eeli, as a master baker, had skills and a marketable trade. He joined a line of tradesmen who were anxiously waiting for leads and advice about employment opportunities. Within two hours he was back at Hilkka's side to tell her that he had been offered a job as an assistant baker in a little Manitoba town called Deloraine, southwest of Winnipeg.

It was a significant first step for the family.

Eeli decided to go ahead of the family to Deloraine and check things out. If for some reason the situation in the little town was unacceptable, then he would return to Winnipeg and they would start a job search all over again. If he thought that this would be the right place for them to begin life in their new country, he would send for them in one week's time. By then he should have been able to find somewhere for them to live, and have bought some furniture—at least some beds for them to sleep upon—and they would be able to settle in as soon as they arrived.

Eeli was satisfied that his family would be safe, warm and dry while he was gone. The Immigration Hall offered protection for his wife and children. The building's dining facilities were similar in style and service to a mission's soup kitchen or an army cafeteria. The dining hall may have been somewhat unfashionable and lacking in grace, but it was functional and economical for both the provider and the recipient. Similarly the food was decidedly in the "plain fare" category but there was lots of it and so they were not hungry. They were grateful for all that they had and eager to discover what lay ahead for them.

Hilkka and the children decided to explore what they could of the city while Eeli was away. They strolled down Main Street, unencumbered by suitcases and washed clean of travel's dust, to soak up the colour and character of the local neighbourhood. They were intrigued by the number of shops on Main Street and by the variety and abundance of fresh fruits on display. They saw bananas for sale in a little grocery store and, never having had the chance to eat bananas before, they stopped and bought a big bag of them … twenty pounds of them, to be exact. They ate every single banana in the bunch, not all at once of course, but the twenty pounds disappeared fairly swiftly, and Hilkka and her children thoroughly enjoyed every bite they took. It was during this week that Hilkka and the children had another first taste experience. They ate spaghetti for the first time, and decided that it too was delicious. Liisa was given her spaghetti in a white china mug with a handle. Not only was the spaghetti something she had never seen before, but being served a meal in a mug was also a new occurrence.

CHAPTER TWO

Deloraine

At the end of the week, Eeli contacted them by telephone and told them to catch the train to Deloraine. Hilkka's heart was pounding as the train took her, Peter and Liisa towards their new home. This was it, the end of their journey, the last of their traveling. They passed small prairie towns and villages, tall grain elevators silhouetted against the endless sky and miles of flat farm land waiting for the spring planting. What would they find when they got where they were going? Oh how she wished she could speak more English! The children sat with their noses pressed to the windows, curious and eager as they always were to discover something new.

Eeli and the bakery owner, his new employer, met them at the little wooden train station in Deloraine. Eeli had a week's growth of beard on his normally clean shaven face, and while he was holding Hilkka in a welcoming embrace he whispered hurriedly in her ear, "Don't say anything about what you see. Just let me do the talking." Hugging his children he quietly reminded them to be polite.

The baker took them immediately to meet his family—a wife and little child—who lived in the back portion of the building in which the bakery store was located. When the baker introduced his wife to them, Liisa curtseyed and Peter bowed, as was the custom for Finnish children when greeting adults, or when expressing thanks for something given to them. The baker's wife was touched by this sign of respect but she shook her head from side to side and raised her hand to indicate "stop" saying as she did so, "No, no,

The train station at Deloraine.

children . . . Only for the Queen. Only for the Queen" referring to the up-coming reign of Elizabeth the Second, who was soon to be crowned Queen of England and as the children knew, of Canada. Hilkka was able to translate this piece of information for her children's benefit, and just as Peter and Liisa were beginning to think that Canadian ways were somewhat strange, the baker's wife offered the family tea or coffee and served them hot dogs—another new taste!—which they ate with enthusiasm and found that there were a lot of strange things that were very much to their liking!

The children thought that this was the place in which they were going to live. Peter quickly took stock of the facilities and noticed that there was a child sleeping in one of the bedrooms. When he asked his father who the child was in "our bedroom" he was disappointed to learn that this was the baker's home, not theirs.

The baker had asked Eeli if Hilkka smoked and Eeli had replied, "Yes, a pipe and sometimes a cigar." When the baker apologized to Hilkka that he had no cigar to offer her, she realized that Eeli had misunderstood the baker's question. Eeli had thought he was being asked if he, Eeli, smoked, which he did . . . a pipe and sometimes a cigar, but it was Hilkka's smoking habits that their host was trying to determine. Hilkka didn't smoke at all, so the absence of some pipe tobacco or a good cigar did not trouble her in the least. What did trouble her, though, was the idea that this Canadian man might think that Finnish women smoked pipes and cigars!

Hilkka, fortunately, had begun to study English in Helsinki the year before. Most people who worked in retail stores in Finland were learning the language in preparation for the 1952 Olympic Games which were going to be held there. Using the limited amount of English she had acquired through her lessons, Hilkka explained to the bakery owner that Eeli was the one who smoked, not her. The ensuing laughter helped everyone relax. The language barrier was being overcome.

Hilkka soon realized why Eeli had asked her not to say anything about what she might see when they visited the baker's home. Coming from a background in which cleanliness was considered to be next to Godliness, Hilkka was fastidious about household cleanliness and sanitation. Her own household was always kept in an immaculate condition, scrubbed and disinfected to its very core. Every corner of her sparkling clean home was dust-free. Dirty dishes and soiled laundry were never allowed to remain unwashed for any length of time. Good housekeeping was both a science and an art, and in her case, her family's tradition.

It was quickly and abundantly apparent to Hilkka that the family so kindly offering them such generous hospitality had a much more casual approach to keeping house than that to which she was accustomed. She turned her eyes away when the host dropped his cigarette butts into the dregs of his coffee cup and saucer, not wanting to see the threads of tobacco floating in the left-over beverage. She had never seen cigarette butts extinguished in food or drink before, and she had a feeling that it was not something that she would easily get used to seeing.

When later on Hilkka offered to help dry the dishes they had used during their visit, she noticed that none of the dishes had been rinsed in clear water, and some still had soap bubbles on them. This was a new experience for her and she felt strange drying the dishes without rinsing them, but she believed that "When in Rome do as the Romans do . . . or get out of Rome." She had no intention of "getting out of Rome," so she dried the soapy dishes, and said nothing; not just because Eeli had asked her not to say anything, but because she was courteous and felt she had no right to judge someone in whose home she was a guest. Every family lived in its own way, and guests should always be polite. With this personal philosophy guiding her, Hilkka instinctively displayed the positive attitude immigrants need to succeed in a new land where so many things were different from those to which they were accustomed.

Not many weeks later, she had occasion to help the baker's wife do her laundry, and for the first time, Hilkka used an automatic washing machine. It was vastly different from the scrub board which she had always used before. Perhaps it was because there was a shortage of water in Deloraine, but still Hilkka found it odd that everything was tossed into the washing machine at the same time and the water was never changed through successive loads. The last load of laundry was washed in water that was decidedly grey. For a woman who boiled her linens separately in order to sterilize them, it was an unusual sight, and one more thing that she needed to understand.

Mrs. Monkman, who lived nearby and had a large two story home, sometimes rented rooms to travelers. She had a storage area at the back of her house, a little thirteen by fifteen foot lean-to shed with a slanted roof that had originally been used to store coal, and she was willing to rent it to the Nygårds for a small amount of money. The shed had a very narrow entranceway with a low doorway and one had to stoop down to go through it. Once through the doorway, there was a tall step which one needed to climb to enter the interior of the structure. It was a bit awkward getting in and out, and the place was small and definitely unsophisticated, but it was private and would do as a shelter to get them started. There had been a coal bin on one side of the shack and a potato bin on the other side and these had been removed to convert the space to living quarters. Fresh new wallpaper had been put on the walls and that helped to brighten the place considerably. (Fifty years later when Hilkka returned to Deloraine, the wallpaper was still there under many layers of paint, and the new owner tore off some remnants of it to give Hilkka for her scrapbook.)

There was a big coal stove in the center of the back wall of the room with a rusty barrel full of melting snow beside it. When the melted snow was boiled in a pot on the stove, they would have warm clean water in which to wash and bathe. Drinking water could be purchased from the owner of a well across the street. There was a window on one of the walls to let in light. They had an outdoor toilet referred to as a "biffy" by the Canadians. Eeli had bought two beds, and each was placed in a separate corner of the room. The children would have to share a bed, with Peter's head at one end of it and Liisa's at the other end. Eeli and Hilkka would also share a bed, but they both had their heads at the same end of it!

Baths were taken in a large square galvanized laundry tub which was placed in front of the stove and filled with water made by melting snow and heating it. The hand washing basin was located in the "kitchen" area.

Hilkka missed her beautiful clean home in Finland, but she knew that living in the shed was only until they became established and she could endure it until then. The children were really good. They seemed to have caught their parents' vision and they never complained. Hilkka told them, "We'll be all right. As long as the four of us stick together, we'll make it." The children understood these words fully and completely, and the saying became a family motto, repeated often when times were tough.

A tall handsome man with white hair and a beautiful voice came to see Hilkka. His name was Ian Harvey and he was the United Church minister in town. In her note papers she had written that "he radiated the goodness of a Godly man," and she instinctively trusted him, making an immediate personal connection with this gracious individual who was to become a mentor and advocate for her family, and a close and dear friend of them all. She was relaxed and comfortable enough in Rev. Harvey's presence to risk undertaking a full conversation in English, not just saying individual words but threading words together into sentences. She was delighted that she managed to communicate, however awkwardly, in this way, and she realized that all those English lessons she had taken in Finland preparing for the 1952 Olympics had actually taught her something!

On a visit to Deloraine in 2002, Hilkka and Liisa returned to the church manse (the former Harvey home) where the Nygårds learned to speak English. From left to right: Laura Lewthwaite, her daughter Claire, Liisa, Hilkka, Jean Harvey and her daughter Marg Smith.

The Harvey family visiting the Nygårds in their Winnipeg home.

Ian Harvey offered to help the Nygård family learn to speak English, and each evening thereafter he patiently taught them the basics of the language in his office, for no reason other than to make their lives easier. Hilkka's rudimentary knowledge of English was helpful, even though she recalled that what she remembered best from her lessons in Finland were the words to "My Bonnie Lies Over the Ocean"—not exactly words that would be especially helpful when trying to buy groceries, but it was a start. Rev. Harvey got them all the books they would need for their lessons, and Hilkka in particular enjoyed getting out of the shack and going over to the minister's office to study.

Peter especially enjoyed the lessons which Rev. Harvey illustrated with tangible examples. He would show them a carrot and an apple, for example, and teach them the words for these objects. Once his earnest pupils had mastered the terminology, they would be given the tangible example to eat. Munching carrots while learning English would become a memory never to be forgotten. Rev. Harvey's willingness to sacrifice his time and offer his creative abilities to teach them was an act of generosity for which the family would forever be deeply grateful.

The Harvey children, Margaret, Louise and Stuart, were among the first friends Peter and Liisa made, and Rev. Harvey and his wife supported Eeli and Hilkka in every possible way. The coffee pot was always on at the Harvey's and there was always room at the dinner table for friends and neighbours.

The Harvey family became a significant part of the Nygård's life during their time in Deloraine, and indeed their influence remained with them throughout the rest of their lives.

After several teaching sessions with the children, Rev. Harvey felt that they should begin to attend school where the opportunity to speak English with others would accelerate their language skills. The first grade teacher, Miss Price, began to teach them how to speak, read and write in this new language. They liked being back in a "real" school, even though they were put back a grade until they could communicate more effectively in English. They weren't worried about catching up in their lessons. Supremely confident and fun-loving, they made friends easily and managed to communicate just fine on the playground.

Mrs. Monkman had a dog named Tippy who took a shine to Peter. The dog would follow him to school and be there waiting for him when school was dismissed. Peter was exceptionally fond of Tippy . . . and Tippy didn't mind a bit that Peter couldn't speak English very well. Boy and dog found pleasure in each other's company, and Tippy remained a happy memory for Peter long after the family moved away from Deloraine. (After the Nygårds moved to Winnipeg, a letter from Hilkka—bravely written in her rapidly improving English—to her friend Jean Harvey in Deloraine revealed that "Pekka has longing for dog Tip and Liisa has longing for your baby John.")

Peter and Liisa began to teach the other children on the playground how to speak Finnish. They also taught them how to play baseball the way it was played in Finland, the Finnish rules being somewhat different than the Canadian ones, and their new playmates seemed happy to learn these things.

It was spring when the Nygård children started school in Deloraine, and the March thaw had turned the winter snow into rivulets of water and created puddles everywhere. Splashing in water is something that children everywhere love to do, and there seems to be no cultural barrier when it comes to playing in puddles. Peter made little wooden boats out of tree bark and he and Liisa and the Harvey children would send the boats floating across the water wherever it ponded. Adventures and explorations could continue in this new land just as they did in the old one. Life in Canada was going to be all right.

While the children were settling in to school and finding friends, Eeli and Hilkka were making their own adjustments. Eeli, like Hilkka, was scrupulously clean. Any bakery in which he worked had to be constantly swept and scrubbed. The first thing he did, therefore, when he started work in Deloraine was to clean the bakery. He cleaned and cleaned until he was satisfied that things could not be made any cleaner. Every morning he would clean again before he put the wood in the ovens to heat them so that he could start to bake. He worked 12 hours a day, 6 days a week, for 35 dollars a week. This was his beginning and it was with an eye to the future that he kept going.

In the meantime, Hilkka turned her penchant for cleanliness into a job. She began to clean other people's houses and her services were soon in demand. Her good work led to more good work. The woman who owned the newspaper had asked Hilkka to clean the newspaper office, and then, pleased with Hilkka's work, hired her to clean the apartment above the office as well.

Hilkka was amazed at how kind everyone was to them. People gave them delicious homemade preserves, eggs and cream, small useful gifts, and even a beautifully handcrafted quilt for their bed. Every day for the first week

In 2002, Hilkka and Liisa returned to visit the building in which the Deloraine bakery was located.

They also paid a visit to *The Deloraine Times* office building, one of the places Hilkka used to clean.

after their arrival, someone would stop by with something to welcome them. Everyone was so good to them that they were completely overwhelmed. What warmth and friendship these Canadian neighbours gave them!

Although Eeli and Hilkka were Lutherans and were not familiar with the United Church, Rev Harvey invited them to worship with his congregation. Arrangements were made for Eeli, Hilkka, Peter and Liisa Nygård to attend a special service at the United Church in Deloraine, Manitoba, as friends of Ian Harvey.

They hadn't been to church in a long time and they looked forward to being in a house of worship again. They were greeted warmly at the door by members of the congregation and were taken to sit in one of the front pews. Both the service and its language may have been unfamiliar, but the spirit that was there was deeply familiar. As she bowed her head in prayer Hilkka felt the presence of God, a universal presence that superseded any language and any rite of service. She was with fellow Christians and she felt peace.

The choir stood and began to sing an anthem which was instantly recognized by every member of the Nygård family. As the haunting beauty of Finnish composer Sibelius's magnificent symphonic poem, "Finlandia", filled the little church, Hilkka, Liisa, Peter—even Eeli—found their eyes welling with water. The choir sang the English words of the hymn, the last lines of which are familiar to so many:

Be still, my soul, the Lord is on thy side;
Bear patiently the cross of grief or pain.
Leave to thy God to order and provide;
In every change He, faithful, will remain.
Be still, my soul, thy best, thy heavenly friend
Through thorny ways leads to a joyful end.

Hilkka was stunned. That people could be so incredibly kind was almost unbelievable. "Finlandia" was one of the most important national songs in Finland, second only to the national anthem, indeed to many Finnish people even more important than the national anthem, and its soaring majesty and power stirred their souls. They were only immigrants and yet they were being treated as if they were special. How kind, how very, very kind. Hilkka's tears flowed freely. Never would they forget the great gift the choir gave them that day. That same day, Peter and Liisa were presented with a copy of the New Testament by members of the Canadian Girls in Training (CGIT) who were part of the congregation. The Bibles were inscribed for each of them and Liisa to this day keeps hers as a treasured part of her personal library.

The friendly warmth and tranquility of this small town and its people was to form the solid foundation of the Canadian way for the Nygård family. A Saturday night stroll on Main Street meant seeing nearly everyone in town. It was like being a member of a big family, with laughing children and friends greeting friends as they shopped for the following week's necessities. Hilkka, Eeli and the children fit right into this way of life, but sadly it was not to last.

Liisa, recalling wonderful memories, visits the United Church in
Deloraine with her sons, Kristopher and David.

Before long, despite his expertise as a baker and his willingness to work long hours, it became obvious that Eeli was having real difficulties in his relationship with his employer. The bakery's owner, who could be a fine fellow when sober, unfortunately had a drinking problem. Eeli's difficulties became obvious when he realized that he had to start picking up his pay cheque as soon as the payroll arrived every Saturday, or the owner would go to the local beer parlour with it. Hilkka and Eeli began to go together, arm in arm, to pick up the pay cheque each week as a way of reminding the owner that Eeli was a family man who needed to be paid. This ensured that Eeli got paid, but it didn't solve his employer's drinking problem.

The situation at the bakery became increasingly stressful until finally one night, the baker, under the influence of alcohol, threw a cake at Eeli, which effectively ended their working relationship. It was the last straw. The excessive drinking had now caused his employer to become physically abusive, and there was no sign that he would be able to stay sober.

Eeli gave his notice on the spot. He would find other work. His boss yelled at him. "Where are you going to go?" he asked, "There aren't any jobs for you any place else!" Eeli shot back, "I go to Winnipeg!" "Hah!" came back the drunken response, "No one in Winnipeg is going to hire you!"

"Then I go to Toronto!" Eeli retorted. "No jobs for you in Toronto either! You have to stay here. No one else will have you!" "Well, maybe then I go Finland again where no drunk boss!"

The exchange had started badly and ended up even more badly, with Eeli quitting his job and his employer berating him for doing so. It was over. What had started so hopefully ended miserably.

Eeli went to see Pastor Harvey for guidance. The bank in town might have been willing to lend Eeli the money to buy the bakery, but the reality of small town living and the fact that everyone knew about the argument at the bakery, made this alternative unworkable and impractical. Eeli decided to go to Winnipeg to see if there were any bakery jobs available. Ian Harvey went to the bus depot with him and gave him a letter of reference saying that Eeli Nygård was a reliable man, a good baker, a hard worker and that he deserved a job. Pastor Harvey advised Eeli to stay at the YMCA and promised him that he and his family would keep watch over Hilkka and the children in Deloraine while Eeli looked for work in the city.

Fate has a way of leading a person to his destination. Ultimately, their unplanned move to Winnipeg would prove to be the right move, and the time they spent in Deloraine would prove to have been the best start the Nygårds could have wished for in their new country. In this quiet prairie town, with its kind people and gentle ways, the family had been able to make their first adjustment to Canada. That adjustment was greatly needed and highly meaningful. Despite their poor circumstances and the unfortunate conflict with the bakery owner, Eeli and Hilkka had been comfortable and happy in Deloraine, the place where they had been able to gain confidence and courage and find their Canadian roots. It was their first Canadian home.

Many years later, the family returned to Deloraine and opened Nygård Park where the flags of many countries are flown as a way of expressing thanks to the town which welcomed them from a land whose flag was flown far away across the ocean. Peter, always remembering and recognizing the importance of the past, had the shed in which they had lived transported to Winnipeg, where it sits as a constant reminder of his family's beginnings.

He also arranged for a replica of the little room which the family had occupied to be constructed on the Monkman's former property. It is his sincere hope that his Deloraine foundation will serve as an inspiration for other newcomers to this country. He believes and often has stated, "In Canada you may start with very little but you have the privilege of soaring to any height imaginable if you have a plan, and if you are prepared to work hard, and pay the price."

On June 23, 1952, the Deloraine Times printed a letter of thanks to the people of Deloraine from the Nygårds, along with an editorial which expressed the warmth and admiration the town's people felt for the Nygård family. The letter and the editorial that accompanied it are included here.

The shed where the Nygård family lived while in Deloraine,
being moved to Winnipeg.

Peter at the opening of Nygård Park.
The park is dedicated "to the people of Deloraine, Manitoba, who welcomed
the Nygård family from their native Finland in 1952."

Feminine . .
Chit - Chat

This week I am going to break away from the orthodox custom of newspaper procedure, and include a thank you note in this column.

Card of Thanks

We would like to say thank you very much to all those people who were kind to us and made us happy during our short stay in Deloraine.— Hillka, Eli, Lisa and Peka Nygard.

Behind this simple thank you lies a human little story.

These four people, father, mother and two children, arrived in our town at the beginning of April from a small country in far-away Europe. In their native Finland they lived in Helsinki, a town approximately the size of Winnipeg. There they had a modern suite, friends and relatives. You can imagine how they felt when they came here. Our language and customs bewildered them. Yet in the space of a few weeks they had endeared themselves to all who knew them. They were prepared to make our town, their town. It was too bad that fate decreed otherwise.

It would have been easy for them to have grumbled and become miserable, for they had little or nothing of material wealth. Here they lived, four in one room, without the comforts they had been used to in their own land, making the best of this small home, with a smile.

I watched the kindness of many folk in town towards them, and faith in my fellow humans reached a new high. A minister gave up a few hours of his precious time each evening to teach them English. His only reward — their grateful thanks. Other people gave them clothes, not old cast-offs, but nice wearable clothes. Other gifts of household utensils and effects came from folks who had learned of their situation. One parcel was left on their table without even a note to identify the donor.

Eli Nygard in his own country was a baker . . . not just an ordinary baker, but a craftsman with twenty years experience in one of the largest bakeries in Helsinki, where he was in charge of a staff of thirty. You are perhaps wondering why he left such a comfortable job to try his luck in a new country? I wondered too, and asked his wife. In her broken English, this is what she told me: "Eli, not like Communists. Communists give Eli papers to sign, Eli say, No. So we come to Canada." Her simple explanation makes me realize how lucky we are. We should be proud that these people selected Canada as a free nation in which to start

The little family struggled along for a while on small wages, the husband working long hours, endeavoring to make ends meet. Hillka did her share to balance the family budget by taking up domestic work in various homes in town. Work of this nature had not been part of her life in Finland, but unlike a lot of other people in her circumstances she took everything in her stride, and mind you, always with a smile. But all the while they knew that this was not the life they had planned. They had dreamed of starting afresh in a new, large, free land, where work was plentiful and wages were paid according to ability. But soon Eli realized this dream could only come true if he worked in the city.

This week, Hillka, Lisa and Peka have joined him in Winnipeg. It seems sad to me that this had to happen. The little family had the real pioneer spirit. They would have made good citizens of our town, and one day without any doubt, they will be good Canadians. I hated to see them leave us, but I'm going to keep in touch with them, and one day I'll let you know how they are, and what they have accomplished.

We Canadians should remember always, the duties and responsibilities of good citizenship, only while we remember this, will our land flourish and grow, offering opportunity to Canadians and immigrants alike. If we fail in our responsibility to these newcomers, democracy will fail also, and other forms of government—totalitarian dictatorships—will have the chance to rise to power.

The question we should ask ourselves, is this: "Where have we, as Canadian citizens, fallen down in our treatment of this family?" In the future we may have other immigrants in our town. How are we going to use them?

* * *

Editorial, "Feminine..Chit-Chat" in
The Deloraine Times,
Manitoba, Canada, June 23, 1952

Section

FOUR

Winnipeg
The building years
1952 – 1997

CHAPTER ONE

Looking For Something That Fits

In Winnipeg, Eeli began to search for bakery work. Although his English was poor, he did manage to figure things out, read signs and find his way around in unfamiliar territory. He happened to see a truck with a picture of a pretty blond girl biting into a slice of white bread painted on its side, delivering bread to houses in one neighbourhood. He tried to follow the truck back to its origin by running after it, thinking he could apply for a job at the bakery from which the delivery truck came, but he couldn't keep up with the vehicle and lost sight of it as it traveled the neighbourhood. He didn't know how to ask anyone where the shop was.

The next morning, he returned to the street where he had seen the truck the day before, and sure enough there it was delivering bread again to the same houses. This time he was able to run behind it all the way back to the bakery, which was called General Bakeries, and there he presented his qualifications and the letter of reference from Pastor Harvey. There was no full time job available at the time, but the company needed someone for the summer months and Eeli was offered the job, which he took. The summer job lasted for fifteen years.

His next task was to find accommodation for his wife and children. After searching the downtown area, he rented two rooms in the upstairs of a rooming house on Bannatyne Avenue for $40.00 a month. The house was owned by a Polish woman, a new Canadian like himself.

Eeli sent a message to Deloraine for Hilkka and his children to come to Winnipeg. Hilkka packed their belongings. She took their two mattresses outside and pounded and banged on them to clean them. Then she rolled them up and tied rope around them for traveling. They could sleep on these mattresses until proper bedroom furniture could be obtained.

Eeli had said that he would be at the train station to meet them when they arrived in Winnipeg, but when they got there Eeli was nowhere to be seen. It was uncharacteristic of Eeli not to keep his word, and Hilkka was worried that something might have happened to him. He had provided her with a phone number as a contact in case she needed to reach him, and so Hilkka asked the clerk at the ticket counter to call the number for her. It turned out that Canada's daylight saving time was the culprit. Eeli was un-aware that the clocks in Manitoba had all been set ahead one hour the night before Hilkka and the children arrived. Hilkka was operating according to the newly adjusted time, and Eeli was still operating on the time used the day be-fore. They were safely reunited, and they added daylight saving time to their increasing understanding of what it meant to be Canadian.

His family's relief at seeing Eeli again became even more pleasurable when he declared that he had a delightful new treat in store for them. Ear-lier in the week, he had discovered a little kiosk at the train station that of-fered customers a unique North American taste experience—cool, creamy, flavourful beverages called milk shakes. Eeli couldn't wait to buy each of them a strawberry milkshake so that they could find out for themselves what wonderful drinks they were. As Hilkka, Peter and Liisa sipped on the thick frothy shakes he bought them, they had to agree that Eeli was right. Milk shakes tasted really good! They were certainly more fun to add to their list of Canadian things than daylight saving time!

The landlady wasn't pleased when Eeli's family showed up. She began to complain about the children the minute they walked through the door. "Too many noisia!" she exclaimed. It was an interesting exchange. There stood Finnish and Polish immigrants trying to communicate with each other in a third language with which neither were totally familiar, and succeeding some-how to make themselves understood. She indicated in her broken English that the children ran around on the floors too much, and the sound they made carried down to her own rooms. Nothing Eeli or Hilkka could do, short of gagging the children and chaining them to bedposts, would satisfy their landlady. Perhaps she had not understood that Eeli would be bringing

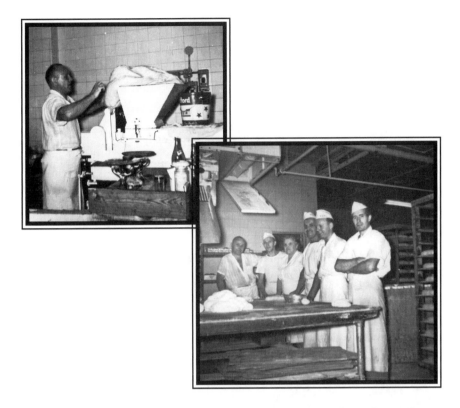

Eeli Nygård becomes a baker in Winnipeg, Manitoba, in the early 1950's.

children with him when he moved in, but it was plain to see that she simply didn't want children living in her upstairs rooms. After two weeks of constant haranguing, Eeli had had enough. They wouldn't stay where they weren't wanted. He gave the woman $20.00 for the two weeks they had spent in her house and told her that she wouldn't have to worry about his noisy children any more. "We rid you of problem," he said . . . and with that notice they made plans to move out as quickly as they could.

The one new thing that Hilkka would carry away with her from the Bannatyne address was a set of blue glass dishes that Eeli had given her on their 12th wedding anniversary. What a beautifully laid table she had been able to present to him on that special occasion! She had cooked pork chops and mounds of vegetables and when the meal was placed on the table with the blue glass, it looked like a picture in a magazine. The blue glass dishes would always be a good memory that overshadowed any recollection of the numerous scoldings they had received during the two weeks they lived with their unhappy landlady.

As for the children, they remembered going from the Bannatyne apartment with Hilkka, past the Coca Cola plant near Main Street, to the big Eaton's Department Store on Portage Avenue where they discovered the array of bargains in Eaton's big basement. Hilkka bought Liisa a skirt and Peter a tie which he has kept to this day. To their delight, she also made a special purchase for each child—a cowboy hat and two cap guns in holsters. Movies about the Wild West (dubbed "westerns") were popular at that time, not just in Canada but around the world, and both Liisa and Peter had often played "Cowboys and Indians" in Finland, re-creating the images they had seen on the big screen. Having cowboy gear of their own was a source of great pride and they wore their new accoutrements whenever they could.

Hilkka and Eeli had heard that there was a place in Winnipeg where Finnish immigrants would gather to visit and share experiences. After they had given their notice to their landlady on Bannatyne Avenue, they discovered where this gathering spot was and went there to see if they could get some information about places to live. Meeting other Finnish immigrants was a wonderful thing for them. What a joyful relief it was to be able to speak

Hilkka and her sister Aili visit their mother Selma's grave.

Eeli, Hilkka & Perkkiön Mummo (Johanna Nygård) visit Eeli's father's grave.

in their mother tongue again, to not have to search and stumble for words, to be able to be understood without having to struggle to make themselves clear! They knew that English would eventually become easy for them, but in these early days in Canada, when everything was so strange to them, not being able to communicate well was extremely stressful.

Hilkka and Eeli had lived only a few months in Canada when they were sent a telegram, starkly worded, "*Äiti kuoli. Terveisin, Aili.*" "Mother has died, Regards, Aili." Selma had lived many years as a widow, and now at the age of seventy-five had succumbed to the assault of an inoperable tumour lodged between her lungs and heart.

Hilkka's grief at her mother's death was painful and intense, because she was unable to go to the funeral. Alone and far away from all that was familiar to her, still a stranger in her new land, Hilkka wept and mourned the loss of her mother. Her mother, the beautiful and unassuming soul who had given Hilkka life, who had loved her deeply and taught her life's lessons so patiently and so wisely . . . it was inconceivable that she would never see her or talk to her or touch her again on this earth! No letters would go back and forth across the ocean between mother and daughter. Hilkka's sorrow engulfed her, overwhelming her completely as she contemplated the day that Selma was buried with Aleksanteri in the Lappeenranta Church Cemetery. She was in agony knowing that she couldn't be there with her family to pay homage to her mother as her earthly body was placed into the ground.

Many years later, Hilkka would visit the Lappeenranta Church Cemetery and stand at the foot of her parents' graves and remember them, not just with love, but also with gratitude and respect for all they had taught her during her wonderful childhood on Lamposaari.

A few short months later, the Nygård children would lose yet another grandparent when Eeli's father passed away. Again, with no means of returning to Finland, the Nygård family mourned and wept alone. Eeli's father was buried in the Alajärvi Church Cemetery, and this graveyard, like the one in Lappeenranta, was also visited many years later by Eeli and Hilkka; only this time it was Eeli who contemplated the past and reflected with respect on his father's life. Eeli was told that on the night his father died he had sung hymns, and his rich powerful voice was still so strong that the music could be heard echoing throughout the hospital, and for Eeli this was a comforting thought to hold.

CHAPTER TWO

Five Children, Two Husbands
&
One Extra Lady

At the Finnish Center in Winnipeg, Hilkka and Eeli had met a couple named the Halinens who had just bought an old house on Albany Street in the St. James community. The husband was a mining engineer and the wife was a doctor. Because she had received her medical degree in a foreign country the wife was required to qualify for Canadian medical standards and she was receiving training at St. Boniface Hospital for that purpose. Her husband couldn't speak English yet, and since many homes did not yet have refrigeration and relied instead upon a household icebox to keep perishable food cold, he was able to obtain a job delivering ice to people's homes. Mr. Halinen would continue his job lifting the huge frozen blocks with sharply pointed giant ice tongs (an implement which fascinated the children) until he was able to communicate well enough to practice his profession once more. Because both husband and wife were working long hours to become professionally established in Canada, they desperately needed someone to help them care for their three children and to take care of the household. The Nygårds felt this would be a perfect arrangement for them, one which would be beneficial for each family; the Halinens wholeheartedly agreed.

Eeli, Hilkka, Peter and Liisa moved into the house on Albany and Hilkka took over the running of the household. "I now have," she thought, "five children, two husbands, one extra lady and a house to look after. I think I will be a busy woman" . . . and so she was.

The house was a fairly large one and after the tiny shed in Deloraine and the small upstairs rooms on Bannatyne, it seemed positively spacious. The Nygårds had a room of their own, which wasn't actually that big, but which had space enough for their beds and personal items. The Halinens had their private quarters upstairs, and both families shared the main floor kitchen, dining and sitting rooms.

Hilkka was given $40.00 a month to buy groceries for the household. On shopping day she would get out the Halinens' red wagon, put a big cardboard box in it, take the five children and walk to the Safeway store at Ferry Road and Portage Avenue, five blocks away. The children were well behaved and a pleasure to be with, and they thoroughly enjoyed going to the store with Hilkka. After the shopping was done, they would help Hilkka carry her purchases to the wagon and load them into the big cardboard box. When the box and wagon were full, the older children would help her pull the red wagon home. In 1952, one could buy a lot of groceries with forty dollars and the wagon load was heavy to pull. It was healthy, useful exercise and the shopping trips were a good outing for all of them.

The Albany house. In front, left to right, Liisa, Inkeri Halinen, Kirsti Halinen, Antti Halinen, Peter. In back, left to right, Eeli, Mr Halinen, a visiting friend, Hilkka. Liisa and Peter are decked out in the "western gear" Hilkka had bought for them when they lived on Bannatyne.

Hilkka did the laundry using a wringer washer which was in the basement. The basement was dark and had a low ceiling and Hilkka didn't like being down there. She also didn't like letting the laundry pile up, so she was in the basement more than she cared to be. She hung the clean laundry on the outside clothesline both winter and summer, letting the bright sun and blowing breezes dry everything naturally. She washed and changed all the bedding every week. Folding the freshly dried sheets and pillowcases and inhaling their fragrance after they had hung all day in the clean outdoor air, gave her great pleasure. Every so often the clothesline would break under the weight of the wet clothes and would fall to the ground. Hilkka would then have to return to the dark basement and re-wash everything, which pained her, not just because she didn't like the basement, but also because she hated to waste hot water.

The hot water tank in the Albany house was small in size, and with nine people now living there, one needed to be aware of who would need hot water and when they would need it. Mr. Halinen, for example, always had a hot shower before he left for work in the early morning, others in the house also had their preferred times to bathe. Hilkka remembers fondly how little Kirsti Halinen would have her bath and then linger in the warmth of the kitchen with Hilkka. Her older brother, Antti, on the other hand would linger in the bathtub until the water was cold. Hilkka had laundry and dishes to wash and many other household chores to complete. As the household manager there were times when Hilkka began to feel that her sole purpose was to be the hot water scheduling coordinator. Whenever she started to be frustrated with the task, however, all she had to do was to remember heating melted snow on the stove in the shed in Deloraine so that her children could wash their hands, to erase any impending aggravation.

There were unique benefits to living with a doctor in the house. When all the children happened to become ill at the same time, the doctor was able to examine and treat them. The treatment often would include a big scary needle shot of penicillin, delivered to the buttocks. The children may not have seen this as a benefit, but their parents knew that it was and their opinion prevailed.

Life in the Halinen's house on Albany Street was good. In the summertime, Liisa and Peter played in nearby Bruce Park with its big shade trees, wide bubbling creek and wading pool. There were little frogs in the creek. Green things and tall grasses grew along its banks and ducks had nests hidden in them.

There was a cenotaph in the park, and the Nygård children knew that a cenotaph was a thing that had to be treated with great respect. It was inscribed: "Their names live on forever . . . Erected to the memory of the men and women of St. James who died in the Great War."

They were told that the people who were memorialized on the cenotaph had died for their country. Their country. Which was now Peter and Liisa's country. Having left Finland to escape the threat of a communist regime, the children understood better than most Canadian children that the freedom they found in Canada had been provided for them at a great price, and that it should never be taken for granted.

The Nygård family took its first Canadian family pictures in the winter of that year, in front of the Bruce Park Cenotaph.

Peter and Liisa got to know other children in the neighbourhood, even though the manner of introduction was on occasion somewhat unorthodox. They met the Jacksons, from down the street, when Peter and Andy got into a scrap. Peter had been climbing a tree and Andy was chasing him. When Andy came up too close behind Peter, Peter kicked him. An angry Mr. Jackson came storming over to the Nygård's and complained that Peter was picking on Andy and he, Mr. Jackson, was going to call the police. Eeli and Hilkka were horrified, since in Finland police were only called for very serious matters dealing with criminals. After that rather shaky start to their relationship, Peter and Andy stopped chasing and kicking each other and began to enjoy a friendly companionship.

In the strange way that life unfolds, through that bizarre introduction the Jacksons and the Nygårds ended up becoming close friends—friends, in fact, for life. Hilkka's English improved rapidly with her companionship with Mrs. Jackson, except for her confusion about the word "milk". It seems that Mrs. Jackson, when asking someone to pass her the milk jug for her coffee, would often say "Please pass the cow"—a common colloquialism referring to the fact that the little jug contained milk. Hilkka, of course, was not familiar with the colloquialism and, taking Mrs. Jackson's words literally, for the longest time she called milk, "cow". The two friends laughed over "the cow in the jug" for years after they figured out the source of Hilkka's confusion.

Laura, Andy's sister, was a Brownie leader. Liisa had been a girl scout in Finland, and so Laura invited her to join her Brownie Pack, and encouraged Liisa to wear her blue Finnish uniform with its many hard-earned badges (which Liisa still keeps in her memory chest) to the Brownie meetings, which

Hilkka, Peter and Liisa sitting at the base of the cenotaph in Bruce Park
during their first winter in Canada, 1952-1953.

made Liisa happy and saved Hilkka some household money! Laura also made
arrangements for Peter to join a local Cub Pack, since he had belonged to a
similar group in Finland. Both children enjoyed the scouting experience with
its positive and healthy emphasis on life and living, and to this day, Liisa can
recite the Brownie Pledge.

Andy, Peter and Liisa and the two older Halinen children, Inkeri and
Antti all went to Linwood School, one of the original school buildings in St.
James, architecturally and historically interesting. Despite its age, Linwood
was a modern educational facility with an up-to-date learning environment.
Liisa and Peter, as always, settled right in.

Hilkka had been cautioned that she would find winter in Winnipeg cold-
er than winter in Helsinki. Helsinki benefited from the moderating influence
of a nearby ocean, whereas Winnipeg, situated on a mid-continental prairie,
received no such benefit. In fact, strong icy winds would streak across the
prairies and come howling into the various wind tunnels created by Winnipeg city corridors, their paralyzing cold penetrating, as some had said, "the
very bones of living creatures." In winter, such harsh winds could bite right
through a person's outer garments and into the flesh. Exposed skin could
freeze in a matter of minutes if fierce winds were accompanied by sub-zero
temperatures, which, in a Manitoba winter, they always were.

Hilkka, remembering how cold she felt at the Halifax harbour, took
these cautions seriously. She took Peter and Liisa downtown on the street

car—which the children loved to ride—to Eaton's Department Store, which had become her favorite place to shop. There she bought them each a thick parka with a fur-lined hood to keep them warm when winter came. Mittens and scarves of course were things that she knit herself, as had her mother Selma so many years before.

Liisa's tenth birthday came in 1952, at the end of October, and with it came the family's introduction to Hallowe'en. Peter and Liisa had never heard of Hallowe'en, and so disguising themselves in costumes and going door to door with friends on their street to get apples and popcorn from the neighbours, was both novel and pleasurable. Popcorn was a brand new treat for Peter and Liisa. They had only seen it for the first time a few weeks earlier, when they had been to the Saturday matinee at the King's movie theatre on Portage Avenue. They had spotted other children eating the white stuff during the movie and they noticed that the others had begun to eat more rapidly when the really scary parts of the film were being shown. Liisa thought that maybe the white stuff had something in it that would help keep people from becoming too frightened at what they were seeing on the big screen.

They lived with the Halinens all through that first winter in Canada. At Christmas they exchanged gifts and Hilkka cooked a traditional Finnish feast for everyone which left them stuffed and satisfied. Eeli, always eager to give his wife something pretty, gave Hilkka a pair of earrings and a matching necklace set exquisitely in rhinestones and deep blue beads—a gift that was not a necessity or of any particular practical use, but rather a gift that was simply lovely to look at. Hilkka was moved that Eeli would give her such a treasure when he was denying himself so much, and because of that, those Christmas earrings were always special to her.

But perhaps the greatest pleasure that first Christmas in Canada was a delightful visit from Eeli's sister Aili and her husband and children from Minnesota, who arrived for the holiday season. As she embraced her sister-in-law, Hilkka thought about the fact that both she and Eeli had sisters named "Aili" and that both her sister and her sister-in-law were loving and loved. How lucky she was to have these wonderful "Aili's" in her life!

The Christmas visit on Albany gave Hilkka and her sister-in-law time to reminisce together—time to remember the flowing wedding veil both of them had worn, to remember how Hilkka, as a young seventeen year old bride, had relied upon Aili so very much the day of her wedding to Eeli. The wedding attire, the flowers, the photographer—all had been arranged for by

Aili. Her thoughtful generosity had helped to make the Nygård's wedding perfect and Hilkka would never forget the love that Aili had shown them.

There was time to remember when Aili's son, Erkki and her daughter Airi, had disguised themselves as gypsy minstrels and sang for coins in the courtyard at Kotkankatu. Oh how angry Uncle Eeli had been with them! How he scolded them and made them return the coins to the tenants, and how charmingly they had sung for the people who tossed coins to them from their balconies! Liisa recalled hiding around the corner to watch her cousins perform and thinking how wonderful they had sounded.

All those thoughts, all those memories, all the adventures they had experienced since those days, caused the house on Albany to overflow with the joy of a sweetly familiar Finnish Christmas in a wonderful new land of opportunity.

A special gift for the Nygård's first Christmas in Canada, 1952.
Eeli's sister Aili and her family visit the house on Albany.

CHAPTER THREE

Hindley

After living for eight months on Albany Street, Eeli had managed to save enough money to buy a small house on Hindley Avenue in St. Vital, in the southern part of Winnipeg. One of the first visitors to their Hindley house was their beloved friend, Rev. Ian Harvey from Deloraine, and his presence in this, their very own home, meant a great deal to them.

Eeli had purchased the Hindley Avenue house for $3,000. It was a very small house indeed, with only one bedroom, a kitchen, a living room with an oil heater in the center, and a bathroom, but it had a front porch and a double lot with potential. Over the course of the years from 1953 to 1960, a continual upgrading of this humble home would transform it into a house of some substance.

With the help of a carpenter friend, Eeli began by turning the front porch into two 8' by 8' rooms . . . separate bedrooms for Peter and Liisa who relished having their own private spaces at last. Following in swift progression, as they could afford them, came a new water and sewer system, a new lawn, a concrete driveway, new all weather exterior siding and numerous other household renovations. Eeli always had a home improvement project on the go, increasing the comfort of their dwelling and adding value to his real estate investment.

They had great neighbours on Hindley, as they had on Albany. The Charettes not only provided Liisa with a steady baby sitting job, but also took her camping, on evening car rides for ice cream cones and generally treated her as one of their own family members. Since the Nygårds had no car (Eeli had, in fact, never felt the need for a driver's license) a ride in a car was a special event.

The children soon became friends with Norman and Raymond Stevenson, who held memorable potato roasts in the fall. Everyone at the Stevenson's roasts would throw fresh garden potatoes into an open fire, and when they were cooked, retrieved and sliced open, the potatoes would emerge white and steaming hot from their blackened and charred outer skins to be devoured with immense pleasure by those who gathered around. It was a delicious and tasty treat that was hard to forget.

Phil Reimer, (later to become a west coast sports announcer) lived next to a vacant lot where the neighbourhood children would hold stock car races in their home made stock cars, with one person pushing and the other driving (Liisa pushed, Peter drove.) In a foreshadowing of the future, Phil would announce the race. It was considered a real find to come across useful items that could help build a stock car. Finding a discarded baby carriage, for example, was especially valuable, because the old wheels and axles, even if rusty, were key components in a well built racing car.

Liisa and her friends Carol Tucker and Audrey Cassidy would spend afternoons in Carol's secret hideout (an old chicken coop) and take turns singing war time songs played on an old gramophone. Linda Chilton and Liisa were good friends who each adored babies, and they would compete with each other to see which of them could become the first to take the new baby in the neighbourhood for a stroll. Such simple pleasures made life beautiful, easy and care free, even though money was scarce.

The Nygårds lived on Hindley Avenue for a few years before sewer pipes were laid there. Two muddy ruts would form on the street during the wet season, and there were no proper sidewalks. The bus stopped running two blocks from Hindley and the long walk to the bus stop during the muddy season was a challenge. Peter was getting close to the age at which he would be eligible to take his driving test. Eeli noted that some of the teenage boys in the area had begun to steal cars, take them for "joyrides" and end up in a lot of trouble. Eeli felt it would be appropriate and timely to avert such potential problems. When the road was finally gravelled after the sewer was laid, Eeli had a concrete driveway laid, bought a 1953 Buick, took driving lessons and the Nygård family became mobile! Peter took his driver's test as soon as he was eligible, and became the family chauffeur.

Hilkka at the doorway of their newly renovated Hindley home.

Liisa and Hilkka in front of the newly acquired Hindley Avenue house.
Peter on ladder. 1953

Irja Suominen skating on "children's" rink on Hindley Ave.

Liisa holding the Nygård's
new puppy "Pal",
in front of the family's
first car, June 1958.

1957 reception at Hindley Avenue
celebrating Liisa's confirmation.

1956 dinner at Hindley Avenue celebrating Peter's confirmation.
Clockwise from far left: Mrs. Astrom, Esko Repo, Anna Repo holding daughter
June, Hilkka, Irja Suominen, Mr. Astrom, Peter, Eeli, Viljo Suominen, Liisa, Miriam
Vallittu holding son Billy, Harri Vallittu.

One day Hilkka met a woman at Eatons whose first words to her were, "Hey, do you speak Finnish?" It didn't take long for this woman, Irene (Irja) Suominen, and her husband Bill (Viljo) to become special family friends. The Suominens who, like the Nygårds, were from Finland, purchased a home on Worthington Avenue, just one street away from Eeli and Hilkka. They had no children of their own, and so they "adopted" Peter and Liisa as theirs, celebrating with them their confirmations, graduations, Christmases and all the things that loving parents would attend. Together the Suominens and the Nygårds flooded the Nygård lawn to make a skating rink for the children in the winter, which gave pleasure to many skaters in the area.

For Hilkka and Eeli, the presence of the Suominens in their lives was as if they had been given a Canadian family. Together they shared everything. When they would have a festive gathering, or a party of some sort which included other people, Eeli and Viljo would carry a kitchen table a block and a half, down sometimes very muddy streets, to ensure that there would be lots of seating for everyone. Hilkka and Irja would bake together and cook meals together for special occasions which were held at one house or the other.

Hilkka will never forget one occasion during the years they lived on Hindley when she tried on her own to cook a turkey for Christmas. Eeli had been given a turkey as a Christmas gift by his employer at the bakery, and it was too big to fit in their kitchen's icebox, so Hilkka decided to cook it right away. Her problem was that in Finland, only the very wealthy people were able to afford turkey, and so it wasn't a common food. She didn't know how to cook the turkey Eeli had been given, nor could she read any recipe that might instruct her. She did her best. Her best wasn't good enough. Hilkka had undercooked the turkey to such a degree that it was virtually raw when her family tried to eat it. The story of Hilkka's first attempt to cook a turkey became another of the family's Hilkka legends.

It took Hilkka many years to try turkey again; in fact she didn't eat her first real turkey dinner until Liisa married Russell Nichol in 1965. She found the wedding meal to be so delicious that she started cooking turkey again herself, and eventually perfected a variety of poultry dishes that were happily received by those who dined at her table. She also wrote to her family and friends back in Finland to tell them that turkey—the rich man's meal—had been served at Liisa's wedding.

Peter and Liisa transferred to Norberry School from Linwood School when they moved to St. Vital. The principal of Norberry School, Victor Wyatt, became a mentor to Peter and Liisa, playing a major role in their lives and profoundly influencing them. He helped them adjust to Canadian ways while they were struggling to better their English language and communication skills, and he followed their learning with sincere interest, always encouraging them and praising their successes. It was no surprise to anyone when this outstanding educator was made the superintendent of the St. Vital School Division, and no surprise when, in 1979, a division school was named the Victor Wyatt School.

The Lutheran Church had always played a pivotal role in the Nygårds' lives. When Pastor Wilbur Sallach, the pastor of Christ Memorial Lutheran Church, came calling on the Nygårds in their new home, Hilkka and Eeli were reminded of the warmth and humanity of their dear friend, Rev. Ian Harvey, from the little United Church in Deloraine. They welcomed the Lutheran clergyman's visit to their house with gladness, and decided to begin attending Christ Memorial, a place of worship that seemed ideally suited to them. Both children began Sunday School and started going to confirmation classes. Christ Memorial Lutheran Church became the family's new church home, filling a void Hilkka had felt since leaving Finland.

Auntie Irene, as Irja Sominen was to become known to Peter and Liisa, worked for Rice Sportswear garment factory. Auntie Irene was able to get Hilkka a job at the factory sewing men's golf jackets and parkas.

Hilkka was taught how to use the commercial sewing machines by a talented tailor at the factory who took traditional pride in his craftsmanship. She and the tailor respected each other, perhaps because they were both perfectionists who valued work of fine quality. His tutoring, enhanced by her own natural abilities, made Hilkka good at her sewing assignments. Being a perfectionist had one drawback, however. She couldn't let herself make a mistake. If the slippery lining of a jacket wasn't smoothly sewn she would rip it out and do it over. This slowed her down somewhat and since they were paid by the piece, not the hour, it meant that she didn't always make as much money as some of the other workers who didn't worry so much about getting every stitch perfectly sewn.

There were a couple of other women who worked close to Hilkka and they were a real source of frustration to her. They were heavy smokers and the air around them was always thick with smoke. These girls worked very rapidly, producing a large amount of piece work, so that they made lots of money, but their work was full of little mistakes here and there—not enough to reject a garment, but not as well made as they could have been. This irked Hilkka, the perfectionist, to no end.

Hilkka with some of her friends at the Rice Sportswear garment factory.

Still the workplace was made pleasant by the presence of Irja, the thought of the money that she was earning and above all, that she had a job. In the garment factory they made clothes for summer in the winter and clothes for winter in the summer, but in the workplace it was always hot and sticky no matter what the season happened to be. Every day, Hilkka would get a headache from the smoke in the air and the oppressive heat. Their employer would give the workers some salt pills when it was really hot to replace the mineral loss their bodies experienced through excessive sweating. They would also give the workers some 222 tablets if they had headaches or eyestrain from the close work at the machines. Sometimes Hilkka and Irja would come home with sore, smarting eyes and headaches . . . and then make supper. Such were the times.

The children saw that it was a privilege to work and they were always thrilled to find summer employment. One summer, Peter got a job in the garment factory as a bundle boy. Watching the workers, he swore that he would never let his mother work like that again. When he himself became a garment manufacturer, he made certain that his own factories were well ventilated, air-conditioned and clean.

Thursdays were paydays at the factory. Since Eeli's entire pay cheque went to pay off the mortgage on the house, Hilkka's earnings, therefore, had to cover everything else the family required. Each Thursday after work, Hilkka would have her children meet her at the Safeway store near their house. They would bring with them a wagon in the summer and a toboggan in the winter. Hilkka would buy groceries—lots of ground beef, oats, canned fruit, butter, eggs, bananas (they still adored bananas), mushrooms, milk and four of each fruit (four apples, four oranges etc.)—one for each person in the family. No one ever took another's portion. Hilkka was able to stretch the food she bought so that she could make ends meet, and as she stretched, she managed to find tasty treats for their palates. On Thursdays, for example, Hilkka would buy a small brick of ice cream and cut it into four pieces, one for each of them. Everyone, including Hilkka, looked forward to Thursday dinner because of it! Besides her homemade desserts, another favourite which she served whenever she could afford it, was a can of fruit cocktail, again divided in to four servings, making sure that each dish had a maraschino cherry in it. Augmented or not by such occasional grocery store treats, Hilkka's nutritious, tasty and creative meals became family favourites, still chosen over other more sophisticated and exotic cuisines later on when money was no object.

Nothing in Hilkka's well-run household was ever wasted. Leftover food formed the basis of delicious dishes for subsequent meals. Guests at her dining room table were sent home with their favourite leftovers packed in some of the many margarine containers that Hilkka had washed and stored to be used again rather than to be thrown away. Re-used plastic containers were jokingly referred to as "Hilkka's Tupperware Collection"—today consumers call such initiatives "re-purposing"! Hilkka's "re-purposing" of things was a thrifty habit that remained with her all of her life. Long after she could afford to buy bags of soft cotton balls for first aid and cosmetic purposes, she continued to save the cotton balls from her medicine bottles, keeping them in a special box on her dressing room table for ready use. Why toss them away when they were still perfectly good? Grocery bags, paper or plastic, which had carried her groceries home, were re-used to hold household garbage. They were not wasted; rather they were used as receptacles for legitimate waste.

To Hilkka, like many in her generation, re-using, re-purposing and re-cycling were natural habits, ingrained since childhood. Those who have lived through major wars and depressions when food and material goods were scarce, seldom, if ever, waste food or discard things that might still prove to be useful in some way. As she became increasingly aware of environmental challenges, Hilkka recognized that her frugal practices also had positive benefits for the world around her. When she started limiting, as best as she could, the number of plastic and other environmentally unfriendly items brought into her home—and when she stopped using margarine altogether—the Hilkka Tupperware Collection diminished dramatically.

Hilkka's attention to efficiently maintaining the family budget didn't stop at stretching the grocery bills. She and Eeli had always operated on a cash-as-you-go pattern. Except for the mortgage (the repayment of which was the highest priority for the family) they had never borrowed. Hilkka was amazed to discover how many people in Canada relied upon credit to maintain their standard of living. This was a foreign concept to her and she had difficulty relating to it, but when she was informed that she could purchase a top-of-the-line winter parka for each of her children by taking advantage of Eaton's Department Store's credit policy, she decided to try it out. At the store's credit office, located in the upper levels of its huge building, they were

Liisa and Peter playing musketeers with the Niemelä children
at Lac du Bonnet.

met and served by an immaculately groomed woman who wore bright red lipstick and had her brown hair pulled back into a fashionable bun on the back of her head. Hilkka never forgot how professional the woman was, in both her appearance and in her manner, and how that factor seemed to underscore that this financing was to be taken seriously. She bought the parkas on credit and paid off her bill as fast as she could. Thereafter her ability to use credit was treated as a convenience to be utilized from time to time—and always to be paid off immediately. She still was much more comfortable paying for things with cash.

During the children's younger years, summers developed a pleasant rhythm of their own. When school was out, Eeli would stay back in Winnipeg and work on his latest renovation project, and Irja and Viljo would take Hilkka, Peter and Liisa to Red Rock Lake in Manitoba's beautiful Whiteshell region to camp in a tent with a number of other new Finnish immigrants. At other times they would take them to Pointe du Bois to cottages owned by the Astrom/Repo families, or to Lac du Bonnet to visit the Niemeläs. Those were peaceful relaxing times, filled with good memories of blueberry picking, sun bathing, swimming and just enjoying fellowship around a camp fire with dear new Finnish-Canadian friends like the Pellinens, Keskikyläs, Ampujas, and Eronens.

The Finnish Canadian club provided the Nygård family the opportunity to become acquainted with yet more new Finnish immigrants. They came to know the Tuominens, Rainonens, Vallittus, Vesas, Jordans, Pikkarainens, Salos, Välimäkis, Harjus, Ovaskainens, Ollis . . . the list of newcomers was long and all of the people in the club formed a type of extended family group in which members shared each others' joys and sorrows, laughter and tears, and supported each other in everything from entrepreneurial efforts to sporting events.

The Finnish Canadian Club would put on theatre productions in which Hilkka and Eeli often had leading roles. The children would participate in the Mothers' Day and Christmas Concerts and Hilkka would often do a reading from *Aleksis Kiven Ajatuksia* or from *Kalevala*, the famous Finnish epic. She loved to perform because she could feel the writer's purpose and sense his mood in the words. Her passion for the cultural richness found in the works of the great Finnish writers and composers stirred her soul and she wanted to instill the same depth of emotion in her children.

Theatre productions at the Finnish Canadian Club:

Eeli starring in play, centre stage.

The cast with Eeli at right, in the mid-nineteen fifties.

Hilkka was blessed to have found wonderful friends, true kindred spirits, in Canada. Irja Sominen and Hilkka supported and cared for each other through thick and thin, enriching their lives and vanquishing the unique kind of loneliness and homesickness so often experienced by immigrant women. Hilkka's sorrow was deep when both Irja and Viljo Sominen died within a year of each other—Viljo in August of 2001, and Irja in December of 2002. With their passing, it was as if two family members had gone. Other sisters of the heart formed bonds in many different ways. Four of the women who were part of the 1950's original group of Finnish Canadian immigrants stayed in touch with each other through the years. Hilkka was one of the four. From wherever they happened to be and in no matter what circumstances they happened to find themselves, Kaino, Annikki, Maire and Hilkka would communicate on a regular basis. In their later years they would talk almost weekly on the phone, laughing and reminiscing, supporting each other and comforting each other as all but one of them became widows. Every one of the four had achieved success in their personal goals, the most important of which was the raising and nurturing of their children. Ironically, three of the four died within two weeks of each other in January 2010. (Annikki died on January 6th, Hilkka on January 12th, and Kaino on January 24th.)

Their friendship had turned out to be lifelong.

The Hindley Avenue house had a little blue radio, and there was no television in the house for many years. On Sunday afternoons there was a classical music program on one of the stations, and Hilkka and the children would lie on the floor, close their eyes and each in turn would describe the picture which they imagined the music was creating. A Sibelius composition would make the game increasingly exciting! To hear the great Finnish composer's work on Canadian radio was a marvelous treat for them. Both Peter and Liisa grew up with a keen appreciation for the performing arts, an appreciation which never left them. For this gift of understanding, they are both grateful to their mother.

Hilkka's wide ranging interests broadened their minds and outlook on life. They saw nothing unusual about their mother eagerly reading the novel *Sinuhe* by Mika Walteri, while at the same time avidly following the racing careers of Formula One racing car champions, Mika Häkkinen and Kimi Raikkanen, in great detail, even to the point of getting up at unusual hours of the night to watch specific car races on television. Mika Walteri, of course, was a Finn, and many of the international racing car competitors were also Finns. Though she was proud to be a Canadian, Hilkka's loyalty to the Finnish people was intense and she was always there in the cheering section to support them in whatever their endeavours happened to be.

This genuine sense of kinship and special respect she felt for Finnish athletes would continue throughout Hilkka's life. She would attend all the Winnipeg Jets' hockey games and her cheers would become especially loud when the Finns were on the ice. After most games, the Nygård home (and sauna) would become a refuge for Finnish Winnipeg Jets' team players, Veli-Pekka Ketola, Hexi Riihiranta, and their families. The fellowship that the Nygårds had provided for Finnish hockey players continued to be offered when Markus Mattson and later Teppo Numminen and Teemu Selänne would receive the same warm Winnipeg welcome in Liisa's home as the others had in Hilkka's. The mutual respect and the friendships thus formed were to last long after the players left Canada.

In later years, every chance she got, whether she happened to be in the Bahamas or at Falcon Lake, Hilkka would be seated in front of the television whenever she heard that Teemu was on the ice or when the Finnish National Team was playing, and in all cases the entire Nygård family would sing the "Maamme Laulu" with misty eyes when a Finnish victory presented the opportunity.

The Hindley Avenue home was a training ground for entrepreneurship. The children, at a very young age, devised their own allowance contract. They allocated a price for each task. Making one's own bed was a five cent task. Making the parents' bed was a ten cent task. Washing dishes? Ten cents. Drying dishes? Five cents. Carrying out the slop pail was a whopping big twenty-five cent job. (When the family first moved in, there was no sewer. The grey water ran into a cistern under the garden but the contents of the toilet had to be carried out to a second dugout further back in the garden. Drinking water was carried from a stand pipe two houses over.) Peter and Liisa liked the rewards and they enjoyed the competition as they raced to see who could get the better paying jobs!

Before long the children expanded their enthusiasm for making money to places outside their own home, and from this time on would not require spending money from their parents.

Liisa found numerous baby-sitting jobs. As well as for the Charettes, she sat for the Fraser family with six children, the Vallittus family with three children, the Stewarts and the Friesens. She began eyeing pregnant women with anticipation and the hope of acquiring yet another job. Peter was the ultimate recycler. He collected pop bottles, and had a couple of paper routes. He sub-contracted to Liisa and paid her a small share of the income.

Although the housework allowance was no longer needed, the work was still expected to be done. Each Saturday, Hilkka expected the children to clean their own rooms. That meant washing the floor, wiping each vein of the venetian blinds, and each base board, dusting, and changing the bed sheets, remembering to make hospital corners and to pull the sheets tight. When Hilkka worked on Saturdays, Liisa did the family wash with the wringer machine.

Whenever her children left for school or for some type of job, Hilkka always sent them off with the words, "Have a good day! Work hard!" Her own work ethic was revealed in her parting words—how very different from the parting words so often used by others, "Don't work too hard!" Hilkka believed that hard work lead to a productive, and therefore rewarding, life. To help her children understand this concept, Peter and Liisa were rewarded for their performance. An "A" on their report cards earned them five dollars. The school was seen as a training ground for the world of work, where an outstanding performance lead to success and a poor performance did not. Mediocrity was not a goal that a Nygård would pursue!

Hilkka and Eeli taught their children to have respect for work. Any job, no matter how lowly, had dignity. It was important to be able to take care of oneself and one's family and not have to depend upon the good will of others to survive. Education was the key ingredient to becoming self-sufficient, and therefore great respect must be accorded the schoolteachers who delivered the education. The teacher, they stressed, was always right and must be obeyed. If a teacher called their home to report that one of their children had misbehaved at school, Eeli and Hilkka made sure that the scolding at school was followed by a scolding at home.

It seemed that only a short time had gone by before the fifties ended, and Peter and Liisa were in high school at St. Vital's Glenlawn Collegiate. Hilkka looked at them and thought, "How could my little babies get to be so old? When did they both become taller than me?"

Both Peter and Liisa were athletic teenagers and both made their school basketball team. They were coached by one of St. Vital's best and most respected Physical Education teachers, Ernie Gaudreau, who inspired them to

Peter graduating from Glenlawn Collegiate 1960, winner of the Sports Award.

Ernie Gaudreau, far right, back row,
and the Norberry Junior High basketball team, 1957-58.
Peter in back row, third from right, number 21.

Liisa graduating from Glenlawn Collegiate in 1961, receiving the
Home Economics Award, presented to her by her mentor, Victor Wyatt.

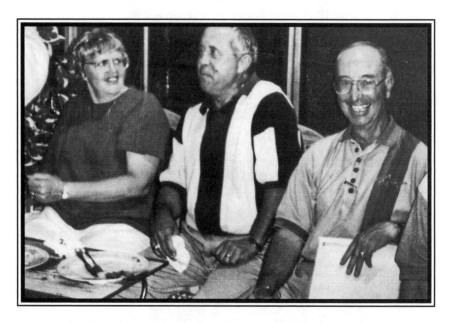

Joanne "Rubberlegs Schultz" Koskie with her husband Ron Koskie and Coach
Ernie Gaudreau at a birthday party for Hilkka.

Liisa and Peter with Victor Wyatt and Ernie Gaudreau,
two of the many educators they especially admired.

put forth their best efforts. Gaudreau was a tough but fair task master, a no nonsense teacher and a coach who never seemed to lose his cool. Liisa said once that Mr. Gaudreau had left a "positive mark on the mosaic of my life." Eeli and Hilkka were again blessed to have a man of integrity influencing the lives of their children.

Basketball, volleyball and track and field were Peter's favourite sports in high school and he was a top performer in all of them. In testament to this, he was presented with the school's Male Athlete Award at graduation.

Liisa loved to play basketball as well, especially for Ernie Gaudreau, for whom she wanted to perform well. She participated as well in the discus throw and gave a credible performance in competitions. She would brag that she came second in the half mile race, only to add with a grin that there were just two runners in her class.

Because Eeli worked the night shift, he was pleased that he was available to be one of the parent spectators at the daytime track meets. He would bring a thermos of egg nog—his homemade mixture of raw eggs, sugar, milk and vanilla—to Peter and Liisa to nourish and refresh them at the track.

Hilkka attended almost every basketball game to watch them play, even traveling to see games played out of town. There were usually only four parents who showed up consistently at the girls' games—Hilkka, the father of Carol Marchysyn and the parents of Joanne Schultz. Joanne was one of Liisa's best friends on the team and is now the wife of Ron Koskie and mother of the well known national team super volleyball athlete Scott Koskie. Hilkka got a big kick out of hearing Liisa called "Elbows Nygård" by her teammates, while Joanne who was tall and agile and bounced like a ball through the defence was named "Rubberlegs Schultz".

When the Glenlawn girls' basketball team made it into the Provincial Championships, Hilkka invited the whole team to come to the Nygård home for a party after the championship game was over. Liisa and her teammates won against Viscount Alexander Collegiate by a hair in the last seconds of the game, but even before knowing the outcome, Hilkka had already made a huge strawberry Victory Cake—she knew that they would win. The Nygård home rocked with happy athletes and fans. Even Coach Gaudreau came. It was a great party!

During the summers when he was going to high school, Peter worked the night shift at a local Loblaws grocery store, stocking shelves. He was learning about retail marketing and being paid to learn. The one summer he had worked in the garment factory taught him a tremendous amount about manufacturing. He saw what he liked, and more importantly, he saw what he didn't like.

Hilkka and Eeli were proud when Peter won the Glenlawn Collegiate Sports Award and Liisa won the Glenlawn Collegiate Home Economics Award. Perhaps the greatest thrill to Liisa was that the award was presented to her by Victor Wyatt! Their children were progressing nicely in this new land.

Hilkka continued working at Rice Sportswear until Peter graduated from High School in 1960, at which point she was offered, and she accepted, a job in the sewing room at Misericordia Hospital. There she mended and shortened uniforms, made and repaired curtains, and did general sewing as requested by the hospital administration. Hilkka was dependable and valued by the hospital and she enjoyed working there.

She took to visiting patients during her lunch hour, and when she was told that her former St. James neighbour, Betty Jackson, had admitted her mother to the hospital, Hilkka made a point of regularly visiting her at her bedside. Betty's mother and another patient who had been badly injured in a motorcycle accident were two people that Hilkka stopped in to see almost every day, and she always found them waiting and looking for her. When Mrs. Jackson's mother died, Hilkka's heart went out to Betty. She had grown very fond of her friend's mother and suffered along with the whole Jackson family in their loss.

Hilkka, third from right, in Misericordia Hospital Sewing Room.

NYGÅRD for Life   AUG 05

The wind beneath our wings

CHAPTER FOUR

A Matter of Degrees

When the decade turned and the sixties began, it seemed that suddenly the whole pace of Hilkka's life went into high gear. In rapid succession, major events took place within the family.

When Peter graduated from Glenlawn Collegiate in 1960, he made plans to attend Hibbing Junior College in Hibbing, Minnesota where Eeli's sister Aili lived. At this time Peter was an avid curler and Hibbing Junior College offered a great curling program. He had only to convince his parents that this would be a good choice for him.

When it came to major family decisions Peter had discovered that it was always best to convince Liisa of the merits of his case first and have her, as his advocate, convince Hilkka. Hilkka in turn would gently suggest to Eeli that it would be a great idea, for example, for Peter to go to Hibbing.

The strategy was successful, to a point. Eeli agreed to send Peter to Hibbing, but he made his decision conditional. He would pay for Peter's tuition as long as he kept up his marks. If he failed any courses, he would have to pay for the balance of his classes, or quit.

Aili promised that she would keep a steady eye on her high-spirited nephew while he studied, and she would provide a room in her home for him. Aunt Aili must have been true to her word, because Peter did well in those studies and after two years at the Junior College, he again had to convince his parents that he should now continue to finish his university education at the University of North Dakota (UND). Again the same negotiations took place. Liisa thought it was a great idea, Hilkka agreed and Eeli again made it conditional on marks. The investment was well worth it. Peter graduated with a Bachelor of Science with a major in Business Administration in January of 1964, and jumped immediately into what would become a dynamic career in business.

Eeli and Hilkka sold the Hindley Avenue house, made a tidy profit from its sale, and moved into the Southbend Apartments on St. Mary's Road. With the profits from the sale of the house they were able to help Peter with his university expenses, and set money aside to save for the eventual purchase of their own bakery and for a visit back to Finland.

Liisa was by then in her last year of high school, graduating from Glenlawn Collegiate in 1961. She went directly into the work force, and was employed by Great West Life Assurance Company in the Group Insurance Department, whose head office was at that time located in Winnipeg. Liisa loved working at Great West. She had a wonderfully satisfying job in a company with a staff association which included sporting activities, a choir, dressmaking contests, charity events and more. Liisa jumped into everything with both feet and flourished. She couldn't have asked for a more effective transition from her active involvement in high school life to the world of work.

Even so, as time went on, she wanted to learn more, to explore theories and acquire credentials that would lead to a stimulating professional career. She had also not forgotten that she had promised Principal Victor Wyatt that she would go to university—a promise which kept surfacing repeatedly in her memory.

She wanted to work with children and knew she could achieve a degree majoring in speech pathology at UND; and so in 1964, Peter's graduation year, Liisa approached her parents with the idea of her beginning her own program of studies. Eeli and Hilkka were delighted at the initiative, and gladly offered their support, with the same rules that were set for Peter now applying to her.

Liisa was at this time in a serious relationship with Russell Nichol, who was also planning to enroll at UND. The two decided to get married and attend UND as married students, where they would augment their meager income by acting as area supervisors for the married students' housing at the university. By attaining good marks in her first year of studies, Liisa was to be awarded a bursary from the Province of Manitoba which would pay for her tuition from her second year on. In exchange for this bursary, Liisa provided a commitment to the province to work in Manitoba as a Speech Pathologist for three years after graduating with her degree. With these sources of revenue, and the earnings they intended to accumulate during the summer, the young couple anticipated that they could adequately cover their necessary costs while at UND.

They planned an August 28, 1965 wedding. Both would work for the summer and be ready to begin university classes in September.

With no tuition to pay, Hilkka and Eeli offered instead to pay for a 250 guest wedding for Liisa and Russell, and so, on the appointed date, the happy couple was married in the warm and loving presence of many dear friends and relatives.

Classes started in September, and the newlyweds had very little time to set up housekeeping. They were going to be living in a Quonset hut that had originally been an army barrack, but which had been converted to student housing. The place needed decorating badly. Hilkka and Eeli, Auntie Irene and her husband Bill, all drove down to North Dakota to help redecorate, paint, sew curtains, and generally clean up, so that Liisa and Russell would have their home in order before their studies began. The older folks slept on the floor in the living room of the Quonset hut—these dear sweet people— and the bride and groom were so grateful to them for their help that it never occurred to them that it was a rather bizarre way to spend a honeymoon.

Liisa and Russ stayed in their nicely turned out Quonset and studied together and in 1966 planned to start their family. The child would have to be born in the summer of 1967 because Liisa had one more semester of student teaching left. On August 26, 1967, Hilkka's first grand daughter, Angela Christi, was born, just in time to move to campus for classes to start on September 13. Liisa graduated Cum Laude on January 28, 1968 with a Bachelor of Science in Education with a major in Speech Pathology and Audiology and a minor in Psychology. Russell received his Bachelor of Science in Business Administration in June of 1968. Liisa would begin her work with the Child Guidance Clinic as a Speech Therapist in the Greater Winnipeg School Division. (Later, in one of life's delicious ironies, Liisa worked in the St. Vital School Division, where her mentor, Victor Wyatt was by then Superintendent of Schools.) Russ was hired by the Hudson's Bay Company to become an executive trainee, and he eventually became Personnel Manager in Winnipeg.

As well as Gramma Hilkka and Grampa Eeli, little Angela had a huge group of aunts and uncles and grand parents on the Nichol side of the family in Winnipeg anxious to hold her.

Hilkka loved this tiny little girl with a heart so full of love that she thought it would burst. She didn't know then that she and Angela would one day share a significant experience that would bond them together forever. She just knew what she had always known . . . a baby is a miraculous gift from God.

Liisa and Russ chose Peter, and Russell's sister Carol, to be Godparents for Angela. Peter was fascinated with Liisa's first born. After the Christening service, he lay across the bed in his parents' apartment with the baby's tiny hand wrapped around his finger, and Liisa saw his eyes welling up as he marveled at the miracle that had come into the family. As the years passed, Peter and Angela would grow ever closer in trust and loyalty and would become a significant part of each other's lives.

Liisa graduating Cum Laude, from University of North Dakota with husband, the late Russ Nichol, and their new baby Angela.

Gramma Hilkka at Liisa's graduation with baby Angela. Angela is wearing a snowsuit given to her for the occasion by Gramma Johanna.

After Peter graduated from university, he returned to Winnipeg and took a management position in the food section at Eaton's. He was an excellent employee, having absorbed his parents' work ethic and possessing a top notch understanding of the retail market. He progressed rapidly with Eaton's and was soon in a commanding position as the youngest Regional Supervisor of eighteen Heavy Goods & Mail Order Stores. He came to the attention of a headhunter who was looking for a person to work for a clothing manufacturer who owned a company called Jacob Fashions. Nathan Jacob, the owner, wanted someone to take over his $800,000 business and none of his four daughters were suited to the industry. Nathan and Peter signed a contract agreeing that, if Peter could double the business in one year, he could buy a one-fifth partnership in Jacob Fashions.

Two months later, after Peter had started to work on the biggest gamble of his life, Nathan Jacobs was diagnosed with terminal cancer. Peter pushed himself harder than ever, and doubled the business in a half a year.

Nathan knew he was dying and he had taken a shine to Peter, who was bringing so much life and energy to the company, and so, as they had previously agreed, he offered Peter a twenty percent partnership in his business. Peter borrowed eight thousand dollars from his family and friends and Nathan himself loaned him the rest of the capital he required. Peter became a one-fifth partner of Jacob Fashions and entered the fashion world.

Peter regretted never having been able to benefit directly from Nathan's twenty-five years of experience. He missed not having the opportunity to consult with him and seek his advice. Still, Peter was bright, enthusiastic, and blessed with a natural instinct and knowledge of appropriate marketing techniques. Using all his energy and ability, he survived the first year on his own. The other family partners saw the success he was having, and wanting to buy Peter out, they offered him a buy/sell deal. At the end of the complex negotiating and maneuvering that ensued, Peter Nygård ended up as the sole owner of Jacob Fashions. To make the business truly his and give it a brand new start Peter recognized that the company needed to have a new name. Wanting to achieve this while still paying homage to Nathan, Peter took the product name, "Tan Jay" ("Tan" being "Nat" spelled backwards, and "Jay" being a shortened form of "Jacob") and made it the name of the company itself. Peter really respected Nathan Jacob. Nathan had respect for Peter in return. "Peter," he advised his young successor, "you will be wealthy by the time you are forty, and you should retire then."

Peter told his mother later that day that he had missed an interview he was supposed to have had that afternoon, but he couldn't make it because he had been too busy buying a company.

Peter was quickly becoming noticed in the corporate world. Although he was still in his twenties, he was being touted as an up and coming business tycoon. In an interview which appeared in the Winnipeg Free Press, Peter was quoted as having stated that he aspired to be a millionaire by the time he was 30. Although the article was a flattering one, Hilkka was embarrassed by it because it sounded as if Peter were in the thralls of an impossible and overly optimistic dream. She wondered what her son was thinking of to say such a thing! Liisa remembers people at the Child Guidance Clinic where she worked expressing skepticism about her brother's ability to achieve his lofty objective. Peter, however, just went ahead and became, not just a millionaire, but a multi-millionaire . . . and he acquired his first million years before he was thirty. The best way, it seems, to prove your credibility is to just go ahead and do the things people say you cannot do. As Peter said, "One thing about striving for the impossible is that you have very little competition."

In 1967, Eeli and Hilkka decided to take a vacation and go to Finland. It had been fifteen years since they had left the land of their birth and they missed it. They wanted to go back and see again all the old places and famil-iar faces that meant so much to them. They bought their tickets and eagerly prepared for an exciting trip back to "the old country."

As they were in the midst of their preparations, a bakery came up for sale on Winnipeg's busy Sargent Avenue. It was the chance that Eeli had been waiting for. Ideally located and fully equipped, he knew right away that this was destined to become *their* bakery. The tickets to Finland were non-refundable and both Liisa and Peter urged their parents not to cancel the journey home that they were so looking forward to taking. The bakery could be bought and the children would oversee anything that needed to be done regarding it while Hilkka and Eeli were away.

Eeli was short the full amount required to buy the business, so Peter sold his car, an Impala of which he was inordinately proud, for $2,500 to get the necessary cash needed to complete the transaction. It was not a sacrifice, he assured his parents. "A sacrifice," he told them, "is when you give up something for someone else." That's not what Peter was doing. He was sell-ing his car so that he, Peter, could have the joy of knowing that his parents had their dream come true.

This exciting opportunity for Eeli and Hilkka had come just as Liisa was nearing the date for delivery of her first baby, and for the final semester to complete her university degree. Despite these upcoming personal events, she held firmly to her promise to help get the bakery ready for business while they were gone. Liisa spent every day overseeing the renovations required in the bakery. Carpentry, cleaning, painting, signage—all came under her efficient supervision. Like her brother, she too shared in the joy of knowing her parents were having their dream come true.

Peter and Liisa standing in front of Peter's car, which he sold to help his parents buy their bakery.

CHAPTER FIVE

New Business

Eeli and Hilkka went to Finland with mixed emotions. They were thrilled to return to the land that had nurtured them when they were young, the land in which they and their children had been born, but they were anxious about leaving their new land and the bakery that was now theirs. They had very little spending money for the trip, having put the balance of their savings into purchasing the business, and so they returned to Finland having to be as frugal as they had been when they lived there! Still it was a wonderful time for Hilkka and Eeli. Although they were temporarily cash-poor, they were wealthy beyond measure in opportunity and optimism. They were extremely confident that if they worked hard (hard work being the key, as it had always been for them) they would have a successful business. Traveling around Finland, knowing that they were truly established now in Canada, made them deeply conscious of their treasured past and exciting future.

The plane ride back to Canada was noisy and uncomfortable and Hilkka was unable to relax. It wasn't just the racket made by the rotation of the propellers outside that made her tense. It was the anticipation of walking into the bakery to begin work that kept her in a high state of restlessness. It was late when they landed in Thunder Bay and most of the other passengers on the plane decided to stay overnight there, but not the Nygårds! They wanted to go home right away.

Despite the late hour, they picked up their car from the parking lot and headed to Winnipeg. They contemplated, very briefly, the idea of stopping

Visiting Hilkka's sisters, Iida and Aili, in Finland.

for a rest at a cottage Peter had rented at Falcon Lake in the Whiteshell Provincial Park. At any other time, Hilkka would have been delighted to stop at Falcon Lake, since the area, with its clear cold waters, tall conifers and granite outcroppings, reminded her so much of Finland, but even the lure of a cottage by a lake couldn't keep her from agreeing with Eeli that they should press on towards home. They arrived back in Winnipeg exhausted and fell into bed and went immediately to sleep.

Eeli's eyes were suspiciously moist when, later on, he stood on the city sidewalk in front of his new establishment and looked up for the first time to read the freshly painted sign that said, "Nygård's Bakery". His dream had come true.

He and Hilkka baked all kinds of bread. Rye, wheat, barley, oat—healthy delicious breads that were rich with flavour and goodness came out of their ovens each day. The trend towards eating full grained breads had not yet caught hold with Canadian consumers, so the Nygårds were seen as specialists offering unique Scandinavian breads and buns in addition to the more commonly requested brown and white loaves. Doughnuts, cinnamon buns, dinner rolls, cakes, cookies—if the consumer wanted to buy it, the Nygårds would bake it. Hilkka and Eeli prospered. They were in charge of their own destiny.

Initially they had no staff. Customers would ask Eeli, "How many employees do you have?" and he would answer, "We have four. My wife works two shifts and I work two shifts." That they were each doing the work of two full time employees meant that they had to work for long hours in the shop, but the rewards were definitely worth it. They were able to keep the overhead expenses down, but more importantly, they were also able to maintain exceptional quality control in the bakery.

Eeli and Hilkka would arrive at the bakery at five a.m. Eeli would begin the dough preparations while Hilkka washed down the store counters and mopped the floor. She would cook the jam busters and help Eeli get the buns on to baking sheets and into the proofer. They would continue baking until one half hour before opening time, at which point Hilkka would go downstairs, freshen up, fix her hair, put on a crisp clean white uniform, apply her makeup and arrive back upstairs to open the door precisely at 9 a.m., often to a long line of waiting customers. She recalls one morning when she was one minute late opening the door only to have a waiting customer comment, "Slept a little late this morning did you?" He had no idea! She said nothing. She just nodded good morning, smiled and welcomed the paying customers in.

The plain fact is that Hilkka loved to work. She didn't rejoice, as most people did, when the work week ended; nor did she groan when Monday mornings came. In fact she eagerly anticipated Monday mornings—the coming alive of the shops and stores, the hustle and bustle on the streets, the many different sounds of business and trade—all of these spoke to productivity, prosperity and success. Hilkka was a lover of Monday mornings, a true entrepreneur.

Eeli and Hilkka attributed the success of their bakery, not just to their hard work, but most significantly to the high quality of their ingredients. They paid a little more to achieve this quality, but Eeli's expertise in achieving perfect texture and flavour in his Danish pastries, jam busters, cinnamon rolls, pecan buns and variety of breads and famous fruit tortes made Nygård's Bakery a popular place. Customers appreciated not only the product, but also the integrity and dependability of the business owners. Liisa recalls how Hilkka ran after a customer who had forgotten five cents change, so important to her was being honest in everything.

They became successful. They began to receive orders from far away. Elite clientele would send taxis from their elegant mansions on Winnipeg's exclusive Wellington Crescent to Nygård's Bakery to pick up breads and baked goods. Regular customers kept track of Eeli and Hilkka's schedules so that they could fill their home freezers up with baked goods before the Nygårds took holidays.

The Lieutenant Governor of Manitoba, the Honourable Pearl McGonigal, liked to order pastries and dainties from Hilkka whenever she entertained groups of women for afternoon tea at Government House. Hilkka would make little buns and pastries, pink Alexanders, chocolate brownies, lemon tarts, for Her Honour, and would even match the colour of the dainties with the colour scheme, flowers and tablecloths selected for the event! Lieutenant-Governor McGonigal asked the Nygårds to consider coming to work for her if and when they decided to retire, with Eeli assuming a position as a butler, and Hilkka as head of the kitchen staff. It was a great honour and a tribute to the level of the Nygård's success in serving the public, but by the time they retired, Hilkka and Eeli had other exciting plans in the making.

Eeli and Hilkka in Nygård's Bakery, in charge of their own destiny.

Hilkka welcoming customers at the Nygård's Bakery, 1967

CHAPTER SIX

Eagles Don't Walk

In 1968 Peter bought the cottage that he had been dreaming of owning for fourteen years—the one he had been renting on that dream point of land at Falcon Lake—and began to renovate it. He was busy building up his business, and like his parents had done before him, he was working night and day to become successful. He spent a lot of time traveling, and even when he was at home he was always working, on the phone, writing up plans, setting up meetings, on the go every minute. It was in his nature, indeed part of his very being and soul, to work hard. He was driven to excel. Asking him to do otherwise would have been like asking eagles to walk instead of fly.

During this period, Peter married briefly, but the marriage didn't last, and Peter was never to marry again. He did go on, however, to have some special relationships which blessed him with children who have given him much joy.

Though still under thirty, Peter had risen rapidly to the top of the fashion industry, was internationally successful, and in an astoundingly short period of time, as predicted by Nathan Jacob, had become a wealthy man.

As his wealth continued to increase, Peter, as a present for his wife Carol, bought the opulent Wellington Crescent mansion previously owned by the Eaton family, of department store fame. The irony of the fact that his first job after graduation had been at Eaton's and that he had been launched into the manufacturing world from there, was not lost on him.

The Eaton house was one of the most magnificent—and expensive— private residences in Winnipeg. For all its splendour, or maybe because of it, the mansion was imposing and intimidating. Designed to be run by a household staff, the residence was overwhelming. Peter took possession of the estate and was ready to move in, but by then he was single again and the residence seemed too large for just one person, so Peter offered his parents the house. Both Hilkka and Eeli were nervous about moving into such a grand residence. "It is too big for us," Hilkka told him, "It is like a palace. We are simple people and we don't know if we could get used to living in a palace."

Hilkka and Eeli were by this time living in Chateau 100, a high rise apartment building overlooking the banks of the Assiniboine River. They had a large suite there, with a sunken living room, white carpets and housekeeping. (The white carpet/housekeeping combination seemed to be a natural fit). Hilkka had discovered a long black hair on her clean pillow one evening and it had upset her. Given that she and Eeli both had very light hair, the black hair meant that someone else had slept, or at least reclined, on her bed. It was an uncomfortable feeling, and while she liked the apartment, she felt a little violated by this intrusion into her private space by a person she didn't know. She was willing to move, but not into a mansion like the edifice on Wellington Crescent.

So Peter reluctantly sold the Eaton house, and instead provided his parents with a sizable down payment on a large and gracious home on Bower Boulevard in Winnipeg's exclusive Tuxedo district. The Bower house was impressive in its own right, but it had been built as a family dwelling and not as a "palace" so Hilkka knew that she could make a home there that her children and grandchildren would enjoy coming to visit.

Their new house was close to Winnipeg's 1,100 acre Assiniboine Park with its lush greenery, formal gardens, reflecting ponds, sculpture garden, art galleries, a tropical conservatory with over 8000 exotic flowers, plants and trees, a ninety acre zoo with over 300 animal species, and countless other attractions. Assiniboine Park is one of the loveliest of Winnipeg's city parks, and Hilkka and Eeli, like so many others who enjoy being outdoors, could stroll on its winding pathways in the summer and traverse them on skis in the winter. For companionship, Peter presented them with a huge Great Dane. They named him Drake, and took him for long walks in the park.

Eeli skiing in Assiniboine Park with Drake.

There was always time for laughter and fun with friends at the Nygård home.

Hilkka, too modest to let people know that she lived in Tuxedo, used to say, when asked where she lived, that she lived "near the Park." People, she felt, whether they were rich or poor, could relate to the park, and hence to her.

Peter had moved into the penthouse in the Park Terrace Apartments, on the other side of the river from his parents.

Eeli and Hilkka continued to work hard, rising at five o'clock each morning and working until seven o'clock each evening, six days a week. During the Christmas season they would receive literally hundreds of orders to be prepared for customers on December 24th. It was important that the baked goods be fresh when they were picked up or delivered, and so Hilkka and Eeli would be joined by Liisa after she got off work on December 23rd (which was Eeli's birthday), and the three of them would bake all night and straight through the next day to fill all the orders on time. Hilkka would take little breaks now and then, and Eeli would sometimes literally fall asleep while standing on his feet. After the work was done, they would take out their own Christmas Eve casseroles from the bakery ovens where they had been slowly cooking for several hours, and carry them home for the Christmas Eve dinner with their family. There they would relax, comforted by the knowledge that all over the city people were enjoying the delicious taste of Nygård's Bakery items.

Christmas Eve on Bower held the same special magic for Hilkka that Christmas had held for her in Finland. Liisa and Russell and their children, Peter, and of course Irja and Viljo, would gather at the big home on Bower Boulevard, and Hilkka, tired but happy, would beam with pleasure in their presence and allow herself to relax from her labours and enjoy her many blessings. Young Kristopher, Liisa's third child, twice tipped over the tall white Christmas tree that Hilkka and Eeli had put up each year, and so eventually Liisa suggested that until the children were a little older, perhaps the family Christmas dinners could be held at her home . . . and so it was. The venue may have changed, but the joy of the Christmas season and the love that flowed around them at that time never changed.

Despite the grueling hours of work, Hilkka and Eeli still had energy to enjoy dancing, watch the Winnipeg Jets play hockey, cheer for the Winnipeg Blue Bomber football team, and host innumerable dinner parties. Many laughter-filled evenings were spent with friends Heikki and Riitta Kelonen, the Suominens, Eronens, Thusbergs, Tuominens, Tuuni and Pekka Voittola and others from all walks of life.

Hilkka and Eeli developed a routine of closing the bakery for one or two weeks each winter and escaping to a warm sunny spot for some rest and relaxation, sometimes traveling alone and at other times with another couple. They visited wonderfully colourful and exotic places like Hawaii, Acapulco, Grand Bahama, and took a boat cruise in the Caribbean. Each time they returned from their holiday refreshed and eager to start working again.

In the early 1970's, just prior to the 1976 Olympics, Peter, an avid and adventurous sailor, provided Eeli and Hilkka with added travel excitement as he invited them to join him as spectators on a sailing circuit of several regattas—among them the North American championships. Peter and his crew won the Tempest class in this race, which thrilled his parents. Later on, they were privileged to watch their son participate as part of the Canadian Olympic Team Trials. Having grown up with water and waves being so much a part of her life, Hilkka reveled in Peter's love of sailing and delighted at his ability to compete at such a high level.

Peter's great love for sailing was overtaken, as were so many things in his life, by his choice to focus on the massive business opportunity in front of him. He knew that the Nygård Company, which was still in its infancy, could climb to unimaginable heights, but for that to happen, he would need to concentrate on that climb to the exclusion of almost everything else in his life. With his unrelenting drive and personal ambition, he was often referred to as a workaholic. He didn't see it that way, of course. When asked about his demanding work ethic, he would only smile and say, "Work is only work when you wish you were somewhere else, and by those standards I don't work very much."

Hilkka and Eeli enjoy well deserved vacation time.

Sharing the sailing experience with Peter.

CHAPTER SEVEN

Pirjo-Liisa

After Liisa graduated in 1968, she had begun having children and had a baby every two years until she had four of them in all. In swift progression the Nichol household added Angela in 1967; David in 1969; Kristopher 1971 and Allison in 1973. These were wonderful babies, and everyone in the family adored them. Russell's mother looked after Angela, David and Kristopher during the day when Liisa was working at the Child Guidance Clinic, but after Allison's birth Liisa decided to quit her job and stay home with her four children rather than try to continue working outside the home.

That first year at home was a trying one for Liisa. All four children got sick one after the other, which was stressful for everyone in the house; on top of that Liisa began to feel guilty that she wasn't contributing to the household income. Her mother had always worked to earn money for the family, managing the dual role of homemaker and income earner with skill. It was a normal way of life for Liisa, and so it was that in 1975 she decided to do it all—be a mom at home and start her own business. It hadn't been *that* many years since she had cut holes in the dress that her grandmother Nygård had sewn, and true to her natural inclinations, Liisa decided to go into the garment industry. Peter was by this time already established in manufacturing and his Tan Jay line was, to put it mildly, doing very well. He encouraged Liisa in her endeavours and advanced her a thirty-day $2000.00 line of credit to get started. It was enough for her to take off like a race horse charging out of the starting gate. She paid off the first $2000.00 in less than thirty days. Sales increased rapidly as Liisa purchased increasing amounts of Tan Jay merchandise, under the same terms as any other retailer. With Peter and Liisa, business was always business. Liisa did not need favours, just opportunity. Seeing her children take pleasure and pride in each other's accomplishments made Hilkka truly happy.

Liisa's company, called Pirjo-Liisa Fashions, was a line of women's clothing which was sold through home parties. Business boomed and more than doubled every year. Before long, Russell left his job and came into the business with her. The two of them ran Pirjo-Liisa, expanding it and consistently increasing the company's profitability.

Pirjo-Liisa Fashions started moving into other Canadian cities, extending from Winnipeg into Calgary, Regina, Saskatoon, Edmonton, Ottawa, Victoria, Vancouver, Oakville and St. Catherines. Liisa became a business woman to be noticed. Her brother felt that she had the potential to build a fashion empire of her own, and with her sales soaring, he was probably right. He encouraged her to strive towards opening one hundred stores.

Liisa, however, despite her growing success, ultimately chose a different pathway. She chose to spend more time with her children and grandchildren, and so she gradually "retired" from running a business, feeling richer (both figuratively and literally) for the experience.

During this same period, Peter continued to prosper at an accelerated rate. His business operations had expanded into the United States, and there was now a woman in his life with whom he had three children—two daughters, Bianca in 1977 and Alia in 1979, followed by a son, Kai, who was born in Los Angeles in 1982 (three more grand children for Hilkka to love and nurture!) Although he was beginning to become a major player on the American stage, Peter still kept his main outlets in Canada—in Toronto and in Winnipeg where he had his beginnings.

Worried that his father was beginning to have health issues, Peter began trying to persuade Eeli to retire—to stop and enjoy life before he wore out, and eventually, in 1978, Eeli and Hilkka did retire and sold the bakery to a couple who planned to turn it into a restaurant.

The Nygårds did not take advantage of any opportunity to sell the bakery to another baker. Their business reputation was imbedded in the bakery and Eeli and Hilkka would not risk any potential deterioration of that business name, or of the quality of their products, by turning the shop over to others who might compromise the high operating standards they had set. Nygård's Bakery itself, therefore, retired with them.

In rapid succession, Liisa and Russell sold their home in Transcona and bought the Bower Boulevard house from Eeli and Hilkka; Eeli and Hilkka in turn bought the Falcon Lake residence from Peter, and Peter moved to the Bahamas. Thereafter, Hilkka and Eeli would winter in the Bahamas, summer at Falcon Lake and stay with Liisa in Winnipeg between times.

They made friends in all of the places they dwelled. At Falcon Lake, a warm friendship grew between the Nygårds and Earl and Peggy Sherman. Earl was a retired Air Canada pilot, and he and Eeli shared a love of flight. The two couples would enjoy saunas at the Nygårds and a hot tub soak at the Shermans, and all treasured the relationship which would remain for a life time.

The boat house at Falcon Lake.
The grass growing on the roof is reminiscent of ancient Finland.

Peggy and Earl Sherman visiting at Falcon Lake.

Hilkka making a saunavihta, the traditional Finnish bouquet of fresh birch branches with their aromatic leaves still attached, for the Falcon Lake sauna. In the heated sauna, the saunavihta is used to slap and scrub the body, helping to stimulate circulation, detox the body and exfoliate the skin.

From humble beginnings in her own home, Liisa Nichol has turned a part-time venture into a multi-million-dollar empire.

The president of Pirjo-Liisa Fashions, she heads a Winnipeg-based company that encompasses two concepts: 16 stores featuring high-quality, discount-priced women's clothing, plus a system of house parties at which those garments are sold.

Since its inception in Liisa's basement, in 1975, Pirjo-Liisa has grown to a point where there are now stores in Ottawa, Thunder Bay, Regina, Saskatoon, Edmonton, Calgary, Vancouver and Sidney, while retaining its operations and head office in Winnipeg.

The 44-year-old University of North Dakota graduate describes the philosophy that's propelled her through life: "Nobody owes me anything. Too many people feel that they're owed a job or that they're owed unemployment insurance. Nobody owes me the privilege of working. I've always known that I had to earn that privilege. Don't expect a lottery to give you your wealth — earn it!"

Liisa Nichol was born in Finland, and came to Winnpeg in 1952 with her family. Liisa's older brother, Peter Nygaard, is also a brilliant entrepreneur: his company is one of the most successful manufacturers of women's clothing in North America. From him, Liisa says that she received a valuable insight into business: "There's no excuse for something going wrong — it's always preventable. Have alternate plans ready. Peter's organization is a dynamite one to emulate!"

However, Liisa's also enough of a maverick to have charted her own fashion house parties because she wanted to find a way to work yet continue to look after her children.

Of her more than 150 employees, only one is male. Most of the people who are now her top executives had no experience when she hired them — they were women, much like herself, who wanted to balance a career and a family. "We also hire young people, because it is a wonderful feeling to watch them grow and develop.

I also like senior citizens wherever possible; age is irrelevant."

One of the extraordinary young people of whom Liisa is especially proud is one of her own progeny. Daughter Angela, now 19, took over the brand-new Vancouvr branch of Pirjo-Liisa in the fall of 1985. Says her beaming mom: "She's doing a great job! We have two stores there now, and plan to open four more within the next year. Angela intends to have her region to earn $1 million in sales this year: she has tenacity."

Liisa Nichol

Sisu is the Finnish word for tenacity and resilience. Liisa was raised on that concept, and says it's a national Finnish characteristic.

The founding of Pirjo-Liisa has led to numerous honors for its namesake, including the title of the YWCA's Businesswoman of the Year; membership on the federal government's Export Trade Development Board, and first female member of the board of directors of the Manitoba Institute of Management.

Quite a difference, one would think, from her previous career as a speech pathologist — but in Liisa's view, the two professions are surprisingly similar: "Speech pathology involves serving people, and so does the retail business."

It's that belief which, in Liisa's view, makes her staff and her business unique "Service seems to be our competitive edge. When a customer walks into your store, she should be treated as though she were a guest in your home. Don't growl at someone who brings in a return, because you wouldn't growl at them in your home! We look for a positive attitude in our staff."

Basics! With intelligence, creativity and business acumen, Liisa Nichol founded her empire on basics: "Clothing is always a great idea, because no matter what the economy, people still buy clothing — especially at reasonable prices."

Those prices are kept reasonable by innovation founded upon yet another basic concept: buy at lower prices and sell at lower prices." We purchase at large volume, particularly at the end of the season, from over 100 Canadian manufacturers. We don't always buy what we want, but we buy it at great savings that we can pass on to our customers. We also produce something new out of manufacturers' end of lines. For example. if a manufacturer has some fabric left over, we'll get them to cut us some blouses to go with a suit that we bought from another manufacturer. The customer gets not only the value, but also a coordinated outfit."

The location of Pirjo Liisa stores, as well, helps to keep prices low: "We choose industrial areas or core areas where rent is inexpensive."

Selling fashions at house parties — the method by which Liisa started — is one more basic premise. "Women like any excuse to get together for a party. Being able to shop in the comfort of a home, and have your friends right there to offer an opinion, is an added bonus. It's also very convenient for a woman on a tight schedule."

Liisa Nichol knows a good deal about tight schedules: In addition to travelling one to two weeks out of every month" ... "to touch every garment in every warehouse in every city," she's mother to four teenagers, and has an enormous volunteer undertaking in her life right now. Liisa is chairperson of the Canadian National Gymnastics Championship, which will be televised across Canada from their Winnipeg location in May, 1987.

Gymnastics is the perfect involvement for this entrepreneur who manages her own balancing act so gracefully.   •

BASEMENT BUSINESS BLOSSOMS INTO MAJOR FASHION EMPIRE

BY BRENLEE CARRINGTON

Article in *Manitoba Business* magazine reporting on Liisa's business acumen.

CHAPTER EIGHT

Bahamas

After they sold the bakery, Hilkka and Eeli took a second trip back to Finland. Unlike the first trip, when they were preoccupied and overcome with the prospect of owning their own bakery, this visit to the homeland was more affordable and less rushed. They had plenty of relaxed time in which to enjoy the companionship of all the relatives and join in fellowship over many "Welcome" cakes and strong cups of coffee.

With delight and pride, Hilkka and Eeli shared the story of Nygård's Bakery with their friends and family. What a pleasure it was to tell how their dreams had been fulfilled in Canada!

Everyone listening to them recognized, however, that it wasn't just Canada that had lead to the Nygård's success. While the freedom and opportunities available in Canada to plan, create, grow and prosper in business were significant, the ultimate success that Hilkka and Eeli had achieved was the result of a concentrated labour of love by them both. Even those few who had expressed skepticism during the Nygårds' first trip back to Finland were now able to witness what the right people with the right work ethic would be able to accomplish in Canada.

Wanting his parents to be able to escape the cold of winter and relax in the sunny tropical climate, Peter flew his parents down to the Bahamas to meet with a real estate agent who would help them select a house that they could enjoy during the winter. Hilkka and Eeli thought this was a wonderful idea and began to dream of a having a huge family gathering in the Bahamas for Christmas, bringing in friends and relatives from Finland and anywhere else they happened to be, to bask in the warmth of the Bahamas for the holiday season. They had difficulty settling on a house that would be right for them. They lost count when the number of houses they were taken to see came close to fifty.

At last they settled on one that they liked, but when Peter came to inspect it, he declared that it wasn't big enough. "You'll need more room," he told them, and so he took them to another house with which Hilkka fell instantly in love. Peter asked her, "Mom, do you like this house?" and Hilkka replied, "*Ja*, I like very much this house." The price of the house Peter showed them was double the price of the one Hilkka and Eeli had selected, and they were conscious of the difference in cost and worried about the expense, but before they could even think about it, Peter had bought the house, which they named Viking Hill, in the beautiful Bahamian city of Nassau.

Ironically they couldn't get possession of the place until after Christmas, and ended up having to rent three houses to have enough room for all the guests who had accepted their invitation to join them for Christmas. Among the many who gathered with the Nygårds that Christmas were Liisa and Russ with their four children, and special friends Aira Samulin, a famous dancer/choreographer and politician, and her husband Ekku Peltomäki, an artistic lighting technician from Finland. Peter was right when he told them they would need more room!

Peter had one other burning desire besides his intense ambition to succeed in business. He wanted to create a haven, an oasis, the ultimate fantasy escape from the everyday world, and when he was able to purchase a six acre parcel of land on a cay (peninsula) in the exclusive gated community of Lyford Cay in Nassau in the Bahamas, he knew that it was the perfect location for his dream home. Bordered by soft sand beaches and the radiant deep blue Atlantic Ocean, the land was a magnificent tropical retreat.

Like all the Nygård family members, Peter had always been drawn to water. As a boy he had fantasized about living in a house on an island, edged by sandy shores and surrounded by turquoise water. Here in the Caribbean, on this wonderful Cay, he could find his Utopia.

Peter did not want to build a Hollywood-Beverly Hills style house in the Bahamas. He wanted to build a *Bahamian* style house in the Bahamas, one that would fit naturally into the atmosphere and ambience of its setting.

Inspired by the great stone structures built by the ancient Mayans, Peter Nygård created a fantasy land which melded perfectly with the breathtaking tropical beauty of his peninsula. He designed and supervised the entire creation himself, and with the help of hundreds of skilled craftsmen and trades people, engineers and architects, he made sure that nothing in the construction phase happened without his hands-on approval.

Churches and temples, he felt, represented some of the finest architecture in the world. His own architectural design reflected his admiration for this type of edifice. Tons of stones were used to create what one observer called "a masterpiece of a Pre-Columbian structure."

The residence itself was a magnificent 150,000 square foot home, which included a 32,000 square foot grand-hall protected from the elements by a 100,000 pound glass ceiling, and many quiet, open-walled suites with thatched roofing and hanging beds. Free ranging exotic birds, parrots and peacocks made their home on the estate, and the open walls allowed guests to enjoy not just the ocean breezes but also the sight and sounds of the birds.

Adding modern luxuries to the primitive ambiance of his home, Peter installed a twenty-four seat movie theatre, countless Jacuzzi whirlpools, a human aquarium, water slides, two volleyball courts, a tennis court, and a basketball court. (Peter, a volleyball fanatic, plays beach volleyball every day when he is home and believes that beach volleyball should be synonymous with the Bahamas. He makes his world class beaches available to competing athletes for practice and strongly supports, in word and deed, the emergence of an Olympic Champion Bahamian Beach Volleyball team.)

Replicas of Mayan temples and statuary, reflecting ponds, pools and waterfalls set amid gloriously splendid gardens, made the landscaping of the Nygård retreat a feast for the eyes.

Peter named his paradise "Nygård Cay".

It didn't take long for Nygård Cay to become known as one of the most unique private residences in the world and it drew many celebrated personalities and athletes to its shores; everyone from Prince Andrew Duke of York, Sarah Ferguson, Michael Jackson, President George Bush Senior, Sean Connery, and Lee Iacocca to Robert De Niro and others have visited Nygård Cay. Oprah Winfrey, after spending time there, said, "After seeing *Nygård Cay*, I am not living large enough!"

Whenever possible, Peter would ask Hilkka to join him at the Cay to welcome special guests. He was proud of his Mom and wanted everyone to know her. He trusted that his mother's presence would contribute positively to any occasion, and he was not mistaken. Hilkka had an amazing ability to put others at ease, in large part because she sincerely liked people and enjoyed their company.

On one occasion, Peter had asked her if she would be good enough to be hostess to Prince Andrew's wife, Sarah Ferguson, the Duchess of York, for afternoon tea at Nygård Cay. Hilkka was more than willing to have tea with "Fergie" as the Duchess was informally known, since she had long held respect and admiration for the Royal Family. She served her traditional *pulla* with pride, but Nygård Cay had no proper English tea set and so the tea itself was served with coffee cups brought over from Viking Hill. Hilkka apologized to the Duchess for the less formal service she provided because of this, but the small detail didn't seem to matter at all to her guest and the two women had a delightful visit. Some time later, after the Royals had returned to England, Hilkka received a large package in the mail. Opening it, she discovered an elegant china tea set, named "Sarah's Garden," a gift and an expression of gratitude from the Duchess of York to Hilkka Nygård for a most enjoyable afternoon. Hilkka was both delighted and humbled by this thoughtful gesture.

Because his ballroom could hold 600 people, Peter was able to host large events to help support a variety of organizations and endeavours, from holding a massive fundraiser to help the Bahamian International Film Festival to hosting the Nygård Cay Annual Song Writers' Festival (giving musicians the opportunity to spend time together in a tranquil setting to compose and perform).

Hilkka always believed that playing beach volleyball, sailing and hosting big events were outlets for Peter's pent-up energy, but even at Nygård Cay, the business was always first in his mind and a day never passed that Peter didn't work.

Hilkka was as comfortable with presidents and princes
as she was with everyone she met.

The Duchess of York, Peter,
Hilkka, Prince Andrew and
the two young princesses,
Beatrice and Eugenie.

Hilkka with American President
George Bush Sr. at Nygård Cay.

Hilkka, Dennis and Verona
(Hilkka's friend and housekeeper for over 22 years)
attending Verona's church
together. Sadly Verona has
since passed away.

Chapter Nine

The Fourth Generation

As they aged, Hilkka and Eeli began to have a few health issues, nothing that really slowed them down too much, but signals all the same that they needed to be watchful over their bodies. High blood pressure, high cholesterol, type 2 diabetes and fading eyesight came along to plague them, but they still maintained a zest for life that was unconquerable. They traveled to Viking Hill in Nassau for the winter, taking Drake along with them to romp in the sun. Eeli worked in the garden, enjoying the miracle of growing things much as his parents had done in Perkkiö many years before. Hilkka took care of the house and Peter's children.

In 1986, Angela had a baby girl whom she named Courtney Leigh. Courtney was Liisa's first grandchild and Hilkka's first great-grandchild. Both grandmother and great-grandmother were ecstatic over the little baby's entrance into the world, but they knew that Angela was going through a difficult period of adjustment. Young and single, Angela needed all the support her family could give her.

It was after the birth of his first grandchild, Angela's baby Courtney, that Russell Nichol decided to steer his life in a new direction; a direction that did not have Liisa in the plans. He went out of Liisa's life, and just like that, she too was single. It was a blow, but Liisa had no interest in looking for a replacement for Russell. There was too much to do. Russell remained a vital part of his children's lives until 2006 when they were devastated by his untimely death from cancer.

Hilkka and Eeli came to help Angela with the baby. The Nygårds were excited about having their first great-grandchild, and they adored Courtney. Babies, they continued to believe wholeheartedly, were gifts from God and should be cherished. Hilkka would get up in the night and hold Courtney and wash her, change her and give her to Angela to feed. She would say, "Angela, don't be late feeding the baby, because if she cries too hard, her navel will pop out." Angela must have been on time with the feedings, because the "baby" grew up to have a perfect navel with a diamond in it. All the while Hilkka and Angela were tending to Courtney's needs, Eeli would be vacuuming and cleaning everything in the house.

Angela matured after Courtney's birth and became very close to Hilkka. She repeatedly expressed gratitude to her grandmother for helping her take care of her precious baby girl, and told Hilkka that her home would always be Hilkka's home too. Angela spent time with Hilkka at Falcon Lake and in Winnipeg and little Courtney, the first baby born to the fourth generation of her family, started going to the Bahamas for extended stays with Hilkka and Eeli when she was only four years old.

Courtney was very much a part of Hilkka's life. They were together so much that Courtney even began to appear in some of the legendary "Hilkka tales". When Hilkka had to have cataract surgery, for example, Courtney was present with Liisa when the now oft-repeated "gurney accident story" took place. Hilkka was being wheeled along the hospital corridor lying on a gurney en route to the operating room when one of the gurney's wheels broke. The gurney tipped and Hilkka rolled off the mattress and on to the floor, where she became wedged between a door frame and the gurney. Jammed tightly, unable to free herself, Hilkka was initially terrified. Her shoulder was bruised and painful and no matter how she struggled she was stuck. Having heard the crash and a scream, Liisa, who had been waiting for her mother with Courtney, ran to the hallway to see Hilkka traumatized and on the verge of panic, pinned under the weight of the tipped gurney. She was eventually rescued by hospital staff, and after a few hours of rest and calming conversation, was able to have her eye surgery.

Hilkka, thereafter, was understandably suspicious about the reliability of gurneys, and any future rides that she had to make on one of them always began with a close inspection of the device, followed by a caution to the person about to maneuver it to be exceedingly careful because . . . and the whole story of her trauma would be told in detail, time and time again. Ultimately she added a touch of humour to soften the tale, but she continued to be relentless about educating medical staff about the perils of gurney-riding. The family added this episode to the many "Hilkka stories" they like to endlessly repeat, and they would tease their mother and laugh together when they did so. Courtney's presence at the hospital on that occasion was only one of the many interesting times she would share with her dear, loving, funny and never boring Gramma Hilkka.

CHAPTER TEN

Solitude

In 1988, Peter asked Liisa if she would take over the presidency of the Nygård Corporation in Los Angeles California. He needed a competent person he could trust to do the job well, and there was no one he trusted more than his sister. It was potentially a 200 million dollar business, and Peter needed new leadership at the top. He believed that Liisa would meet the challenge.

Liisa took the job and waded in to face uncharted waters. The challenge of re-structuring a large enterprise with hundreds of employees was made more difficult because many of those employees were unilingual Spanish speaking people. Putting Pirjo-Liisa Fashions into the capable hands of her daughter, Angela Nichol, and her trusted friend, business woman Linda Gerrard, Liisa flew to New York and hired highly paid professionals to form a competent management team. With this team's help she worked to ensure the prosperity of the California company.

Peter's son Mika was born in 1987, another grandchild for Hilkka and Eeli. In 1988, being in California, Liisa had the privilege of being present in Los Angeles to witness the birth of Peter's son, Jessar. Because she lived nearby, Liisa had been chosen to be the birth coach and support person for her nephew's entrance into the world. It was a thrilling experience for her, and because of it Liisa developed an immediate bond with baby Jessar, another gift from God for Hilkka's brood of grandchildren!

After two and a half years of sixteen to eighteen hour work days, of constant world-wide travel, and of fast paced, hard driving corporate decision making, Liisa felt that the reorganization she had been tasked to create for her brother had been done. Things were running smoothly in California, and she longed to wind down her operations, get out of the big city atmosphere and return to a more natural setting. And after ensuring that proper leadership was in place for Peter's company, she did just that.

When she finished her stint with Nygård, Liisa cast off all the trappings of society and headed, literally, for the hills. Buying a home in the mountains of British Columbia she isolated herself from the hectic pace and relentless tension of the corporate world and changed her life style completely. She kept a few animals, grew a simple garden, and walked in the forests by herself. She opened herself to the contemplative life, to solitude and to prayer. She knew peace.

Chapter Eleven

Fifty Years, Six Cities

The year 1990 was one of celebration. It had been fifty years since Hilkka had stood beside Eeli in the Lutheran Cathedral in Helsinki, wearing the long white dress, and feeling Aili's soft billowing veil float about her face as she walked; fifty years since they had become husband and wife, with all their life's adventures as a couple ahead of them.

Peter and Liisa wanted to mark this occasion by creating a truly spectacular memory for their parents. Liisa came up with several ideas for events, each meaningful and significant in their own right. She took the list to her brother to discuss the options. He looked at the list and said, "These are great ideas. Let's do them all!" And thus was born what was eventually called "The Tour of Tribute."

That year the Nygård family had no fewer than six major anniversary celebrations in as many different cities. Guests were invited to attend one, all, or as many as possible, of the events planned.

The first of these was held at the Nygård beach house in Marina del Rey, California, where a huge reception and dance was held, with guests coming from all across North America and as far away as Finland. The next morning, the whole family and many of the guests traveled to Garden Grove, California, where Hilkka and Eeli renewed their wedding vows at the Crystal Cathedral (which Liisa had been attending during her time in California). After the service there, the Rev. Dr. Robert Schuler, minister of the Crystal Cathedral congregation, dedicated a stepping stone in the Walk of Faith sidewalk outside the cathedral to Hilkka and Eeli, in honour of their fifty loving years as man and wife. The stone stands as a testament to their marriage, with an inscription from First Corinthians, 13:7, "Love bears all things, believes all things, hopes all things, endures all things." The group then headed north east to the University of North Dakota. During the celebration there, Eeli and Hilkka were made honourary alumni of the university, and Peter announced the establishment of an Endowment Fund in their honour. The next stop was Winnipeg, and the Scandinavian Centre on Erin Street. As a surprise to their parents, Peter and Liisa had the old lobby of the building completely refurbished—a gift to the Centre as well as to Hilkka and Eeli! At this event, their children presented Hilkka and Eeli, to their great delight, with a 1990 BMW. On to Toronto, Ontario for the fifth event: a Gala Fashion Show with dancing under the stars revealed to the guests below by the Nygård Building's retractable glass roof. In Toronto, they were given a portrait of themselves painted by Winnipeg artist, Helen Granger Young. The last stop on the tour was at Hancock, Michigan to attend the FinnFest celebrations in that town. The Nygårds took the whole Toronto Fashion Show with them to Hancock. For this show, however, Nygård family members and members of the Hancock Finnish community were added to the show as models, and at a dinner held at Hancock's Suomi College (Finnish College) they were presented with the Lion Award. (The lion is a symbol of Finland.)

Their children did indeed give their parents a spectacular memory! The Tour of Tribute was an extravaganza unlike anything Hilkka and Eeli could ever have imagined. They still felt like newlyweds in so many ways, but when they considered all that had happened in their lives since they walked hand in hand in their wedding finery down the street in Helsinki, it was hard to deny that half a century had gone by. Never had they dreamed that they would prosper so abundantly in a new land, and that their children could not only afford to give them such an incredible honour, but more importantly, that they should want to do so! Truly, they were blessed!

Hilkka and Eeli celebrating 50 years of marriage,
with their children Peter and Liisa at the University of North Dakota.

Renewal of wedding
vows on the campus of
the Crystal Cathedral, in
front of the statue of the
Good Shepherd.

Eeli's sister Aili, Peter, Rev. Dr. Robert Schuler, Hilkka, Eeli, Liisa, Hilkka's
sister Aili at the Crystal Cathedral, Garden Grove CA, where Hilkka and Eeli
renewed their wedding vows.

CHAPTER TWELVE

Dennis

Liisa had spent the year after her parents' spectacular Anniversary Tour in her peaceful mountain retreat, soothed and calmed by the serene life style she had adopted after leaving the hectic Los Angeles years behind her. Periodically she would travel to Winnipeg to tend to Pirjo-Liisa business and would visit there with Linda Gerrard and Linda's husband Wayne. Linda had continued to manage and, at Liisa's request, downsize Pirjo-Liisa after Liisa left Los Angeles, and the two women were in frequent touch with each other.

In September, 1992, Liisa joined Linda and Wayne for dinner at D-Jay's Restaurant, a popular Winnipeg dining establishment which was one of the Gerrard's favourite restaurants. Linda often scheduled business meetings and events at D-Jay's and as a result she and Wayne had become quite friendly with its owners, Dennis and Jeannette Johnson.

Liisa recalled that earlier that year, Linda had taken some time off work to attend the funeral of a friend who had multiple sclerosis and had passed away. That friend, she remembered, was Jeannette Johnson. It happened that Dennis Johnson, who had been devastated by his wife's death and had been in mourning and a deep depression for many months, had recently returned to work and was now greeting his customers at their tables as had been his custom. He ended up sitting with the group at Liisa's table and the conversation began and never ceased.

Linda and Wayne eventually readied themselves to leave, but Dennis and Liisa kept right on talking. They talked all the way to the restaurant's door, and they talked all the way across the parking lot and they talked all the way to Liisa's car. In fact they talked the night away. They laughed and wept together. They discussed family, friends, hurts and healing from hurts, music and faith.

Liisa was impressed by the devotion and loyalty Dennis had shown his first wife during their thirty-two years of marriage and by his faithful caring of her during her long and painful illness. At one point Dennis exclaimed, "Are you some kind of psychiatrist or something? I've never told any one all this about my feelings!" It all seemed so natural and right . . . each needed the other . . . a mutual and genuine caring seemed to have leapt into existence between them with the speed of light.

They communicated by phone for the next few months and in the early spring of 1993 they met for a lingering dinner date. Dennis had been so nervous about this first date that he had circled the block twice before he finally gained enough courage to go to her door. Liisa's heart filled with love. She knew that she must return to Manitoba to be with this man. She was called to him and he to her. She trusted him completely.

Dennis Johnson and Liisa Nygård were married in 1994, and anyone watching them knows that they were meant to be together. Hilkka grew to love Dennis immensely and let him completely into her heart. Liisa in turn embraced Dennis's family, which included Jeanette's mother, Doris Fraser (who became an integral part of Dennis and Liisa's home until her death in 2008), and Dennis and Jeanette's adult children Mike, Heather and Robert. Liisa's children had immediate respect, love and appreciation for Dennis; and Peter continues to declare that Dennis is the best thing that ever happened to Liisa. Hilkka rejoiced that her daughter's marriage was obviously a good one.

Liisa marries Dennis Johnson at First Lutheran Church in Winnipeg, 1994. (L to R) Front row: Robert Johnson, Chris Johnson, Scott Johnson, Angela (Nichol) Dyborn, David Nichol; Middle row: Heather (Johnson) Kristjansson, Courtney Nichol, Allison (Nichol) Stewart, Kristopher Nichol; Back Row: Michael Johnson, Liisa and Dennis

CHAPTER THIRTEEN

An Amazing & Wondrous Thing

Hilkka had looked after Peter's three children, Bianca, Alia and Kai, for a few years in the Bahamas. She had been firm with them, but she had showered them with an abundance of love that was evident to all. She would be forever grateful that she was able to spend so much time with them when they were little. She would read them stories, changing the names of the characters to the names of the children. The children loved this game, loved to hear the characters re-named; and if Hilkka occasionally "forgot" and read the name as it was actually written in the book, they would call out to her to correct herself. All of them liked the scent of the Oil of Olay moisturizing skin cream that Hilkka used at night. In the minds of her family it was a fragrance that would remain uniquely hers.

The most fun the children had, however, was only found out after the fact. They used to sneak into their grandfather's room when he was napping and try out his false teeth. The teeth were kept in a glass beside Eeli's bed and it took real talent to be able to get them out of the glass, put them in their own mouths, make faces, and return the teeth to the glass without waking Eeli.

Hilkka was very happy being "Nanny" to Peter's children.

Alia, Bianca, Kai and their mother lived in the Bahamas with the Nygårds for several years, and as time went on they would often spend summers with Liisa and her family in Winnipeg and with Hilkka and Eeli at Falcon Lake. These were joyful times for them all.

For many summers Gramma Hilkka would escort at least one of her grandchildren to Kenora to catch the boat to the YMCA's Camp Stevens, and after two weeks, she would be back there standing on the dock, waiting to pick up her tired, suntanned campers and take them to Falcon Lake where spinach soup, *pulla*, pancakes and meat pies would be waiting.

Hilkka was exceptionally proud of her children. Peter and Liisa had both been recipients of the prestigious Sioux Award for Distinguished Service and Outstanding Achievements from their university, and they had both kept on winning recognitions and awards for their efforts after embarking upon their respective careers. They had taken Hilkka's cheery, "Have a good day and don't forget to work hard!" to heart. Despite their hectic schedules and no matter how busy they might be, her children were consistently "there" for their parents. Their devotion was, to Hilkka, an amazing and wondrous thing. She would sometimes wonder what she had done to deserve so much love. The answer to that was clear to Liisa and Peter. She had first loved them.

Hilkka kept scrapbooks and mementoes of her children's accomplishments. Their mother had been proud to see them both flourish in the new land to which she and Eeli had brought them and she took pleasure in saving the mementoes and souvenirs she had collected through the years. A partial listing of Liisa's many successes is indicated earlier in this book, and some of Peter's awards and achievements, highlighted in Hilkka's collection of mementoes, are listed immediately below.

Peter was North American Yachting Champion and a member of the Canadian Olympic Yachting Training team, 1976. He has received numerous awards which include the following: Outstanding Canadian Distinction, Manitoba Chamber of Commerce, 1981; Winnipeg's Community Service Award, 1986; Commemorative Medal Award, Government of Canada, 1993; AIM All Star Award, 1998; City of Toronto Award, 2001; Patriot Award, The Royal Military Institute, 2002; Keeping America Strong Award, 2002; Queen Elizabeth 11 Golden Jubilee Medal, 2003; Medal of Merit, Finnish War Veterans' Association, 2003; Entrepreneur Hall of Fame, UND, 2004; Best of Scene Award, Dallas Fashion Awards, 2004; Honourary Captain to the Fort Garry Horse Regiment and elected Senator of its regimental senate, "For Unequalled Civilian Support of the Military and His Outstanding Philanthropic Humanitarian Efforts", 2005.

Perhaps Peter Nygård's most significant contribution to Canada has been the role he played in the establishment of the North American Free Trade Agreement. In 1982, Peter wrote a strategic position paper to initiate a Free Trade Agreement between Canada and the United States which was presented to the federal government. He was subsequently appointed to chair the Advisory Committee on Future Canadian Long-Term Industrial Strategy, and from that position he became involved with the development of the North American Free Trade Agreement. In 1984, he served as the Co-Chair of the fifteen member Task Force appointed to make recommendations to the Federal government about long-term industrial strategies for Canada's textile and clothing industries. He was later appointed (in 1985) to the International Trade Advisory Committee, and in 1986 to the Sectoral Advisory Group on International Trade as Chairman of the Committee on Apparel and Fur. His participation in various aspects of international trade has been ongoing, and his opinions and expertise on such matters is highly regarded. Hilkka was justifiably and especially proud of her son's achievements in this international arena.

The family continued to expand. Liisa's oldest daughter Angela married her husband Marten Dyborn in 1995, and her second daughter Allison married Cameron Stewart the following year, and the ever growing extended family became richer by two.

Eeli by then had begun to visibly weaken physically, and Peter, noticing his father's decreasing mobility, began construction of an elevator in the Viking Hill home, which regretfully, Eeli would never use. Hilkka, however, was later to benefit greatly from this addition to the house when the spiral staircase to the upper floor became too difficult for her to manage.

Hilkka and Irja Suominen at the ceremony awarding Peter the Patriot Award from the Royal Military Institute.

Liisa receiving the Sioux Award for Distinguished Service and Outstanding Achievement from the late Dr. Thomas Clifford, then president of the University of North Dakota. President Clifford maintained ties with the Nygårds for many years and developed a warm relationship with them.

SECTION
FIVE

ALL RIGHT TOGETHER
1997 - 2010

CHAPTER ONE

Eeli's Great Going

In 1997, Hilkka had an angioplasty done, the first of many medical procedures she was to undergo in the decade to come, and a relatively minor one considering the serious life-threatening procedures that lay ahead of her. But in 1997 none of that was contemplated and all that Hilkka knew or cared about was that her darling Eeli was about to die.

Eeli had been sick for four years, battling what he would later find out was bone cancer. During this period, he had begun to decline. His strong body had become less strong; his razor-sharp mind had become less sharp; his zest for life had become less vibrant; he had begun to fade in all aspects of his being. Hilkka, often battling her own health problems, looked after him with a fierce devotion. She took over making decisions that in the past she and Eeli had made together. She began managing new tasks involving wheelchairs and transportation. She learned how to ease his discomfort and frustration over his increasing weakness. Her dedication to her husband was passionate and intense. He meant the world to her, and even though she had health challenges of her own to face, it was for Eeli that she had concern. He had suffered greatly, but he had held on until now when the ferocity of the disease finally hit him with the force of a hurricane. There was nothing that could be done to stop it from rushing in to carry Eeli away. The cancer had spread to his lungs and his brain and his fading body was riddled with it. It was no longer a question of how many years or months he might have left. It was a matter of how many days. Eeli and Hilkka were prepared for the inevitable. Doctors in the Bahamas had first alerted Eeli to the fact that he might be in jeopardy, when they told him he had a broken bone, and told him as well that he had to catch the first plane he could get to take him back to Canada, where he should see his own doctor right away.

Eeli did as he was told and he and Hilkka were at the Grace Hospital in Winnipeg within the week. The diagnosis at the Grace Hospital was alarming. Eeli appeared to have cancer and the doctors were sending him over to the St. Boniface Hospital for a biopsy and complete diagnosis. There the worst was confirmed. Bone cancer, inoperable, terminal.

Hilkka's blood ran cold. Her knees were shaking and she felt weak all over. This couldn't be happening. Eeli was stoic as he always was, but the blow was a hard one to take. No matter what the age or the circumstances, the knowledge that one's death is near is a dreadful thing to know. The first revelation of such a fact is surreal, because nothing will ever again be like it was before. Expectations and reality will have been forever altered.

Death, however, is part of nature's cycle. Once they got over the shock of the diagnosis, they began to ready themselves for the journey ahead of them. Goodness knows they had already traveled a long way together, and they knew how to cover any distance they had to cover. "As long as we stick together," Hilkka had said as they had stood in their little shack in Deloraine, "we'll make it." They would stick together until the end.

As soon as he was finished the procedures at the hospital, Eeli wanted to go to Falcon Lake, so that's where they went. How fortunate they were to have this beautiful restful place! A hospital bed had been set up for him there. A nurse was in attendance. How wonderful that he had such good care! Liisa and her children were there when he came home. She lay down beside her dad and told him how much she appreciated all the things he had done to show her that he loved her. Liisa recalled how he used to bring her eggnog when she was competing in track and field meets, or warm onion milk when her throat was sore in the middle of the night, or how he had worried and waited for her to return home after some of those first dates—all those little things that let her know that her father loved her very much. She had time to tell him that. He smiled at her and he mouthed "I love you" to her, and with that, the assurance of an everlasting love between father and daughter was confirmed.

Eeli's attention was drawn to something that wasn't visible to the others in the room. He softly murmured a litany, repeating it over and over with his speechless voice, "*Jumala armahda minua. Jumala armahda minua.*" (God be merciful to me. God be merciful to me.) He reached up at one point as if trying to grasp something and Liisa asked him, "What are you reaching for, Dad?" and he said one word that could be faintly heard. He said, "Jesus."

Peter and some of his children arrived next. Peter sat by his father and gently held his hand and stroked his head. Eeli would not go until Peter had arrived and now that he had come, it was enough to just have him near. He could go now. His son was here.

For the days to come, the family members kept up a vigil for him, taking turns beside his bed. As the days passed, Eeli became unable to swallow or talk, so he was given suppositories to ease the pain.

Hilkka never left his side.

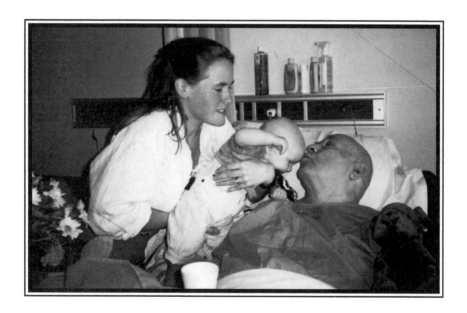

Allison holding Angela's baby Anders for Eeli to kiss, 1997.

Hilkka lay in bed beside her husband and reached out and took his hand into hers. How many years had they spent lying side by side like this? She knew that his body, so intimately familiar to her, was shutting down. She could sense it happening, but still she thought for one brief moment that he might turn to wrap her in one last sleepy embrace. With his hand in hers, she fell asleep. When she woke up she was still holding his hand, and it felt unnaturally still. It wasn't cold, at least not yet. There was still warmth in him. It was lined and well used, that hand. How often she had felt its caress, its gentle touch. She looked at their two old hands joined in a last clasp and she saw them as they had been in that first clasp so long ago on the white linen table cloth amidst the sparkling glasses and polished silverware at Restaurant Tenho: their young hands, unlined, that had filled them with so much wonder; the feel of him, of his strength and power, how he had made her blood race and her heart pound. He hadn't been able to speak then either, she mused, because he was so overcome. "Dear husband, darling Eeli! How I will miss your hand in mine. You have been the love of my life and you will be with me yet."

Peter was sleeping in a reclining chair beside the bed. At last Hilkka gently laid her lover's hand down and went to Peter, "Peter," she said touching him lightly, "Peter, Dad is gone." Peter rose and went to his father's side. He touched the pillow, and then, passing his big hand slowly down the length of his father's face he closed Eeli's eyes and sealed his lips.

Eeli Nygård was gone. His great going had been peaceful, one might even say beautiful. It had been a perfect ending to a life bravely lived.

The funeral home came and the family was asked to leave the room while they prepared to move the body. It was "the body" now, not "Eeli" any more. Hilkka, Peter and the grandchildren who were there went outside to wait. Peter called all the Nygård offices and told them to put the flags at half mast. Hilkka and Peter left with the hearse and the grandchildren stayed behind to lock up the house, following their grandmother later in another car. Liisa was there at the funeral home when Hilkka arrived. Hilkka didn't do much to help with deciding the final details of the funeral. Her heart was broken. She could only sit and stare at the ground. But Liisa and Peter were excellent planners. They would make a nice funeral for their father, which they did. It was a large funeral attended by hundreds. Here they were—so many, many people, turning out to pay their respects to Eeli Nygård, baker, who came to Canada with only two suitcases, a trunk and his little family.

CHAPTER TWO

Aili

In 1996, the year prior to Eeli's death, Peter's daughter, Scarlet, was born. Shortly after Scarlet's birth, Hilkka and Eeli became great-grandparents for the second time when Angela and Marten had a son, Anders in 1997. In 1998 a third great-grandchild was born when Allison and Cam had their first child, Makayla.

Having grandchildren and great-grandchildren made Hilkka happy and lessened the weight of her grief. Despite having a series of health issues, she kept up her busy pace. She was living now for the children she and Eeli had brought into the world, for the grandchildren and great-grandchildren, and if God willed it, for their children yet to be. The baptisms, the birthdays, the confirmations, the innumerable concerts and performances, filled her life with purpose and meaning. Hilkka had faith that all things would work out well.

In 1998, the year after Eeli died, Hilkka and her younger sister Aili attended the one hundredth anniversary celebrations for their old school, Muukonniemen Koulu, on the mainland across from their beloved Lamposaari. The sisters loved visiting old familiar places together, and they laughed uproariously and gleefully over the silliest things. Neither time nor circumstances had lessened their capacity to find immense pleasure in life and in living. Indeed they held the precious moments they enjoyed more closely to their hearts and memories during this trip than they had done when they were young. They appreciated the good things around them more deeply because they could be contested against a lifetime of experience

Hilkka and Aili, visiting Muukonniemen Koulu in 1998,
remembering when they were little.

Muukonniemen Koulu 100th anniversary reunion 1998.
Only four men were left after the war.

Hilkka was excited to see her former classmates and childhood friends at the reunion. Everyone, it seemed, had experienced his or her share of sorrows and joys, and the old friends couldn't get enough of hugging each other and sharing both laughter and tears as they told each other of all that had taken place in their lives since they had been young. Only four men were left from the war. The rest had been killed or so badly injured that they were invalids. They mourned the loss of these men, whose lives had been so brutally ended or ruined.

Memories of her childhood days blazed brightly during that reunion, and when she and Aili took a boat across to Lamposaari, Hilkka was overcome with bittersweet emotion. Here she could see shadowy glimpses of her parents, her mother scrubbing the braided rugs at the dock, her father stirring his hot toddy with the little silver spoon. She could see her sister Iida climbing down from her loft in the shed, and little Aili putting on her woolen leggings. Over there on the beach the rowboats lay neatly on the sand while her playmates went floating through the air on the giant swing . . . .

Looking around, she was amazed at how small the houses and buildings were. The manager's house, especially, which had always been so big to her, was actually not very large at all. Hilkka saw that there were cottages on the island now, part-time residents and vacationers with summer saunas who enjoyed Lamposaari, but called someplace else home. There was no real community there anymore, and the children were no longer running freely about exploring and playing on their own. "It was a good place in which to grow up," Hilkka thought, "a happy place filled with people who knew and helped each other." She noticed that many houses needed painting and it was sad to see so many signs of neglect, and yet . . . and yet . . . Lamposaari still had its magic. There was something about the place that could never be altered or taken away. The spirit of Lamposaari would linger with Hilkka until the end of her days. No matter how much the world around her changed, she would always be a child of Lamposaari.

After the anniversary, Aili and Hilkka attended a health spa called Naantali, on the south west seashore of Finland, where they luxuriated in the pampering of their bodies. Next they spent four incredibly satisfying days at Aili's summer cottage on a small island on Lake Saimaa, reliving, remembering, and reflecting on their past . . . always with laughter.

It was to be the last time that the sisters would see each other. Aili died a few years later, of complications from diabetes.

CHAPTER THREE

Heart Beats

The new millennium dawned when the calendar clicked over to the year 2000 and Peter's son, Xar, was the first millennium baby in the Nygård family. Xar's Aunt Liisa was present at his birth in the Bahamas, and shared in the excitement of the event. Prior to the big day, Peter—true to his meticulous nature in which everything must have a plan and a back up plan—had arranged for several practice trips to be taken to the hospital, with alternate routes being identified and timed in case of traffic problems on the main roads on the actual day! Once more Hilkka rejoiced in the birth of a child. In rapid succession, yet more millennium babies entered her life. Allison had Annika in 2000, David became father to Morgan in 2001, Kristopher to Max in 2005 and Jackson in 2007; Angela had Ava in 2004—a little sister for Courtney and Anders—and Bianca had Saylor in 2002 and Maddex in 2006. Peter's son Trey was born in 2003. Hilkka counted each child as a treasure.

Almost without notice various ailments had begun to affect Hilkka's health as the years passed. For many of those ailments yet another pharmaceutical prescription had been added to her daily intake, until she eventually ended up taking thirteen different medications. Several times the combination of so many drugs in her system created a toxic "soup" that had caused her to become severely ill. Both Hilkka and Liisa worried about the side effects of so many synthetics and chemicals being put into Hilkka's body. Natural remedies had kept Hilkka healthy as a child, and she was concerned that her arsenal of drugs could end up doing her more harm than good. Liisa shared her concern and began to seek out more natural solutions to alleviate her mother's problems and essentially, as she put it, "reduce her pharmaceutical load." She took delight in discovering new and interesting menu items that promoted healthy living and were full of flavour and goodness. Both mother and daughter benefited from these enjoyable meals and established a habit of choosing nutritional foods rather than consuming foods which they knew could put a person at risk. Visitors to their table took immense pleasure in the exquisitely prepared entrees placed before them without even realizing that they were dining on "health food."

Hilkka had been having problems for some time with the functioning of her heart and her condition finally deteriorated to the point that surgery became necessary in order to save her life, and so in 2001, Peter arranged for her to enter the Mayo Clinic in Rochester, Minnesota, for a massive operation that included three valve repairs, one bypass, and other adjustments including the insertion of a pace-maker. Major surgery is always a source of concern for both patient and doctor, but Hilkka's attitude was so positive and her faith so strong that her doctors had great confidence in her ability to make it through the trauma that her body would have to endure on the operating table.

Peter and Liisa sat in the family waiting room outside the surgical theatre while their mother was in surgery.

Remembering the many times he had been enveloped in his mother's love, Peter enveloped her now in his. Liisa prayed for her mother, for her to have strength of body and spirit, for it to be God's will to let Hilkka remain with them on earth, and for her to be free from suffering. If love and prayers were needed to bring Hilkka safely through, then these she had been given in abundance, from her children and from many others who cared about her. Hilkka learned later that the doctors there would not even have done the surgery had her own attitude not been so positive.

Hilkka was put on the heart-lung machine while the surgeons worked swiftly and expertly to repair her heart. The operation was successfully completed and she was taken to the recovery room where she would be carefully monitored by the nursing staff until it was safe to take her to her own room. All was well.

When she became conscious and saw Liisa standing beside her bed, Hilkka tried to tell her not to let anyone else see her because she didn't have her teeth in. "I don't have my teeth in," she tried to say, "I don't want anyone to see me like this." Liisa managed to make out what she was trying to say, but with some difficulty, because her mother had just had the tubes removed that had been down her throat during the surgery, and she was still groggy from the anesthetic. "Mom," she told her, "your tongue is all tangled up and you're talking oddly because of it, but I know what you've said, and don't worry. Only Peter and I will see you like this." Liisa took her mother's concern over her looks and appearance as a good sign that she was still "with it."

"Mom," Liisa informed her mother, "I'm going out of the room to get Peter." "Am I dying?" Hilkka asked in alarm. "No, no, Mom," Liisa reassured her, "you're all right. You're just fine. Peter is downstairs in the cafeteria and he asked me to come and get him if you woke up while he was there."

When Liisa saw Peter she put her two thumbs up in a gesture of success. Peter sent the "two thumbs up" signal back to her and together they went to be with Hilkka until she was fully conscious . . . and able to put her teeth back in.

The day after her heart surgery, a blood clot formed in Hilkka's leg and within a very short space of time, the limb became alarmingly swollen. The nursing staff monitoring Hilkka immediately notified the doctor on duty about the sudden change in her condition, but Liisa and Peter were frightened by the look of the leg and were terribly worried that it might continue to swell. They had enough medical knowledge to know that this was a signal that something was terribly wrong, and that their mother was in grave danger.

It was a Friday afternoon, and the surgeon who had performed Hilkka's surgery was planning to go away for the weekend. There were of course other doctors available, but Peter and Liisa wanted Hilkka's own surgeon to see her before he left, and they wanted it to be him who made the final decision about what action needed to be taken to help her.

Knowing that the surgeon was on his way out of the clinic, Liisa stationed herself at the elevator doors and Peter took up a position by the doctor's exit door, both ready to approach the surgeon with concerns about their mother's condition. There was no way that the good doctor would be able to miss the Nygård kids—not that he would have tried to escape them. He was a caring man who stopped without hesitation when Liisa met him as he came out of the elevator. "Doctor!" she had called to him, "Please don't leave yet. My brother and I need to talk to you!" When he learned of the clot and the ominous swelling, the doctor took the time to personally make arrangements to have Hilkka's leg thoroughly examined and treated. Peter and Liisa's love for their mother had created a bond so strong between the two of them that they often worked as one entity to ensure Hilkka's safety and well being.

Hilkka required additional surgery to deal with the blood clot. After the surgery, she was taken to the recovery room for post-operative observation, and an oxygen mask was placed over her nostrils and mouth to help her breathe. Hilkka was in the process of coming out of the anesthetic and, although she was mostly conscious, she was still a bit disoriented and groggy. The oxygen mask annoyed her so she ripped it off and tossed it aside. "I don't want this thing on me," she groused. As always, her children were by her side. "Mom," Peter said firmly, "You have to wear the mask." Hilkka was frustrated and confused. Her irritation intensified. "Why should I have to wear this thing?" she asked Peter angrily. "You don't have to wear one of these things!" So Peter reached over, took the oxygen mask and put it on himself. Hilkka thought he looked awfully funny. Relaxing, she allowed the mask to be put back on her own face. In years to come she would tell others the 'Peter in the mask" story with joyful laughter in her voice, remembering how comical her son had looked, and understanding that he would do whatever it took to help her.

Hilkka's condition improved as anticipated to the point that doctors were able to remove the temporary external pace maker and test out the newly repaired heart. After a day of observation without the device, it became obvious that her heart was beating too slowly on its own, and that a permanent pacemaker would have to be inserted.

Her pacemaker was put in by Doctor David Hayes, who had written a medical textbook on pacemakers. Hilkka's nurse back in Winnipeg was extremely excited to be nursing one of this esteemed doctor's patients. "He wrote my textbook!" she exclaimed. Indeed at the Mayo Clinic there were top notch medical experts in a wide variety of disciplines. For Peter and Liisa, it was the only place they had wanted their mother to be. A patient could come in for diagnosis on a Monday and by the end of the week, if surgery was required, be in the operating room. There were no long waiting periods to see a specialist or have surgery, as there were in Canada, and since private health care was legal in the United States, the family was allowed to pay to receive medical care. The Nygårds were grateful for their financial success and good fortune. Such blessings were able to assist Hilkka in obtaining a healthier existence.

Peter, Liisa, Hilkka's granddaughter Angela, and one of Hilkka's closet friends, Tiina Tulikorpi, took turns being by Hilkka's bedside. When Liisa came to stay overnight, Hilkka was able to fully relax and get the rest she needed to recuperate. Once, when Angela came in from outside, her hands were icy cold and she placed them on her grandmother's sore hot back, giving Hilkka such instant and complete relief that she remembered it clearly and with gratitude after she recovered.

Her recovery from all this trauma was truly amazing. She was up and about in record time, feeling better than ever, resuming her normal exercise regime and swimming her usual ten lengths of the pool every day. Her children and grandchildren were vastly relieved and extremely grateful for the return of Hilkka's good health . . . and so was Hilkka! She left the Mayo Clinic needing only two prescription medications.

CHAPTER FOUR

Summers Lost, Summers Gained

It seemed, however, that the fates were intent on keeping Hilkka from enjoying her returning vitality and energy. More than any other time of the year, she loved summer. She constantly followed the sun, traveling back and fourth from the Tropic of Cancer to the 50th parallel, moving along the earth's lines of longitude as the seasons changed. A series of misfortunes complicated several precious summers for her.

Hilkka was immensely creative with wool and thread. Her uniquely fashioned woolen slippers ("booties") were popular gift items, and the many wearers of these warm and intricately crocheted booties include well-known residents of both Canada and the United States. The cloth garments she had sewn in the past were worthy of the Nygård name, and she took pleasure in the quality of her work. Wherever Hilkka was, knitting needles, a crochet hook and a sewing machine were sure to be nearby.

Early one summer, while wandering around in her bare feet in the Falcon Lake cottage, Hilkka stepped on a sewing machine needle. It penetrated her foot at a peculiar angle and no one was able to pull it out, no matter how hard anyone tried. After many discouraging attempts to rid Hilkka's foot of the offending sliver of steel, it became clear that medical intervention was required, and so she had to be taken to the hospital in Kenora, Ontario, where manual attempts to remove the needle also proved to be unsuccessful. To everyone's relief, the following day the needle was finally extracted surgically.

It was expected that Hilkka would have a relatively short period of recovery while the puncture wound on her foot healed, but she had picked up an infection during her few days in the hospital and the foot soon became the lesser of her problems. The antibiotics she had been given to fight off the infection weren't helping to eliminate it. It continued to run its rampant course through her body. She developed a fever as her body fought to rid itself of the aggressive pathogen. Hilkka became very ill. She was sent to Winnipeg, where antibiotics were administered intravenously.

The summer that Hilkka had been so eagerly anticipating turned into a nightmare for her and all those who loved her. It took a long time for the infection to subside and finally disappear, but while she had missed her summer swimming and outdoor exercise, she had continued to receive summer visitors with genuine pleasure at being able to welcome them to Falcon Lake. She was well again when it became time to follow the sun back to the Bahamas and to Peter.

In May 2003, during her annual medical checkup, a manual examination revealed a lump in Hilkka's breast. It had developed rapidly, since a mammogram taken just eight months earlier in September had shown no sign of any growth. "I think," her physician told her, "that we'd better check this out." It was cancer.

Cancer. The very word strikes dread into the hearts of inflicted patients and their families. Eeli's suffering and death had been caused by this sinister disease. Hilkka did not want her children to have to see their mother go through the same ghastly process that they had witnessed their father endure. She was calm and brave as always, but extremely worried. She prayed, and placed her worries and her earthly body in God's care. With trust and faith in Him, she prepared herself for whatever might come her way.

What first came her way was immediate surgery to remove the malignant cancer and nine lymph nodes which turned out not to be involved in the malignancy. She returned to the Mayo Clinic to have the operation performed, and once again her son and daughter were by her side, ready to do whatever they could to help and comfort their beleaguered mother.

Hilkka was confident that the surgery would go well, but she didn't look forward to coming out of the anesthetic after the operation was over. She remembered how disorienting that twilight zone between consciousness and unconsciousness could be, how reality and delirium could seem to merge into one as a soul made its way back into the material world from those airy ethereal regions. She was concerned that she would act in some embarrassing manner, or upset those trying to look after her.

As it turned out Hilkka's fears proved to be well grounded, for in the recovery room she became wildly delirious, ripped out her tubes, vomited profusely and generally acted as if she had gone stark-raving mad. As she gradually surfaced from the effects of the anesthetic and became more and more aware of her physical surroundings she became depressed. The nurses, she felt, were angry with her because of her disruptive behaviour, and this added to her misery. In the final analysis, however, all was well. She was not the first patient to have experienced adverse reactions upon waking up after surgery and she wouldn't be the last.

Step one in her battle against breast cancer had been successful.

Step two was to follow the surgery with twenty-five radiation treatments, which she had in Winnipeg. These treatments were also successful, albeit somewhat unpleasant.

Once again Hilkka's life had been saved, and once again her children and grandchildren rejoiced with her.

Peter, in gratitude and with increased understanding and awareness, took it upon himself to begin his own personal campaign to educate the public about breast cancer and to help those who had already been diagnosed with the disease.

Peter had become an international celebrity, famous for his business empire and luxurious life style. Like many wealthy men, he supported a variety of worthy causes, but none was more significant to him than his commitment to helping women who, like his mother Hilkka, had been affected by breast cancer.

Along with title sponsor CIBC, and supporting sponsors Ford of Canada, Running Room Canada Inc., McCain Foods (Canada) Ltd., Ganong Bros. Ltd., New Balance Canada, Revlon Canada and Canpar Transport L.P., Nygård International became a sponsor of the Canadian Run for the Cure which raises millions of dollars each year to support a wide range of studies in the areas of prevention, diagnosis and improved treatment of breast cancer, as well as quality of life research that focuses on helping survivors return to as normal a life as possible.

Hilkka joined him in his support, and was proud to be part of the annual 'Nygård for Life' Pink and White Charity Ball sponsored by Peter and held at the Winnipeg Convention Centre in Manitoba. Part of this large fundraising event included a fashion show in which the models were breast cancer survivors, and they hit the runway triumphantly exuding confidence and looking terrific . . . and usually earning themselves a standing ovation! When one year Hilkka appeared on stage in a glistening floor length pink gown with rhinestones sparkling in her hair, she wowed the audience. It was hard to believe that this attractive, vivacious woman, on the arm of her handsome son, was a breast cancer survivor in her eighties!

Breast cancer is no longer hidden and talked about in whispers, and as a result women are taking note of the signs and treatment required to be safe from this killer disease.

The radiation Hilkka had received had prevented her deadly cancer from spreading, but there was a most unfortunate side effect to the treatments. Her skin, lungs and the heart valves repaired in 2001 had been damaged by the radiation, and many of the symptoms she had experienced prior to her heart surgery returned.

Being short of breath was an uncomfortably familiar and unwelcome sensation, but she could adjust to it and live with it. It was, after all, better than dying of cancer. The unbearable itching that she felt all over her skin, however, was less easy to accept. Desperately trying not to scratch right through the upper layers of her skin in her frantic attempts to find relief, Hilkka was nearly driven to distraction by the unrelenting agony of her irritated skin. She was given soothing ointments by her doctor which she slathered generously over her skin until it cooled and calmed down. After many weeks of consistently applying medicated creams and ointments and using all of her self discipline to suppress her natural scratching reflex, the horrible itching finally subsided and Hilkka was able to function again.

Gone, also, of course, was the summer.

All these illnesses and traumas interrupted the natural progression of her life, but they never defeated her. She triumphed again and again over the many assaults to her body and carried on. Her own Finnish *sisu* provided her with the strength to endure, and Liisa and Peter reinforced that strength by consistently displaying their sincere conviction that their mother would continue to overcome obstacles set in her way. Hilkka was empowered by Liisa's confidence in her mother's natural ability to heal, and by Peter's firm belief that others could rise to challenges and succeed by drawing on strengths, knowledge and abilities that they often didn't realize they possessed. Meeting challenges of all types had become a way of life for Hilkka. She and Liisa often reflected on the opportunities and challenges presented by Peter, not only to them, but also to others—family members, employees, athletes—with his absolute confidence that they could indeed rise to meet the challenge. Over the years Hilkka, especially, had surpassed even Peter's high expectations, in every way. His trust in her uncanny ability to "read" people, and her fundamental understanding of the way in which business works, made her his most trusted confidant. She accompanied him at his request to meetings, and she fit comfortably and agreeably into any setting and any conversation. She would always take a personal hand made gift with her to give to the individuals with whom they would meet, and as a result VIPs from all around the world wear a pair of her unique trademark knitted "booties." She took notes and minutes at meetings and was observant of anomalies and signals that Peter needed to know. Hilkka and others performed at peak efficiency around Peter because he expected that they would naturally do so. Hilkka was proud of her son's leadership abilities and loved to see Peter inspire others and bring out their best.

Peter in turn was proud of his mother's ability and strength to endure adversity with dignity and grace. No matter what her circumstances happened to be, Hilkka continued to find great joy in life. It seemed that her "bad" experiences were not completely bad because each one was also a learning experience and thus contained some inherent value. It was Hilkka's nature to turn stumbling blocks into stepping stones.

CHAPTER FIVE

Green Smoothies & Cranberries

Around this time, Hilkka was diagnosed with pulmonary hypertension (high blood pressure in permanently damaged capillaries of the lungs), and she was given another prescription. The list of medications she was taking was beginning to get long again. Hilkka hated taking so many pills. She hadn't grown up taking pills and she had enjoyed the respite she had been granted from them ever since she and Liisa had begun to use nutrition as a basic tool for health and wellness. Good food was the new medication—or was it the ancient medication? Once again Hilkka and Liisa began to look for the safest and most effective way to downsize Hilkka's medications.

A new skin irritation flared up, only this time it was not itching but rather overwhelming pain that brought her to her knees. Deep, burning, searing, and stabbing pain in her skin caused Hilkka to become virtually incapacitated. She was diagnosed with shingles, a viral infection that causes chicken pox in its first incarnation, and shingles in subsequent eruptions. Shingles appears most often in older people whose immune systems have been weakened. A patient who has had aggressive treatment, such as chemotherapy or radiation, to kill cancer cells, or who has taken certain other pharmaceutical drugs may have an immune system that has been left temporarily weakened. Such a patient is more susceptible to infections. Hilkka suffered the tortures of the infection for the better part of the summer, aching and praying for the rash and the pain to go away, which it finally did.

Liisa and Hilkka decided to analyze everything that went into Hilkka's body. It was a fascinating and revealing exercise! With Liisa's extensive knowledge of foods and nutrition, and Hilkka's ongoing desire for more natural solutions to her medical problems, they laid out a strategy for healthy living designed especially for Hilkka. Building upon the foundation they had laid earlier when they had decided to make good food the medication, they began by eliminating some of her less essential medications and found that Hilkka began to feel much better, more energized and less fatigued. Next they made some major dietary changes, getting rid of things such as white sugar, salt, monosodium glutamate and aspartame. She cut back on the amount of red meat she ate and consumed fish or chicken instead. She found new delight in fresh fruits and vegetables, snacks of cranberries and asparagus, and continued delight in whole grained breads and baked items. With Liisa's help she began to learn about enzymes, probiotics, herbs, olive oil and coconut oil.

Liisa made her mother "green smoothies" to drink. Green smoothies were concoctions made with organic greens, cucumber, celery, orange juice, lemon juice, hemp oil, cilantro, pineapple, and bananas. Liisa would blend these ingredients in her Vita Mix processor, add some Avena Original vegetable protein powder called "Toco" and pour the mixture into a tall glass. Green smoothies, with their unusual combination of fruits and vegetables, were surprisingly tasty and chock full of goodness. Hilkka loved them. It was hard to believe that such delicious foods were designed for anything other than good taste!

Hilkka lowered her bad cholesterol, reduced her blood glucose level, brought down her blood pressure, and before long was able to reduce the number of medications she was taking. She and Liisa continued to work together to maintain a natural balanced diet with high nutritional standards for themselves, and both enjoyed improved health and vitality because they did so. Hilkka for example, very rarely had the flu or common cold, despite not having a flu shot. In addition to her daily food regime, she also took a number of vitamin supplements, including 2000 milligrams of Vitamin C, daily. During the winter in the Bahamas, Peter provided ample opportunity for his mother to swim, her favourite physical activity. Added to all of this, in both the Bahamas and at Falcon Lake, were weekly massage therapy sessions which proved to be highly beneficial for Hilkka. At Falcon Lake she looked forward to these sessions not just for the relief the massage provided but also because of her fellowship with the therapists, Dave and Evelyn Willison from Betula Lake. Each week in the summer, for over a decade, Hilkka would plan and prepare a dinner for the three of them, and after praying together and sharing a meal, a stimulating game of UNO was invariably played. The entire afternoon and evening would be given over to these pleasurable pursuits, lifting stress and relaxing the body. With a concentrated emphasis on good nutrition, regular exercise and weekly massages, Hilkka was able to return to a healthy and active life style.

Some ongoing medical challenges still plagued Hilkka, and she still had to take some medication to keep them at bay. She continued to have diabetes, but it was well controlled without medication. She continued to have pulmonary hypertension and edema, but she began to take her vital signs each morning, monitoring and analyzing the readings. She became healthier in mind and body.

Whatever her physical ailments happened to be, Hilkka seldom if ever complained. Life was to be enjoyed. She smiled and laughed and cooked dinners for her family and friends. She spent time with her grandchildren and traveled with Peter to interesting places. She swam and played UNO and backgammon. Most importantly, Hilkka kept her sense of humour. Her merry laugh was contagious and her jokes were really funny. In her presence people soon forgot that she was elderly and sometimes in pain. They laughed right along with her.

Hilkka had two more frustrating and troublesome events that caused her children concern. Once she fell at home when she tripped getting off her scale, and hit her head on the marble floor of her bathroom. On another occasion she turned the lights off in the hallway, and missing the wall in the dark, she fell into the entrance way and hit her head on the door. Falling was not an experience she wanted to repeat. The bumps on the head hurt a lot. Her children were upset and she was embarrassed. She made sure that she didn't fall a third time. She didn't want her children to start treating her as if she were frail.

CHAPTER SIX

Legacies

Through everything that had happened to her, Hilkka Nygård had always found solace in her family. Her parents, her sisters, her husband and children—all had given great meaning and depth to her life, and they mattered more than anything else in the world to her. Hilkka, who had always loved children, treasured her grandchildren and great-grandchildren. When they were all brought together, as they often were for special occasions, she was totally delighted.

These people had come into the world because she had loved Eeli. They were the manifestation and legacy of their love.

The great family gatherings that took place in the summer at Falcon Lake were splendid affairs, with as many grandchildren as could come all seated around a huge table sharing one of Hilkka's fabulous, colourful, healthy meals. The laughter, the fresh scent of pines and cedars and the clear shining lake all conspired to create the perfect atmosphere for siblings and cousins to spend time together under the beaming eyes of their doting grandmother. Peter and Liisa cherished such occasions and the great pleasure that Hilkka received from them.

The family's Christmas gatherings at Viking Hill, the home which Peter had purchased for Hilkka and Eeli in the Bahamas, were equally impressive. Peter would assemble all of his children—or at least as many as were able to make it—and any other invited guests, and with Hilkka as the matriarch, the ancient traditions of Finland would be honoured along with the modern

North American practices. When the children were small, Peter established a family custom of having everyone at the table give an after-dinner speech. As soon as they could talk, each child was encouraged to stand up and make a little speech after special meals. This practice encouraged the sharing of thoughts and developed self-confidence at the same time. It was a custom which the children enjoyed, and Hilkka laughed when little Courtney, at the age of four, with the last bite of dinner still in her mouth, asked "Now can we have our speeches?"

At Christmas time, children were everywhere in the mammoth house. Hilkka would think to herself that the kids just seemed to pop up like mushrooms in the forest. They were all unique, all different sizes and colours, and all of them were growing up far too quickly. Gifts would be piled in abundance around a huge Christmas tree and the children would have to wait until Santa appeared to open them. Hilkka would spend hours cooking for the ever growing family, making traditional Finnish Christmas foods just the way her mother Selma had done so long ago on Lamposaari.

After the Christmas festivities were over and the rest of the family had departed for home, Hilkka would remain in the sun drenched Bahamas where she would exercise daily in the swimming pool, stroll through the gardens and make delicious dinners for Peter and his many guests. Hilkka was always pleased to serve as hostess at her son's table, and she loved the after dinner card games that were often played when she dined with Peter and his companions. She would frequently win at backgammon and she was no slouch in any major UNO tournament. She looked forward with enthusiasm to the annual visit their family friend and attorney, Zoltan Milhaly, made to Viking Hill. Zoltan was an expert backgammon player who never failed to rise to the challenge of a game. He and Hilkka were well matched, both enjoying the thrill of playing against a talented adversary. Each considered a win against the other a major victory. Hilkka would prepare Viking Hill for Zoltan Milhaly's visits with enthusiasm, making sure that everything was just the way he might like it to be. Worthy opponents deserved and received exactly the kind of accommodation they desired.

Liisa and Dennis would come to spend several weeks with Hilkka each winter in her Bahamian paradise and those were happy, wonderful days for all three of them.

When she found the stairs to the house from the pool becoming more difficult for her and her guests to climb when nature called, Hilkka asked

Peter if he could build a little washroom near the pool deck for her convenience. Peter loved to design and he loved to please his mother. Before she could turn around, Hilkka found that she had a brand new wing added to Viking Hill which contained a full sized washroom, shower and changing room, a sauna, an outside kitchen and entertainment center, all handicapped accessible. Dubbed the "East Wing", Hilkka held a grand opening for the addition in March of 2009, with every part of the East Wing in full use. The kitchen offered up barbequed foods, the sauna was visited by each of the family members, and Hilkka even enjoyed a rare night time swim with Liisa, Saylor and Maddex. The "little washroom"—the only thing that she had originally requested—was used as intended.

Hilkka would have less than a year left to enjoy her new facilities.

Hilkka concentrating on a backgammon game with great-granddaughter Makayla . . .

and winning yet another Summit UNO tournament trophy.

Liisa and Dennis with Hilkka and Liisa's children, left to right,
Angela, Kristopher, Allison and David.

[Centre] Hilkka and Peter with four of Peter's children.
Left to right: Mika, Kai, Alia, Peter, Hilkka, Jessar.
[Bottom Left] Peter with his daughter Bianca.
[Bottom Right] Peter with his daughter Scarlet.

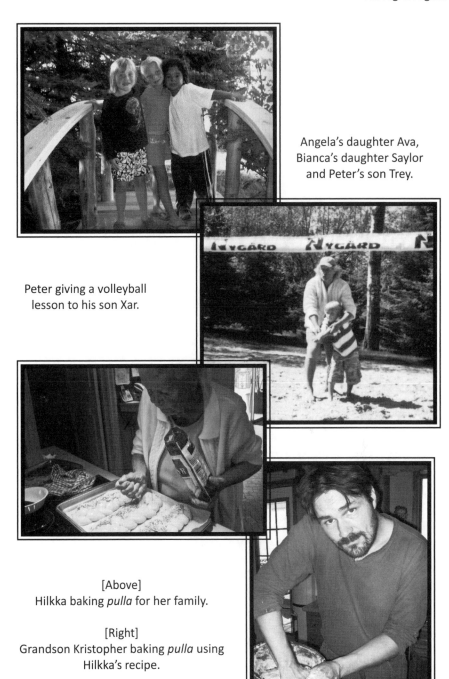

Angela's daughter Ava,
Bianca's daughter Saylor
and Peter's son Trey.

Peter giving a volleyball
lesson to his son Xar.

[Above]
Hilkka baking *pulla* for her family.

[Right]
Grandson Kristopher baking *pulla* using
Hilkka's recipe.

Hilkka arranging flowers for a dinner table centerpiece at Falcon Lake in August, 2009.

Hilkka making Finnish pancakes for her brood at Falcon Lake, August 2009.

August 2009 dinner at Falcon Lake; Alia at the end of the table, Dennis in the forefront.

Hilkka's grandchildren and great-grandchildren enjoying
Hilkka's cooking at Falcon Lake, Manitoba, August 2009.
Maryann and Penny, Hilkka's friends and helpers,
standing at left.

Makayla, Morgan
and Annika hav-
ing a candlelight
dinner with
Great Gramma
Hilkka at Viking
Hill, Bahamas.

Formal dinner
party with great-
grandchildren
at Viking Hill,
Bahamas.

Hilkka, age 86, staying fit in the pool in the Bahamas.

Peter and Hilkka enjoying the sauna in the new East Wing, March 2009.

Chapter Seven

Just a Simple Procedure

In reflective moments, when her many blessings caused her heart to swell with gratitude for the amazing life she had been given, Hilkka would sometimes ask Liisa, "This is all like a dream, when will it all come crashing down?" Liisa would console her mother by reassuring her that they would be all right. "Mom," she would say, "We know how to live humbly. We've been there. We'll just live in my camper if we have to, or wherever we can, and we'll start all over again. We've learned from you, Mom . . . nothing is impossible, and life is an adventure."

Hilkka found peace and serenity at Falcon Lake, in Winnipeg and at her home, Viking Hill, in Nassau. She received love and comfort in full measure from her daughter Pirjo-Liisa and her son Pekka, and she loved both unconditionally and without reservation.

In the summer of 2009, despite having to manage minor health ailments, Hilkka enjoyed many weeks at Falcon Lake.

When Liisa's family and a dozen other guests gathered at the cottage to celebrate both Hilkka's and Angela's birthdays, Hilkka was in her glory. Nothing made her happier than being surrounded by her grandchildren and great-grandchildren. She made her famous strawberry shortcake—an all round family favorite—to top off the delicious dinner for the noisy group of happy diners. It was a good memory and would be the last time that the group dined with its matriarch.

Always present was Hilkka's famous Strawberry Shortcake. No birthday went by without one! The delicious mouth watering recipe was handed down to Hilkka from her mother Selma, and was popular with everyone who ever bit into a piece of it. Each layer of the cake was filled with sweet juicy strawberries and mounds of freshly whipped cream. No matter what, nothing ever stood in the way of Hilkka baking that strawberry shortcake for each birthday that she attended—even if that birthday took place on a desert island!

Allison on her third birthday on a desert island in the tropical sea, with Gramma Hilkka's strawberry birthday cake, 1976.

Saylor on her seventh birthday with Gramma Hilkka's strawberry birthday cake, March 2009.

Tiina and Angela celebrate their birthdays together, waiting for Gramma Hilkka's strawberry birthday cake.

Eeli, another birthday and another of Hilkka's delicious strawberry cakes. Peter and his children Alia and Jessar looking on.

Nine days before the 27th of August, when she was scheduled to have her pacemaker battery changed, Hilkka baked nine loaves of *pulla*, Finnish coffee bread, to have on hand for everyone, because she had been told that the kneading of dough would be difficult for her after the minor surgery required to change the batteries.

When she arrived at the St Boniface Hospital for the battery change, Liisa noticed that Hilkka was out of breath and when pressed, Hilkka admitted that she had been retaining fluid, as evidenced by a sudden weight gain and shortness of breath. Normally reluctant to use a wheelchair in the hospital, on this occasion she chose to have one.

Liisa pointed out the fluid retention to the medical staff and expressed her concern. Hilkka was given the diuretic, Lasix, with no significant results. Her breathing did not improve, but the surgical procedure went ahead as planned, delayed only by an hour or so.

When Hilkka came out of surgery, she didn't know Liisa and "spoke silly" until the effects of the drugs administered for the procedure dissipated. Within hours, they sent her home without any further attention to her breathlessness.

Just before midnight, Hilkka called Liisa to her bedroom, showing her a large swelling over the surgical area and indicating that her breathing problem had become worse. Liisa called 911 and was impressed by the prompt professional help which was demonstrated by the paramedics. This rapid and competent response was reassuring to both mother and daughter.

The Grace Hospital Emergency Room was yet another comforting place where compassionate, capable caregivers quickly assessed the situation, removed some of the fluid from around Hilkka's lungs with a syringe, and admitted her to the hospital.

She was placed into a four bed ward. Having just been given a diuretic and not being able to get to the washroom easily, Hilkka felt somewhat stressed. She was a private person by nature and she was uncomfortable having her personal problems so obviously on display to others.

Private rooms were not available on the ward, so Liisa urged Hilkka to turn her thoughts in another direction. "Perhaps," she said, "we should ask ourselves 'Why are we here?' Perhaps there is someone in this room with us who needs our encouragement."

Without knowing it, Liisa and Hilkka had reversed roles. Liisa was now the one guiding her mother, just as her mother had always guided her.

Hilkka's medical prognosis was not good. The fluid around her lungs

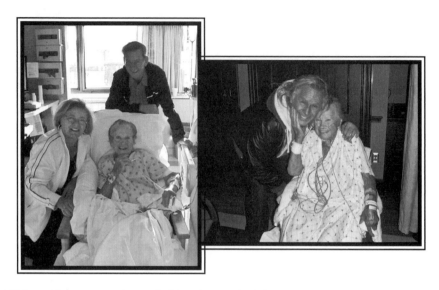

Hilkka, with Dennis and Liisa (left) and Peter (right), improving in the Mayo Clinic.

required the insertion of a chest tube. With the massive doses of diuretics, her body chemistry was out of control. Her life was in danger.

The Mayo Clinic had helped Hilkka to recover in the past, and so Peter ordered an air ambulance and made arrangements with the Cardiology department at the Mayo Clinic to receive her. Then he put together a twenty four/seven support group—Bianca, Angela, Courtney, Alia and Derek—and flew them to Rochester to join Liisa. Within hours of her arrival, numerous tests and procedures indicated that as well as pulmonary hypertension, Hilkka had severe stenosis of her aortic valve. Her condition was serious.

Dr. Chet Rihal performed a valvoplasty to alleviate the situation, but indicated that this would be only a temporary fix. There was a new procedure being studied, he told them, in which a valve could be inserted with a catheter, and while unfortunately Hilkka did not meet the criteria for this procedure in the United States, she did meet it in Canada. The "guru" of this procedure worked in St Paul's Hospital in Vancouver, British Columbia. Dr. Rihal indicated that he would make a referral there for Hilkka, but in the mean time, she needed to recover and become stronger.

While she was still in the Intensive Care Unit at the Mayo Clinic, Hilkka told Liisa that Eeli had come to her in a dream. With his hands reaching out to her, he had asked her: "Why are you suffering down there? It is so beautiful here. Come with me." . . . and Hilkka had answered, "I'm not ready yet." Liisa felt goose bumps on her arms and whispered softly to her mom. "I'm glad you said no."

In each of these scenarios there had been moments of crisis. Each time the family had prepared for Hilkka's possible death, but each time her tenacity and God's great mercy saw her improve and live to fight yet another day.

Peter arranged for Hilkka's recuperation to take place in the sun and warmth of the Bahamas, where he had set up round the clock nursing care, having fully equipped her room at Viking Hill. Accompanied by medical staff and her loving family, Hilkka was able to be transported in Peter's big plane back to the place she loved and was placed under the care of her long time friend and Cardiologist Dr. Dean Tseretopoulos.

She made progress. She started to sound like herself when she talked to Liisa on the phone. Although the fluid buildup in her body was ever present, she managed to have a few UNO games and even hosted a dinner party (orchestrated by her, but prepared by her helpers).

By the end of October, however, it was evident that Hilkka's fluid retention was unmanageable, and she was beginning to have serious breathing problems. Peter was in the final week of preparing to open his Times Square Store in New York. Liisa was to attend the event as a guest . . . but Hilkka needed immediate help. Again, Peter arranged for an air ambulance transport to the Mayo Clinic where the final preparations for the valve procedure were to be made.

Hilkka's favourite nurses from the Bahamas as well as Dennis and Liisa's daughter-in-law Chantal, and Rene Law, a close friend of Hilkka's, were sent to be with Hilkka to ensure a twenty-four/seven vigil. Peter and Liisa were to join them immediately after the store event was complete.

One can only imagine the devastation that the family felt when on November 11, 2009, a blazing fire swept through Nygård Cay, causing millions of dollars of property damage and destroying many of the structures and buildings. Peter was still in New York when the fire broke out, having completed the opening of his flagship store on Broadway in Times Square. It was a dreadful juxtaposition of events, the celebration of the heralded construction of a prestigious retail store versus the tragedy of the fiery destruction of a magnificent home . . . but overriding the significance of both of those events was the increasing concern that the family was beginning to feel about Hilkka's failing health.

Mayo Clinic Nurse Tammi, Hilkka, and Nurse Judy.

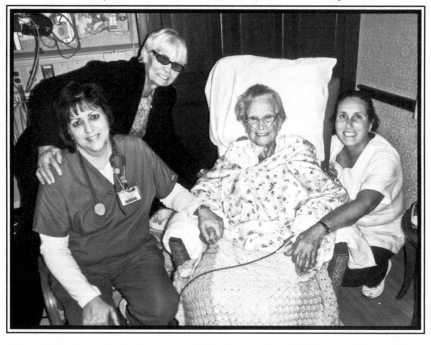

Mayo Clinic Nurse Ruth; Rene Law, Hilkka's dear friend; Hilkka and Nurse Diana Crossgill from the Bahamas, preparing to leave for Vancouver, British Columbia.

Peter sitting vigil in family waiting room at St Paul's Hospital, Vancouver, British Columbia with daughters Scarlet and Alia, and Alia's boyfriend, Derek Daneault.

Liisa was by now at the Mayo Clinic in Rochester, Minnesota with Hilkka. Opening her e-mail she was stunned to read a stark message from her brother, "Lost Nygård Cay. Burnt down last night." The message was both brief and poignant. What else could one say? Liisa felt Peter's grief. Nygård Cay had been much more than just a place on the map. It was the manifestation of Peter's dreams. He had poured his talent, his creativity and his heart into its creation, and it had been unique. No other place like it existed on earth.

Hilkka was at high risk medically, so the family decided not to tell her about the massive fire at Peter's residence until she was stronger, for fear of upsetting her while she was struggling to overcome adversity and become well.

Dr. John Webb of St Paul's Hospital in Vancouver, accepted Hilkka as a candidate to receive the new heart valve, and so Peter booked yet another air ambulance to take his mother to British Columbia. She traveled to Vancouver with Rene Law and was met by another entourage of her own twenty-four/seven support team, arranged for by Peter, which included Nurse Nenita and Courtney, assistant Mary Anne and four of Peter's children, Bianca, Kai, Jessar and Scarlet, who were joined later by their sister Alia and Derek Daneault, Alia's boyfriend, as well as Liisa and Peter. This devoted group was unparalleled to anything the hospital had ever seen.

After examining and interviewing Hilkka, Dr. Webb confirmed that he would proceed with the surgery. During the operation, Hilkka's anxious family waited in the visitors' room with other families who were as anxious as they were. There is a strange and compelling comradeship that exists among people who sit anxiously in hospital waiting rooms. They recognize in each other the fear of illness, of pain, of loss. Their everyday concerns and worries are rendered to the petty and mundane. They are dealing with basic elemental human emotions and they relate one to the other with both sympathy and empathy. In the hospital visitors' room, people are dealing with the big picture. Peter spent a long time comforting a woman, approximately Hilkka's age, while her husband was in surgery. They were all in this together.

Finally, the surgeon came out and told them that the valve was in place and working! Such relief and gratitude they all felt! . . . But not more than an hour later, their joy was dampened when they learned that Hilkka was bleeding inside because a vein had ruptured. She required seven units of blood to replace that which was lost. Her condition was grave. The repair was completed and Hilkka was put on full life support and moved to the intensive care unit.

In true form, and to the utter surprise of many, Hilkka rallied back. Much of the life support had been removed—even the dialysis—and all that remained to be taken away was the breathing tube. She needed some training to remember how to breathe properly (her brain needed to be able to recall how to send down the proper signals to her lungs), and she needed to gain the strength to draw air into her lungs and push it out again.

Liisa had continually warned the nursing staff and doctors that Hilkka was extremely sensitive to most pharmaceuticals. Morphine (or almost any sedative) would literally knock her out, and because of this Hilkka rarely took any pain medications.

Liisa was puzzled and more than a little upset when, after having been given this caution, the medical staff went ahead and gave her mother morphine anyway. "Why do this," she questioned, "when morphine suppresses breathing, the very thing we want to strengthen?!" But despite her worries, Hilkka was progressing well and was in fact considered to be one of the "healthiest" people in the ICU. She was communicating on paper, doing some physiotherapy, her kidneys had recovered from the contrast dye damage and she would happily practice breathing without the use of the breathing machine for increased periods of time. She asked for water, for porridge

. . . and for sausages! . . . which of course she could not have because of the tubes in her throat. The signals she was sending forth were those of a woman about to recuperate. It was clearly living that she wanted, not a decline towards death.

Buoyed by Hilkka's apparent improved condition, Liisa went home for Christmas, knowing that Hilkka would be attended to by Peter and his children who were gathering in Vancouver for their traditional Christmas with Gramma Hilkka. Peter and his children and grandchildren Bianca, Saylor, Maddex, Alia, Derek, Kai, Jessar, and Scarlet were either there or en route. A Bahamian Christmas had come to the hospital and with it came a sunny warmth and gentle atmosphere which soothed and comforted those exposed to it.

According to their Christmas custom, each child in turn gave a little speech of endearment, this time standing around the bed instead of sitting around the table. They showed a video made by Bianca for the occasion and after the little celebration, each took a turn sitting with Hilkka while the rest opened their gifts in the family waiting room. The little speeches made by the children fell on Hilkka's ears. She smiled when she heard them, and she told them that she adored them all, her precious little ones, growing up so fast, so sweet, so clever. But no one heard her say those things. No one heard her speak. Perhaps they saw her lips move slightly and her head turn to look at them, but they didn't know that she had spoken. They kissed her and embraced her and sat with her while she lay there under the covers. They told her little things about their day, and their voices were muffled and seemed to come from far away. It mattered not what they said. It was the reassuring murmur of their voices that soothed and warmed her. "They've turned out well, Hilkka, wouldn't you agree?" Eeli asked her. "Oh yes," Hilkka answered, "they have indeed." No one else heard Eeli and Hilkka speak to each other.

Hilkka had become increasingly sleepy and ultimately comatose. Earlier in the week, she had been given morphine and Tylenol as well as a sleeping pill with devastating consequences. In an effort to revive her she was given anti-narcotics and she had received aspirin, which Liisa had warned might cause a stomach bleed. When stomach bleeding subsequently occurred, other medications were added to counteract it. Hilkka's kidneys began to fail. Signs of small seizures began to be noted.

One day, Hilkka raised her forearm and held it there for a long time. She wasn't reaching or pointing. The gesture was rather one of offering, as if her hand was being held out to be received by someone. She would sometimes gaze off, focusing at a point beyond her vision range, seemingly comfortable and content, but drifting dreamily to another place.

Liisa had returned to Vancouver just as the hospital staff indicated that it would no longer consider dialysis as a lifesaving treatment for Hilkka. Peter and Liisa begged them to do dialysis and give their mother blood because the bleeding in her stomach and the bleeding on the branch of her bronchi which had been irritated by the suctioning tube, were causing Hilkka to lose blood.

Instead, one of the doctors took Scarlet, Peter's thirteen year old daughter, aside and said, "Your Grandmother is dying. I will do everything I can to make it peaceful for her. The hardest part is not her dying. You need to go and tell your father to let her die in peace." The child was thirteen years old, and while she was mature for her age, the message was still a hard one for her to carry.

Peter and Liisa did not accept the death sentence as inevitable. Hilkka had not wished to die, and she had a powerful spirit. She had not provided a "Do Not Resuscitate" order, even when she had had a chance to do so. She was giving written messages asking for food, wanting to know when her surgery was to take place (not realizing that it had already been done), and didn't want anyone to see her without her teeth in. These were signs of a person who wanted to carry on, not cave in.

Their mother was loaded with morphine, Tylenol, sleeping pills, and a cocktail of at least seven to ten drugs to which she was hypersensitive. She had had no solid food for some time. Only a few weeks ago she had baked nine loaves of bread, entertained ten people for dinner, played UNO and backgammon, had attended to her own financial affairs, took her own vital signs and set out her medications. Everything her children knew about her gave them ample cause to believe that she wanted to live. They were not prepared to give up and let Hilkka go. She had never given up on anything in her life. Why should her children give up on her behalf?

The two illnesses that had threatened Hilkka, besides the problems that had precipitated the crisis before them, had been pulmonary hypertension and the aortic stenosis. The new valve was in place and working but the pulmonary hypertension still needed correcting. Peter and his oldest son Kai began researching possible procedures that might help her. They found out that a major conference was being held nearby, which would, among other things, have a session about a Stem Cell technique for Pulmonary Hypertension. Peter and Kai took time out to attend the session and were decidedly intrigued by what they learned. While still in its infancy, this technique had already shown several positive outcomes. It was not yet approved for use in the United States or Canada, but was being successfully performed in the Dominican Republic by American doctors. They relayed their findings to the family. Possibly this could be a treatment that would help Hilkka.

Since the treatment they sought for Hilkka was not available to them in Canada, Peter and Liisa felt that they needed to take a chance and medivac Hilkka to the Dominican Republic. In the Dominican Republic, she would have a team of doctors willing to do dialysis, give her blood and intravenous nourishment and, most importantly, the innovative stem cell procedure to possibly alleviate her pulmonary hypertension. The Canadian doctors expressed concern about moving Hilkka, believing that she would die in transit, which her children found to be a curious comment given that they had said that she was dying anyway.

She was such a fighter! She arrived alive despite unscheduled stops, airplane breakdowns and delays of all sorts. A team of specialists met her at her arrival and began treatment immediately. All of them said, "If only you could have brought her earlier!"

The next night when the sky darkened, Dennis and Liisa went up to the hills overlooking Santiago and the medical centre where Hilkka was being tested and treated. There, standing in the stillness and tranquility of the tropical night, Liisa prayed for her mother. She thought of the love that had flowed so freely between them and of her mother's generous and uncompromising devotion to her family. Hilkka had been to the edge so many times and she had always returned. She had always fought her way back. Why should this time be any different? Yet Liisa sensed that this time was, in fact, very different and that her submission to God had to be, as it had been before, "Nevertheless, not my will, but Thy will be done."

As hard as they tried for several days, the doctors could not save Hilkka. Her hemoglobin had dropped to 50 by the time she had arrived in the Dominican Republic and an EEG indicated that subsequent untreated seizures and lack of oxygen had severely damaged the dominant hemisphere of her brain. She could not be revived. Dr. Leonel Liriano told them that she was going very fast. She lay quietly as if apart from them already. Her distraught family gathered at her bedside to be with her, sticking together, as they had always done, right to the end.

She had no final words, no dramatic farewell. She simply stopped. Stunned by Hilkka's unexpected slide towards death, the family was even more overcome by the speed at which the end of her life actually occurred. How could this happen? Hilkka had gone. Hilkka, who always came back, wasn't coming back this time. What started out as a simple procedure to change a pacemaker battery had spiraled downward to a deadly conclusion. If only . . . if only . . . they had moved her before Christmas, would the final outcome have been different? The family knew that Hilkka would not want them to "if only" or "what if" themselves into a state of despair. It was not her style. She had fought to stay with them as long as she could; she had been reluctant to leave them to travel on, but in the final analysis she had allowed herself to go. She would now be on the greatest adventure of her existence. Who knew what wonders she was experiencing? She would now have come to the full understanding that God had promised His people.

Hilkka had finished her earthly travels.

Hilkka in hospital, August 28, 2009, holding roses received from her children to celebrate her 87th birthday, which would turn out to be her final birthday.

CHAPTER EIGHT

The Last Chapter
"Always a Child of Lamposaari"

Hilkka made her final journey, this time to her Heavenly Home, on January 12, 2010, one day before her scheduled stem cell procedure was due to take place.

Later that afternoon, the people of Haiti were to suffer the worst earthquake in history. The effects of the earth shuddering were felt in Haiti's neighbouring country, the Dominican Republic, where Peter, Liisa, Dennis and children sat in a shock of their own, mourning the loss of their beloved Mother, the pillar of their family, the Nygård family matriarch.

The kindness and talent of the doctors in the Dominican Republic, working as they do on the leading edge of science and technology while incorporating natural healing techniques into their research and development, greatly impressed Peter. Listening to Dr. Mitchell Ghen describe his dream of creating an all encompassing clinic, which will lead the way in integrative medicine, combining conventional medicine with natural healing, intravenous nutrition, and stem cell research and therapy, Peter became convinced that such a dream should come to fruition. There is little doubt but that he will follow the development of this venture with great interest.

Peter's big airplane took the group with Hilkka's ashes to Nassau where a service of Christian burial was conducted by Pastor Sam Boodle of Nassau Lutheran Church at Viking Hill where Hilkka had known such happiness. It was a beautiful service filled with rousing Gospel music, soloists and instrumentalists assembled by King Eric, a family friend for over three decades, who was well known for his Caribbean music and entertainment in Nassau. So much glorious and joy-filled music! Such a wonderful sun-drenched day! What a festive celebration! Oh my, how Hilkka would have loved that day!

At the time of this writing, the family plans to arrange a second service for a future date to commit Hilkka's ashes to the ground, in Winnipeg where she will take her place beside her beloved Eeli.

Hilkka Valtonen Nygård's faith in her heavenly Father remained real and strong to the end. A few months before she died, while reflecting upon her faith, she told this writer, "I believe even more now than I did when I was younger. I believe in God and I pray to Him every day and all the time. I never go to bed without praying. I say, 'Thank you for the good life I have. Please take care of my dear children and grandchildren and great-grandchildren and don't let Peter have a heart attack and many thanks', and then I say the Lord's Prayer."

Her "good life" included living in the land to which she bravely came so many decades ago. Like other immigrant mothers, she endured, and gave to Canada a lasting heritage and legacy. She was the glue that held her large and diverse family together, instilling in its individual members love and loyalty towards each of the others. She made things right. Her son Peter once referred to the slogan used by the American Express company when talking about his mother's impact on events. If you want things to turn out right, he said, "you don't leave home without her."

King Eric, front center, on steel drums,
playing at Hilkka's Memorial Service in the Bahamas.

Hilkka loved Canada, loved the Whiteshell lakes and the evergreen forests, loved the sun-drenched tropical Bahamas, but always in her heart she was a child of Lamposaari. On Lamposaari she was an innocent, carefree and full of joy, to whom trouble meant a spanking because of some impulsive childish mischief, not war and pain or ruthless political regimes, not poverty and fear and sickness and cruel places. Lamposaari shaped her. It was always with her, and perhaps if God is as kind and as good as she believed Him to be, Lamposaari as it was in her youth, exists in a corner of Heaven for all eternity just for her, and sitting there on the big swing in the woods, she will once more hold hands with Eeli.

Kanteleeni

Mun kanteleeni kauniimmin taivaassa kerran soi,
mun kanteleeni kauniimmin taivaassa kerran soi,
siell' uusin äänin suloisin mun suuni laulaa voi,
siell' uusin äänin suloisin mun suuni laulaa voi.
Oi Halleluja rakkaalle mun Jeesukselleni!
Oi Halleluja rakkaalle mun Jeesukselleni!
Ah, autuas on päivä se, kun pääsen luoksesi!
Ah, autuas on päivä se, kun pääsen luoksesi!

My Kantele most beautifully
In Heaven will once again ring
There with a sweet voice renewed
My mouth can once again sing
Now Halleluiah sing I can
To Jesus Christ my Lord
Ahh! Blessed is the day to me
When with you I can be!

Hilkka, Liisa and Dennis attend the Lutheran Church of Nassau
with Pastor Sam Boodle.
Pastor Boodle was later to officiate at Hilkka's Memorial Service at Viking Hill.

Paster Sam Boodle gives the final blessing at
Hilkka's Memorial Service at Viking Hill.

Memorial wall at Viking Hill.

APPENDICES

APPENDIX A

Hilkka's Final Journey
E-mails from Peter and Liisa

E-mail messages from Liisa to the author.

Original message sent Friday August 29, 2009:

. . . Mom did have her procedure done . . . that part went fairly well (still has lots of swelling). When she arrived in Winnipeg that a.m. she was very badly out of breath . . . her weight indicated fluid retention which she had been unable to reduce with her water pills . . . I had noticed her shortness of breath on the phone all week.

In any event, I expressed my concern to the people about to do the surgical procedure and indicated that she needs the fluids reduced and needs her electrolytes checked . . . they did the procedure anyway . . . they gave her some diuretic intravenously and gave her oxygen . . . eventually sent us home . . . she was very out of breath . . . but somewhat better . . . went to bed . . . and called to me around midnight and said her wound was really swollen and she had trouble breathing . . . . Knowing she should see a doctor I decided to call an ambulance . . . they were more worried about her breathing than they were about her wound, which they said was probably normal . . . . They took us to Grace Hospital. She is there now. They removed 1 and 1/2 litres of fluid from between her lungs and her rib cage . . . relieved the pressure a lot . . . but she is still wheezing and can not seem to do too long without the oxygen . . . also her sodium is low . . . but she is coherent (unlike she was after the fluid removal . . . then 5 hours straight of sleeping . . . on waking did

- 261 -

not know where she was or who I was . . . so many drugs combined that she had not used before ???) I thought she might have had a stroke . . . her speech was slurry . . . but she came out of it and last night was totally coherent.

. . . we are going to church and then I will go to see mom . . .

Blessings, Liisa

Original message sent Wednesday, September 23, 2009:

. . . Mom is taking small steps forward each morning but by p.m. is exhausted . . . with her in shifts around the clock . . .

talk soon . . . Love Liisa

Original message sent Monday, November 02, 2009:

. . . Mom may be heading back to Mayo any day to have some more fluid removed and to get a permanent catheter in the chest area . . . . She has not really regained her stamina and keeps collecting fluid . . . . My life has been just more of a roller coaster . . . she has 24/7 nursing care and is well looked after . . . but not her happy self.

I was supposed to go with Heather to New York this Wed. for the opening of the Nygård store at Times Square.

We shall see what happens.

Blessings,

Liisa

Original message sent Monday, November 09, 2009:

. . . Here I am on an airplane . . . heading to Rochester where Mom was taken by Air Ambulance . . . Thursday . . . Same problems . . . . I will call you from there . . . . I am coming from NY . . . where Peter just opened a new store in Times Square . . . I must close up for landing . . . .

Blessings Liisa

Original message sent Wednesday, November 25, 2009:

In Vancouver with Mom . . . not really telling anyone much about it as do not want visitors to tell her about Nygård Cay fire . . . would upset her too much . . . .

Original message sent Saturday, November 28, 2009:

. . . The procedure was successful but many other complications have set in . . . she is in an induced coma because of some bleeding and her blood pressure is controlled with meds to keep it from crashing . . . we can just wait to see what happens???? I trust God will let us know what he has in mind... will keep you posted . . . .

Blessings . . .

Original message sent Monday, November 30, 2009:

. . . Hilkka is in very serious shape. The valve is working and in place but she has a problem with her kidneys . . . because of the contrast used in the procedure as well she probably has pneumonia in her right lung . . . she is retaining a lot of fluid for this reason. She has woken and responds to commands but they are keeping her sedated to keep her from getting agitated. I will keep you posted . . . .

As always, Liisa

* * *

E-mail message from Liisa to her friends.

Original message sent December, 2009:

Hello Dear Friends; Just a quick update on Mom. As you might know, just a summary: Mom went by air ambulance to Mayo Clinic on November 6 . . . with shortness of breath & fluid around her lungs . . . . She was destined for a special aortic valve replacement to be done in Vancouver through a special catheter procedure . . . a new procedure pioneered by a Canadian Dr. Webb in Vancouver. After 2 weeks at Mayo . . . she was accepted in Vancouver for this procedure in which the valve was successfully placed . . . . Complications from the surgery, including a severe bleed, kidney failure due to contrast dye and severe water retention followed . . . she has now been in ICU in Vancouver for over 3 weeks. Initially she was on complete life support but now she is trying to wean off the breathing machine. She was on the way up many times, only to suffer setbacks . . . and currently is more drowsy and low on energy . . . in a very delicate condition.

Her grandchildren, who usually spend Christmas in the Bahamas with her, are going to be in Vancouver instead to spend Christmas with her there. Each, with the two hired nurses, will take a turn to sit with her 24/7, as we have for the past 3 months.

We are not certain what the good Lord has in mind for her but we will continue to support her as long as she continues to strive to get better and stay among us.

Keep us in your prayers.

Lots of love and Good Wishes for a great Christmas and a Blessed New Year. . . . Love, Liisa and Dennis

* * *

E-mail messages between Liisa and Peter, New Years Day, 2010.

From: Liisa Johnson
To: Peter Nygård
Sent: Friday, January 01, 2010 5:52 PM
Subject: Mom update New Years Day

1. Dennis and I spent the night and took in the new year with Mom . . . we had an honorary UNO game with/for Mom and kept her posted on the progress of the game . . . Mom and I won!

2. Sadly, she really showed no overt sign of understanding, nor has she shown any more when I phoned for an update this morning.

3. Yesterday they did a CAT scan of her brain to see if she has had a stroke... from what I understand no sign showed up.

4. She has had a fever off and on, and blood cultures which came back did not grow anything.

5. Blood pressure and heart rate remain the same.

6. The ventilator was increased to 10 for the night as she had some difficulty with mucous but this morning they are planning for 6 hours without the assist today.

7. Her urine output seems satisfactory but her creatinine levels are in 170 (although kidney doctor said many people walk around with those levels and she says perhaps with the damage her kidneys have had, she may establish that as her new norm).

8. She continues to have puffy feet, hands and belly with many lesions that seep out pinkish water.

9. No response from Dr. Boyd about our written response to increased nutrition plan . . . I believe he wanted to consult with the nutritionist.

10. I understand other nutrition experts are coming . . .
    Liisa

From: Peter Nygård
To: Liisa Johnson
Sent: Thursday, December 31, 2009 11:50 PM

Mom is still with us—she is a warrior—Finnish SISU.
We both are helping her to cling onto her precious life—we still have a chance—we need 2 more weeks—let's fight on—Happy New year to you 'n Mom
    Peter

* * *

E-mail messages from Liisa to her friends, New Years Day, 2010

Subject: New Years Wish and Update on Hilkka

Happy New Year to all! God's blessings for a healthy happy 2010. We continue to sit with Mom. Her condition is not good. She has been in a type of coma for the past 5 days, opening her eyes only once in a while with a blank stare. They are trying to figure out why she is so drowsy. Her blood pressure and heart rate are normal and her kidneys are working fairly well. She has had a low fever but no bacteria was grown. She is still on a ventilator but is taken off 6 hours at a time. She continues to retain fluid in her feet, arms and belly. Her muscles are wasting from inactivity. We are trying to convince them to allow us to feed her added nutrients which have kept her in good shape in the past . . . . As she is being fed with a feed tube this is a challenge.

    Blessings, Liisa

* * *

Dear friends, We are so sad to report that Hilkka, our dear Mother, has gone to her Heavenly home, January 12, 2010 while awaiting a lifesaving procedure to possibly extend her life, here in the Dominican Republic. While the facilities are not fancy, the staff and doctors are first class. I will forward further information as it becomes available . . . .

    Love, Liisa

APPENDIX B

Hilkka's Recipes
The Ones the Kids Just Love

A collection of favourite family recipes continually requested by Hilkka's grandchildren and great-grandchildren.

A legacy of delicious recipes is passed on to the next generation. Hilkka's great-granddaughters, Annika and Makayla, baking Hilkka's traditional *pulla* bread.

Hilkka's Recipes

Mojakka or Lihasoppa • Meat Soup • p.269

Hilkka's Spinach Soup • p.270

Hilkka's Pulla • Finnish Coffee Bread • p.271

Cinnamon Buns • p.272

Mustikka Piirakka • Blueberry Slice • p.272

Hilkka's Karjalanpaisti • Karelian Roast • p.273

Riisi/Liha Piirakka • Rice and Meat Pie • p.273

Joulu Tortut or Luumu Tortut • Christmas Prune Tarts • p.274

Apple Crisp • p.275

Nygård Baked Fish • p.276

Hilkka's Mashed Potatoes • p.276

Meat Balls • p.277

Riisi/Porkkana Laatikko • Rice and Carrot Casserole • p.277

Makaroonilaatikko • Macaroni and Meat Casserole • p.278

Lettuja • Gramma Hilkka's Pancakes • p.278

Finnish Squeaky Cheese • p.279

Mojakka or Lihasoppa

This clear broth meat soup is great when a liquid diet is required. This soup can be pureed into baby food but check the puree for peppercorns. The broth is a great beverage with little meat pies after a winter outing.

Ingredients:
8   cups water
3   4-5 inch beef shanks (with round bone in) or 1 ½ lb. stewing beef
1   medium onion
1   tbsp. peppercorns
1   Bay leaf
1   tbsp. sea salt
4   celery stalks
4   large carrots
4   medium potatoes
fresh or dried minced parsley

In a large stewing pot or a dutch oven, pour 8 cups of fresh water. After allowing meat to sit at room temperature for an hour or so, rinse it and place into water. Boil at medium heat, skimming off the froth that forms as meat boils. When no more froth is noticed, add salt, peppercorns, bay leaf, 2 celery stalks (can be cut in half), onion quartered, 2 peeled carrots quartered. Bring to a low boil, turn heat down to low or simmer, cover and allow to stew at least 3 hours or up to 5 hours.

When meat breaks with a fork it is ready for the next step. Remove the onion, celery, carrot pieces and bay leaf. Remove the bone and any tendon, leaving the meat in half inch pieces. Return meat to broth, slice remaining celery and carrots, peel potatoes and cube into about 1" pieces, and add all of this to broth. Bring to a boil and cook on low heat until tender. Season to taste with sea salt.

Ladle into soup bowls ensuring a nice variety of contents with the broth and sprinkle with parsley. Serve with a hardy multigrain or rye bread and fresh organic butter. Enjoy!

Hilkka's Spinach Soup

A favourite of all the grand children.

Ingredients:
- 2   tbsp. olive oil
- 1   medium onion, chopped
- 1   package of frozen chopped spinach or 1 large bag of fresh spinach
- 3   heaping tbsp. unbleached white flour
- 8   cups of milk (can use skim, 2%, or whole milk)
- 1   tsp. white pepper
- 1   tbsp. sea salt
- 8   boiled eggs

Heat the olive oil in a large frying pan, on medium heat. Add onion and chopped spinach, (if using frozen, squeeze water out.) Sauté until onions clear and are slightly tender. Sprinkle with the flour and sauté until flour is all blended in. Mix in white pepper and salt. Slowly add milk, stirring continually until mixture becomes soupy. Pour into a dutch oven or large pot and continue adding milk and stirring until mixture begins to boil slightly, scraping bottom continually. Do not allow to burn.

Place pot into a pan with about 1 inch of water; turn heat to simmer or low, cover pot, stirring periodically. Simmer for up to 3 hours until ready to eat.

Cover 8 eggs with cold water, bring to a boil and remove at exactly 10 minutes. Remove from heat, pour out hot water, and run cold water over them to stop cooking. Peel, cut into quarters length wise, (egg boats as Hilkka called them.) Set aside. (This section is for the grand children, who do not know how to cook eggs.)

When ready to serve, season to taste with sea salt. Ladle soup, and add 4 "egg boats" to centre of soup in the bowl. Garnish with a sprig of parsley. Serve and enjoy.

Hilkka's Pulla

Hilkka's famous braided Finnish coffee bread! If you choose, you may want to add a cup of raisins into the mix. You may also choose to make round little pulla buns by rolling golf ball sized balls, setting them on a cookie sheet, letting them rise, and brushing with egg wash and a sprinkle of sugar.

Ingredients for dough:

2   tbsp. of crushed cardamom pods or ground cardamom
4   cups of milk
2   packages of active dry yeast or fast acting yeast
4   eggs (free range preferably)
1   cup of organic cane sugar
1   cup of soft butter
4   tsp. of sea salt
11- 12 cups of unbleached all purpose flour

Ingredients for glaze:

2   eggs beaten
1   cup of sliced almonds
¼   cup of coarse sugar

Crack open cardamom pods and heat in a pan for several minutes. Grind or pound seeds and set aside. Heat milk until lukewarm. Add yeast to 1 cup of the heated milk and stir; let stand until dissolved and foamy. In a very large bowl beat eggs and sugar until foamy. Add the milk, the yeast, and the cardamom. Add 2 cups of flour gradually. Stir in half of the softened butter, salt and continue adding flour until dough is still very soft and slightly sticky. Squeeze remaining butter into the dough with your hand. Continue adding flour very gradually until the dough no longer sticks to your hands. Knead for 5 more minutes.

Brush the top with melted butter, cover and let rise in a warm spot until doubled in size. Pour on to a floured surface and divide dough into 6 parts. Divide each sixth into two parts. Rolling with both hands, form each part into a strip about 16 inches, fold both in half and pinch the centre to join them. Line up the resulting four pieces, and braid each loaf sealing the ends. (See below for instructions on braiding four strands.)

Place on a cookie sheet lined with parchment paper, cover loosely and let rise about 30 minutes until less than doubled in size. You should be able to fit three loaves sideways on each cookie sheet leaving space between them to allow them to rise.

Brush loaves with beaten egg, sprinkle with almonds and sugar. Bake at 375°F for 20 to 25 minutes. Pulla is done when the bottom is golden brown and it sounds slightly hollow when you tap the top with finger tips.

Cinnamon Buns

Another pulla alternative is to roll out the dough, spread it with butter, and sprinkle it with cinnamon and sugar. Then roll the dough like a jelly roll and cut into $1^{1/2}$ inch slices. Push down on the top of each slice with your thumbs to fan out the roll, brush with egg wash, sprinkle with sugar and bake.

Mustikka Piirakka

This blueberry slice was one of our old favourites. The pulla dough is rolled into a rectangle. Blueberry filling is made by mixing 2 cups of blueberries, 4 tbsp. of organic cane sugar, 1 tbsp. of lemon juice, 1 tbsp. of grated lemon rind, ½ a tsp. cardamom, and ½ a tsp. cinnamon, 2 tbsp. of corn starch and ½ a tsp. of salt. This mixture is poured on the rolled pulla dough (which has been placed on a parchment covered cookie sheet) and the sides are folded in about 1 inch to form a frame. The sides are brushed with egg wash and the piirakka is baked for 25 to 30 minutes in a 375°F oven. When slightly cooled, the piirakka can be sliced into squares and sprinkled with a dusting of icing sugar.

Instructions for Braiding Bread with Four Strands

First, practice the braiding technique on something else besides the dough, such as with string or on a friend's hair. This form of braiding takes a lot of hand coordination. You need to master the technique before you begin to braid the bread dough.

Here is how to braid with four parts:

Separate your hair into four strands, or cut four strings and secure the top with a knot. Count the strings from one to four, from left to right. Begin by crossing the second string over the first and the third string over the fourth. You should see two "X" patterns formed with the four strings. Now cross the new second strand over the new third strand to create an "X" in the middle of the four strings and then begin the pattern again.

Be patient, as this technique takes lots of practice. Many people find that it is easiest to slip the strands between the thumb and index fingers and the index and middle fingers and then use a twist to make the first two crosses. You can then maintain a grip on the hair or string as you make the middle cross and begin again.

Hilkka's Karjalanpaisti

The original recipe method of cooking this Karalian roast or stew was modified over the years by adding all ingredients (with the exception of the water) to a crock-pot left to simmer on low. The original recipe calls for 1 lb. each of beef, veal and pork but Hilkka stopped eating pork so chose to do it entirely with beef.

Ingredients:
3   lbs. stewing beef, cleaned and cut
1   medium onion, chopped
salt, pepper, seasoning salt, and garlic

Begin by pre-heating the oven to 400-450°F. Combine meat and onions in a roasting pan and roast until brown. After browning, add water to roasting pan until ¾ full. Cover and cook at 300°F for 4 hours.

Riisi/Liha Piirakka

When making these rice and meat pies always follow dough ingredients to the letter and make sure you chill the dough long enough. The pastry will always turn out if you do. Filling can be modified to personal taste. Try adding minced mushrooms to the meat mixture when browning.

Ingredients for dough:
1   lb. butter
1   lb. cottage cheese (1%, creamed)
4   cups unbleached flour
1   tsp. baking powder

Cream together butter and cottage cheese. Stir or sift flour and baking powder, and add slowly to creamed mixture. Mix ingredients until dough will not stick to your hand. Let sit overnight or 6-8 hours.

Ingredients for meat filling:
1   cup beef broth
1   lb. ground beef
1   medium onion, diced
1   cup brown rice, cooked as per directions
3   hard-boiled eggs, pealed and chopped
salt, pepper, garlic powder

Brown together ground beef and onion, draining off the fat. Sprinkle with salt, pepper & garlic powder. Set aside.

Combine browned beef and eggs, and add cooked rice a little at a time, adding only as much rice as desired. Drizzle the beef broth into the mixture until it becomes tacky, sticky but not wet! Set aside to roll out dough.

Preheat oven to 350°F. Roll out dough until less than a ¼ inch thick. Using a cookie cutter, cut dough into circles 2" in diameter. Fill the center of each dough circle with a teaspoon of meat mixture, seal the edge with water or beaten egg, and pinch closed. Place half moons on a cookie sheet (line with parchment paper) and brush tops with beaten raw egg.

Bake for 20 min. at 350°F until golden brown and puffy. Cool slightly and serve with ketchup and dill pickles or with a cup of beef broth (see Mojakka recipe.)

Joulu Tortut or Luumu Tortut

Christmas prune tarts.

Ingredients:
1   batch of meat pie dough (see above)
½   lb. prunes
1   cup water
¼   tsp. ground cardamom
⅛   tsp. cream of tartar
½   cup of organic cane sugar

Prepare one batch of the meat pie dough as per the instructions noted above. Make a prune filling by combining prunes and water in a pot and bringing to a boil. Simmer until prunes are tender. Remove the pits, and add the cardamom, cream of tartar, and the organic cane sugar. Cook until thick then mash with fork into a puree.

Prepare the tarts the same way as the meat pies above, placing a teaspoon of filling into each shell, and folding it over to make crescents. Bake tarts for 20 min. at 350°F until golden brown and puffy, and then cool. To serve, warm tarts in oven and dust with icing sugar.

Apple Crisp

Everybody's favourite dessert and so nutritious!

Ingredients for filling:
8   apples, cored, peeled and sliced
1   tbsp. of cinnamon
½   tsp. of ground cardamom
1   tbsp. vanilla extract
½   tsp. salt
¼   cup of organic cane sugar
2   tbsp. corn starch
juice of half a lemon

Ingredients for topping:
2   cups of rolled oats
1   cup of spelt flour (or white unbleached flour)
1   cup of brown sugar
½   tsp. salt
1   tbsp. cinnamon
a third to half a pound of butter

Into a buttered Pyrex or corning ware pan, place all filling ingredients and toss with your hand to mix well and coat all the apples. In a mixing bowl add oats, flour, brown sugar, salt, and cinnamon. With a pastry cutter, cut in the butter until nice crumbs form. Top the apples with the crumb mixture and bake at 350°F until apples soften.

Serve with a scoop of vanilla ice cream.

Nygård Baked Fish

This recipe originates from Liisa's Home Economics class at Glenlawn Collegiate.

Ingredients:
1   package of cod fillets, thawed
1   tbsp. Worcestershire sauce
1   tsp. mustard
1   tbsp. lemon juice
¾   cup melted butter
2   cups crushed Corn Flakes or Ritz Crackers
salt & pepper.

Crush up cracker or corn flakes and set aside.

Thaw fish and pat off excess moisture with paper towel. Salt and pepper the fillets and place in a baking dish. Sprinkle fillets with crushed corn flakes or Ritz crackers. Mix all other ingredients together and pour over top of coated fish.
Bake for 20-30 min. in oven pre-heated to 400°F. Check fish after 15 min. as completely thawed fish may only require 15-20 min. of baking time.

Hilkka's Mashed Potatoes

Ingredients:
10   medium potatoes
¼   lb. butter
1   cup of warmed milk
2   tsp. salt

Peel potatoes, ensuring all of the peel is removed and potatoes are clean. Cut into 1" pieces and add water to cover the potatoes. Add salt, cover and bring to a boil. Cook at a low boil until fork tender. Drain water. Warm the milk. Add the butter to the hot potatoes and mash with a potato masher. Add warm milk and beat with a hand blender until soft, creamy, and fluffy. (Add milk gradually until the right texture is found.) Taste for salt and add if needed, beating continually. Cover until ready to serve.

Meat Balls

Ingredients:

1   lb. lean ground beef
1   onion, minced
1   egg, slightly beaten
1½ tsp. salt
½   tsp. allspice
2   tbsp. butter for frying
2   tbsp. unbleached flour
1½ cups of beef broth
½   cup of bread crumbs

Sauté onion, salt and all spice in olive oil until onions become translucent. Mix beef, egg, bread crumbs and ½ a cup of beef broth, then add the onion mixture. Mix thoroughly until the consistency is suitable to form balls.

Roll into 1" balls and fry in butter a few at a time, shake pan to cook all sides evenly. Remove from pan, add flour to the drippings in the pan and brown over medium heat. Slowly add beef broth, stirring continuously. Add more water if sauce is too thick. Add salt and pepper if needed. Strain sauce if lumps have formed and return to pan.
Add meatballs, cover and simmer for 25 minutes. Serves 6

Riisi/Porkkana Laatikko

This rice and carrot casserole is one of the traditional Christmas casseroles and a very attractive and suitable dish for all ages. Our babies loved it as one of their first solids. Great heated up in a frying pan the next day!

Ingredients:

1   cup cooked brown rice
2   cups of milk
5   large carrots, peeled and cooked
1   tsp. salt
1   tbsp. of maple syrup
2   eggs
3   tbsp. of butter
⅓   cup of bread crumbs

Cook carrots and mash with a potato masher. Whisk together eggs and milk, add salt and syrup. Combine with other ingredients and pour into a buttered one-quart casserole. Melt butter in a pan and stir in crumbs. Sprinkle over top of casserole. Bake at 375°F for 40 minutes or until top is lightly browned.

Makaroonilaatikko

This macaroni and meat casserole is delicious the second day when warmed in a buttered frying pan. The casserole is an all time favourite with all the children, especially with grand daughter Angela. Most of them like to eat it with ketchup. Many new immigrants used this economical dish as a part of their weekly menu.

Ingredients:
1   cup of elbow macaroni
1   lb. of ground beef
1   onion, chopped
2   cups of milk
1-2 eggs
1   tsp. salt
1   tsp. allspice
2   tbsp. butter
2   tbsp. shredded cheese

Cook macaroni according to package directions, drain and set aside. Brown meat and onion in frying pan. Remove from heat and mix with macaroni. Place in greased three-quart baking dish. Mix eggs, milk, salt and allspice, and pour over the casserole. Sprinkle top with cheese and bake at 350°F for 45 minutes. Serve with dill pickles and tomato slices on the side.

Lettuja

No visit to Gramma Hilkka's was complete without a helping of her famous Finnish pancakes. The recipe has been modified in recent years by using a hearty spelt flour in combination with white unbleached flour.

Ingredients:
6   eggs, slightly beaten
4   cups of milk
2   cups of unbleached white flour or 1 cup of white and 1 cup of
     spelt flour

2   tsp. sea salt
2   tbsp. cane sugar or maple syrup
For added flavour, a teaspoon of cinnamon may be added

In a mixing bowl beat eggs slightly. Add milk, salt, sugar, and cinnamon, beating continuously. Add flour gradually. The consistency should be that of syrup as you drop it from a ladle. If too thin, add flour very gradually, one tablespoon at a time. Let the batter sit for half an hour before cooking. Taste for salt.

In a cast iron pan or a griddle set on just below high heat, with butter or organic coconut oil, ladle batter creating approximately 6" round pancakes. They are ready to turn when small bubbles form on top.

Serve with maple syrup or strawberries and whipped cream. Sliced fruit like bananas or blueberries can also be used. For a hearty option, top with ground flax seed and then maple syrup.

Finnish Squeaky Cheese

While Hilkka did not make squeaky cheese, she enjoyed visiting Eeli's sisters and mother who did. It was a favourite of Liisa's also.

Ingredients:
3   gallons of milk
¼   of a rennet tablet
2   tbsp. salt

Heat milk to just 100°F. Dissolve the rennet in a tablespoon of water and add it and the salt to the warmed milk. Stir together. Cover with a towel and let set for at least an hour until the mixture starts to form curds. Do not stir or touch during this time.

After an hour or so, when the curd has jelled, it can be tested by placing a spoon in the center to see whether a hole is left when removing the spoon. Pour the mass that forms onto the center of a large towel that has been draped over a pail or large dishpan and bring the corners of the towel together to make a bag. Let drain and keep squeezing and shaping the mass until it is fairly dry. Never touch the cheese with your hands, only with the outside of the towel. Place one hand underneath, open the towel and invert onto an ungreased pizza pan. Let set again and drain and discard the whey that separates from the cheese.

Sprinkle salt on the cheese and place under broiler. Have another pizza pan available so that the cheese can be flipped over on to the other pan. Again sprinkle salt on top side and return to the broiler for another 15 minutes. It should be watched very closely to avoid over browning and burning. Keep the pail or dishpan close by so that you can keep draining and discarding the whey that keeps separating from the cheese. Again remember not to touch the cheese with your hands. When lightly browned, remove from the oven again draining off the whey. Let cool.

APPENDIX C

Thoughts & Reflections

"Her is old. Her is wrinkled. But her
can still talk."
[Observation made about his great-
grandmother Hilkka by Anders
when he was three years old.]

"She was my everything. She always
smiled. She called me '*Kulta*' (precious piece of gold.) She never forgot my birthday, and always kicked
my butt in UNO."
[Scarlet]

When I asked Maddex what he would like to say about Gramma in her book, he said that he wanted to tell Gramma that he loves her so much and that "they should put that in the book." He also said to write that he didn't want her to die and that we should make sure to put that in the book too.

Saylor said that every time she goes in the pool, she checks her fingers to see if they get wrinkly . . . if they are wrinkled then that was her and Gramma's queue to get out of the pool and make pancakes. She said that she gets out of the pool now and just thinks of Gramma—her pancakes and their times together.

[From three year old Maddex and eight year old Saylor,
message forwarded by mom Bianca.]

"She never forgot a birthday or had to raise
her voice. Gramma could laugh at herself
and she truly cared about others."
[Kai]

"Gramma was always friendly to others, and continuously welcomed new people to her house."
[Makayla]

"She was loving, kind, gentle, and always
a bright star in everybody's life."
[Annika]

"Truth, stability and elegance . . . Hilkka's heart was filled with unconditional love and acceptance . . . wisdom, tenacity and strength
which went far beyond the norm . . . she was very special . . . she
was my best friend."
[Tiina]

Jan 12, 2010,
Tonight my mom told Kian and I about Hilkka . . . and I am having a really
hard time dealing with it. Ever since I was a baby, I always loved listening to her stories. She made everything so real. The stories of little Miss
Valtonen from the little island in Finland . . . . Being with Hilkka meant
always feeling safe, eating great food, and having the best conversations!
Hilkka's words of wisdom and her example will be a big part in carrying
me through my life . . . . Kian is also super sad, she was so good with him
. . . calling him 'Mr. Smiles.'
[Paulina and Kian]

Liisa's son David always called Hilkka by a name of endearment which she had taught to him, "*Kulta*" implying a precious piece of gold; so when asked to come up with a word that made him think of Gramma, he instantly answered, '*Kulta!*' When asked for a memory, he said they would always end their conversations with Gramma saying in Finnish, "*Minun suu maistuu hyvältä kun sain puhua kanssasi.*" My mouth tastes good now that I was able to talk to you. David always had a special, tender spot in his heart for Gramma Hilkka.

"She was a beautiful friend and grandma that always had time to laugh, share stories, and give advice when needed."
[Allison]

"Gramma had a heart full of love and kindness, and she was a woman who always put others before herself."
[Jessar]

"Gramma Hilkka was the strongest, most loving and selfless person. I strive to be like her everyday, and if I can become half the woman she was, I will be completely satisfied."
[Angela's daughter Courtney, Hilkka's first great-grandchild.]

"Gramma Hilkka was so nice. She used to make me pancakes and omelets. Yeah! . . . I will miss her. We need to send her a note in heaven! The note would say 'I love you, Gramma Hilkka' . . . and that's so she doesn't forget."
[Max]

Gramma Hilkka always said "Love you, love you" when she was saying good bye. Morgan remembers this as a tender and moving expression of affection.

Liisa's side note: "Love you, love you" was adopted by Hilkka from Eeli who always said good bye that way. The words are now echoed by almost all the family members and by close family friends like Alice Dunford who to this day uses "Love you, love you" as her email sign off.

"Gramma was a woman of the greatest integrity and
she was the most tolerant person I have ever met."
[Alia]

Like so many of the young ones, having pancakes at
Falcon Lake with Gramma Hilkka is a really lasting,
good, happy memory for Trey.

"Gramma!!! Your teeth are broken! My Dad
will glue them back in for you!"
[Ava at age three, upon seeing false teeth
for the first time when Hilkka removed her
dentures for cleansing.]

Gramma Hilkka, always sang to me, "Patty cake, patty cake, baker's man..."
in her strong but warm Finnish accent when I was very young. She also
sang many different Finnish lullabies to me. She taught me how to cut my
meat for the very first time. She told my Mom when I was born that she
made the tiniest knitted blue booties she'd ever made just for me. I still
have them. She was one of the first people I met in the world when I was
just born at the hospital and she was there. I loved it when she would say,
"I love you" to both me and my Mom. I still have the Christening gown and
shoes she bought for me for my Baptism, and she threw a nice Baptismal
party for me too. I remember her eyes were always very bright and blue,
and she always made the BEST pancakes. My Mom makes them now. So
when my Mom asks what I would like for breakfast on Sunday mornings, I
always just say, "Hilkka pancakes!" Right this minute she's probably making Hilkka pancakes in heaven or knitting everyone booties or kicking their
butt at UNO. Miss you, love you Gramma Hilkka!!! . . . Love Xar

Oh the things she used to say!

Top five family favourites

1. Hilkka, on the order of prominence in the family, "First you feed the husband, then you feed the children, then you feed the dog and then you feed yourself."

2. Hilkka, after talking to her grandchildren: *"Minun suu maistuu hyvältä kun sain puhua kanssasi."* My mouth tastes good now that I was able to talk to you.

3. Hilkka on how to make your marriage last a lifetime, "Never have a headache."

4. Hilkka, when it was time for a visit to end, musing aloud: *"Koska vieras olis kotona jos hän lähtis nyt."* I wonder what time our guests would get home if they left right now.

5. Hilkka's advice to couples: "Love each other like crazy."

Child of Lamposaari

COLOUR COLLAGE INSERT

Photo Details

Page 1

Peter and Hilkka walk the ramp to the tune of "Wind Beneath My Wings" at a Nygård Gala to raise funds for breast cancer research.

Page 2 & 3

1. "Dennis, will you put my eyebrows on?" Dennis and Hilkka enjoy a moment of hilarious laughter.
2. Hilkka with treasured friends Paulina and Kean Tulikorpi in Nassau, Bahamas.
3. Grandson David with a new hair discovery; Dennis and Hilkka enjoy a "serious" UNO game.
4. Liisa celebrating Hilkka's 87th birthday at the Grace Hospital in Winnipeg.
5. Hilkka holding Peter's new born son Xar, newly arrived home from the hospital in the Bahamas.
6. Hilkka with Liisa and great-granddaughter Morgan.
7. Hilkka and great-granddaughter Ava baking Hilkka's famous *pulla*.
8. Hilkka enjoying a great reunion with children, grandchildren and great-grandchildren; from left to right, Angela, Hilkka, Mika, Kai, Jessar, Liisa, David, Allison and Annika.
9. Hilkka's great-grandson Anders Dyborn with Paulina Tulikorpi dressed up for a special date.

10. Eeli and Hilkka celebrating their 50th wedding anniversary in Winnipeg with granddaughter Alia.
11. Peter's son Kai, sent to the corner by Gramma Hilkka after misbehaving.
12. Christmas celebration in the Bahamas with Hilkka and grandchildren Trey, Xar, great-grandchild Saylor and dear friends Aira Samulin and Ekku Peltomalki visiting from Finland.
13. Peter's daughter Scarlet having a traditional sleep over with Gramma Hilkka.
14. Great-granddaughter Annika trying on hat and scarf made with love for her by Gramma Hilkka.
15. Hilkka with first born granddaughters, Liisa's daughter Angela and Peter's daughter Bianca.
16. Hilkka with grandson David sharing time together at Falcon Lake.
17. Hilkka with first great-granddaughter Courtney sharing a traditional cheek to cheek moment.
18. Peter and Hilkka wear genuine smiles as they enjoy a warm Caribbean evening.
19. Hilkka and great-grandson Anders at Falcon Lake.
20. Hilkka's granddaughter Alia with fiancé Derek Daneault.
21. Hilkka with a warm hug from grandson Kai.
22. Hilkka and granddaughter Bianca at a wedding celebration in the Bahamas.
23. Hilkka at the wedding of Liisa and Dennis, flanked by grandsons David and Kristopher.
24. Hilkka receiving a hug from great-grandson Max at Falcon Lake.
25. Group hug with the always happy girls, Hilkka, Allison, Makayla and Annika.
26. Hilkka holding her new born great-grandson, Bianca's son Maddex.
27. Four generations with Hilkka, Liisa, Liisa's daughter Allison and her daughter Makayla.
28. The family's Great Danes, Drake and Dutchess, guard sleeping Bianca at Viking Hill, Hilkka's residence in the Bahamas.

Page 4 & 5

1. Hilkka cooling off in the pool at Viking Hill with granddaughter Bianca and great-grandchildren, Saylor and Maddex.
2. Friend, helper and swimming partner in the Bahamas, Marg Mullin, joins Hilkka in her Falcon Lake exercise pool.

3. Hilkka and Liisa celebrating the opening of the new East Wing and sauna at Viking Hill with a night time dip in the pool in March 2009.
4. Peter and son Kai pose for Gramma Hilkka after a daily volley ball match.
5. Can't keep them out of the water! Bianca, Saylor and Hilkka enjoy their daily swim.
6. Hilkka and guest Aira Samulin from Finland taking part in Hilkka's daily exercise program in the Bahamas.
7. March, 2009 saw Peter and Liisa with their families join Hilkka at the Grand Opening of the sauna at Viking Hill.
8. October 2009, Hilkka receives a get well kiss from great-grandson Maddex as she returned to Viking Hill hoping to recuperate. (Sadly, this would be her last time at Viking Hill before her passing.)
9. Hilkka's grandson Trey and great-granddaughter Ava preparing for a ride in a stretch limo.
10. Dennis and Hilkka try to cheer up Hilkka's great-grandson Jackson.
11. Bianca, Saylor and baby Maddex visiting Gramma Hilkka.
12. Yorkie Tasha, Hilkka's companion, poses after her haircut.
13. Much loved pets, Wrinkles and Parrot Danny Bird, share a kiss.
14. Aunt Liisa and Hilkka's grandson Xar celebrating Xar's 10th birthday.
15. Hilkka poses at Falcon Lake with Julia and Justin, children of Robert, Dennis' son.
16. Liisa's grandchildren, Annika, Jackson, Anders, Max, Makayla and Ava just hanging out at Gramma Hilkka's at Falcon Lake.
17. Hilkka's dearest friend Kaino Tuominen (who passed away just a week after Hilkka) is visited by Liisa in Victoria, BC.
18. Peter and daughter Alia are jubilant at Alia's graduation.
19. Gramma Hilkka meets Kai and Courtney at the Kenora, Ontario docks on their return from Camp Stevens.
20. Hilkka and Peter relax at Nygård Cay as little Courtney dozes on Peter's shoulder.
21. Two games of UNO and we're home! Hilkka, Peter, and Kai jetting to Winnipeg from the Bahamas.
22. Love and cuddles from first great-grandchild Courtney.
23. Nothing was more fun than baking with Gramma Hilkka . . . as Bianca rolls out the dough.
24. Annika has mastered the preparation of a family favourite, apple crisp.
25. Great-granddaughter Annika making *pulla* with Gramma Hilkka.
26. The cooking contest is on. "Gramma Hilkka, who can make the best apple crisp?" asks Makayla.
27. After one of Hilkka's delicious dinners . . . what else but an UNO game?

Page 6 & 7

1. Hilkka attends a Nygård event in Toronto with long time friend Maire Keskikyla and close family friend and confidant, Tiina Tulikorpi.
2. Hilkka and her great-granddaughter Courtney visit with Hilkka's long time admired and respected friend, attorney Zoltan Mihaly.
3. Peter, Liisa and Carlos Mackey (their Bahamian "brother") at Viking Hill.
4. Heikki and Riitta Kelonen, long time close friends of Hilkka and Eeli.
5. President and CEO of Nygård Fashion, Jim Bennett, with Her Honour Pearl McGonigal, former Lieutenant Governor of Manitoba, and her daughter Kim McGonigal, at a Nygård Fashion Event.
6. A Deloraine friend, Grant Cassils, delivers a surprise bouquet to Hilkka at Mayo Clinic in November 2009.
7. Nygård executives Jim Bennett, Pat Chapdelaine, Len Nicolas, along with Jim's wife Shirley, surround Hilkka with good wishes at Viking Hill during her annual hosting of the Summit Dinner.
8. Peter and his niece Allison attend a reunion of the Nygård relatives in North Central Finland.
9. Her massage therapists and dear friends David and Evelyn Willison enjoy a dinner out with Hilkka.
10. Pictured at the Nygård 50th Anniversary Celebration at the University of North Dakota are Ivan and Laura (Jackson) Cronsberry, and the Nygård's first Finnish friends in Canada, Viljo (Uncle Bill) and Irja (Aunty Irene) Suominen.
11. "GiGi" and Edmund, Hilkka's helpers and friends, with their son Emmanuel and daughter Ella Marie, visit Hilkka at Winnipeg's Grace Hospital in September 2009.
12. Hilkka and Peter attend a special dinner with dignitaries in Finland.
13. Celebrating Hilkka's birthday with her are long time friends Mirjam Vallittu and Maire Rainonen.
14. Hilkka has a smile of gratitude for her kitchen assistant and good friend, Kendall, at Viking Hill.
15. Hilkka joins Peter for his key note speech at a major Trade Conference in Helsinki, Finland.
16. Arturo Balcita and his wife Penny, long time friends and helpers of the Nygård family, surprise Hilkka on her 87th birthday at Grace Hospital with a magnificent bouquet of home grown gladiolas and giant mums.

17. Hilkka is surprised on her 60th birthday by her Albany Street friend, Betty Jackson, and granddaughter Allison with her friend Sophia Macrodimitris.
18. Hilkka enjoys a Nygård Fashion Show with close friends Tiina Tulikorpi and Lynn Horrill, a long time Nygård employee.
19. Long time friend of the Nygård family, Tanya Tucker, and her daughters Presley and Layla, visit Hilkka at Viking Hill.
20. Dennis and Liisa pose with special friends Wayne and Linda Gerrard and Hilkka to show off their Nygård Summit jackets.
21. Hilkka accompanies Peter to Montreal gala store opening event.
22. Gary Collins and his wife Mary Ann Mobley join Peter, Liisa and Hilkka at the Marina del Rey celebration of Eeli and Hilkka's 50th Anniversary.
23. George and Tannis Richardson of Winnipeg visit Peter and Hilkka at Viking Hill in the Bahamas.
24. Hilkka hosts Nygård Executives, Rick Wanzel and his wife Martha House (at left) and Dennis Lapointe and wife Cindy (at right) at a Nygård Summit dinner.
25. Erik and Tiina Tulikorpi, who are like her own children to Hilkka, pose with daughter Paulina and son Kean.
26. Construction engineer and Nygård Cay Project Manager Mike Moore at Viking Hill.
27. Long time friends Annikki Eronen, her husband Jokke and Sandra Thusberg, visit at Hilkka's birthday celebration. (Annikki passed away one week before Hilkka died.)
28. Hilkka with friend and housekeeper Sedoni Nairn at Viking Hill in the Bahamas.
29. Hilkka and Eeli attend the wedding of Kirsi (Kelonen) Gray.
30. Posing on the steps of the Mayan Temple at Nygård Cay are Nygård family members celebrating Eeli's sister Aili's 90th Birthday. Peter is flanked by Hilkka on the left and his Aunt Aili on the right.

Page 8

1. Hilkka, Eeli, Peter and Liisa at Viking Hill, Nassau, Bahamas in 1990.
2. Liisa's children become Godparents to Angela's baby Courtney; from the left, Kristopher, David, and Allison.
3. Hilkka enjoys her birthday dinner at Liisa and Dennis' home.
4. Hilkka and Eeli celebrate their 25th wedding anniversary.
5. A great team! Hilkka and Peter at a Nygård fashion event.

6. A memorable family event; the wedding of Hilkka's granddaughter Allison to Cameron Stewart, August 1996.
7. A very emotional moment for Peter, Liisa, Hilkka and Alia (Peter's daughter) visiting the room in Deloraine, Manitoba which had been the Nygård's first home in Canada.
8. Hilkka, Liisa and Peter's daughter Alia attend the First Communion of Peter's daughter Scarlet.
9. Hilkka, Peter and Liisa celebrate at a Nygård Cancer Research Fundraiser.
10. Hilkka and Eeli celebrate their 45th anniversary.
11. Hilkka admires her gifts on her 50th birthday while Eeli looks on.
12. Long time family friends, the Dunfords, Noel, Alice, Carrie and Tyler are joined by Liisa and Kristopher at the wedding of Tyler and his new bride Kim.
13. Celebrating the Baptism of Peter's daughter Bianca at Viking Hill in the Bahamas are Eeli and Hilkka and Liisa's children Allison, Kristopher, David and Angela.